SNIPER

Also by Jon Wells

Heat: A Firefighter's Story
Poison
Post-Mortem
Vanished
Death's Shadow
Some Kind of Wonderful (with John Ellison)

SNIPER

THE TRUE STORY OF ANTI-ABORTION KILLER JAMES KOPP

JON WELLS

HarperCollins*Publishers*Ltd

*To Dana Robbins, with gratitude for his
encouragement, guidance and friendship*

Sniper
Copyright © 2008 by The Hamilton Spectator,
a division of Metroland Media Group Ltd.
All rights reserved.

Published by HarperCollins Publishers Ltd

Originally published by John Wiley & Sons Canada, Ltd.: 2008

First published by HarperCollins Publishers Ltd in an e-pub edition: 2013
This HarperCollisn trade paperback edition: 2015

HarperCollins books may be purchased for educational, business, or
sales promotional use through our Special Markets Department.

HarperCollins Publishers Ltd
2 Bloor Street East, 20th Floor
Toronto, Ontario, Canada
M4W 1A8

www.harpercollins.ca

Library and Archives Canada Cataloguing in Publication
information is available upon request

ISBN 978-1-44343-833-9

Printed and bound in the United States of America

RRD 9 8 7 6 5 4 3 2 1

TABLE OF CONTENTS

Introduction 1

1   A Burning Cross 5
2   Atomic Dog 16
3   Don Quixote 25
4   Silent Scream 36
5   Victim Soul 48
6   *Romanita* 57
7   Loretta 67
8   Remembrance Day 78
9   Sneaky Bastard 88
10 "I'm Hemorrhaging Here" . . . 101
11 Decidedly Distasteful 115
12 Are you James Kopp? 131
13 On the Lam 142
14 Wanted 153
15 Tim Guttler 164
16 A Moral Impossibility 177
17 Partial Success 185
18 Worried Big-Time 194
19 Sayonara 205
20 St. Paul 4:18 214
21 "A Pro-life Scalp" 233

22 The Usual Suspects 243
23 Biblical Figures. 254
24 Grace and Ammunition 267
25 Supernaturally Wicked 278
26 A Complex Martyrdom 289
27 Free Conscience. 299
28 *The Maltese Falcon* 311

    Epilogue 321
    Acknowledgments 325

SNIPER

INTRODUCTION

Dark, early evening in Dublin. Wet cobblestone glistens under street-lights, a damp, bracing nip in the air. The writer checked his watch. Six o'clock. It had been 72 hours since he met the sniper for the first time, back in the United States. James Charles Kopp. "What was ... the weather like, this morning, where you live?" was the first thing Kopp had said, quietly, deliberately, as though expecting some kind of code phrase in reply. And now, across the Atlantic, the writer ducked into a crowded Dublin cybercafe and checked email. Finally, the message was in. Subject: From Jim.

That was how I led the opening chapter of an early draft of *Sniper*. The true story of anti-abortion doctor killer James Kopp ran every day in the *Hamilton Spectator* over the course of seven weeks in 2004. I have now polished, updated and edited the narrative for this book. Looking back, my writer-in-Dublin theme no doubt reflected my fascination as I chased Kopp's shadow far and wide. Research over a ten-month period took me from crime scenes in Hamilton, Ontario, Winnipeg, Vancouver, and Amherst, New York, to New York City, San Francisco, Ireland and France.

Sniper's length and narrative voice were, and remain, unusual in the world of print journalism, but it was not my first project of that nature—that was *Poison*, a series which won a National Newspaper Award in Canada. I note that while *Poison*, *Sniper*, and my other serials to date are written in a novelistic style, all of

1

the detail, dialogue, and thoughts of the characters are true, based entirely on reportage.

In order to craft the story of James Kopp's life and crimes I interviewed nearly 100 people, ranging from those he went to high school with, to prosecutors and defense lawyers at home and abroad, more than a dozen law enforcement officers ranging from FBI agents to city detectives, and individuals on the radical fringe of the anti-abortion movement. I studied hundreds of pages of court transcripts and FBI search warrant documents—and loaded and fired an SKS assault rifle at a shooting range. In large measure what made *Sniper* such a compelling and at times disturbing creative journey for me was the access I gained to James Charles Kopp. To my knowledge, while the paranoid Kopp has been sought by print and TV journalists in Canada and the United States over the years, he has never engaged in any in-depth contact with any of them. As it happened, I was able to exchange many letters with him and meet for several hours of face-to-face interviews. This access allowed me to better retrace his early life in the San Francisco area, and his steps while on the lam from police and the FBI overseas. It also provided opportunity to get inside his head, understand the way he talked and thought. Immersing myself in his world was at times difficult to take, but it did help me write *Sniper* with more authority and color than otherwise would have been possible. I have told this story using different voices—Kopp's most notably, but also those of law enforcement and anti-abortion activists all along the spectrum. A note to the reader: I don't always telegraph when the voice changes, and the language used when visiting the fringe of the anti-abortion/pro-life movement is often quite graphic.

I have told colleagues the story of my unprecedented experience interviewing Kopp in person. He agreed to talk but also refused to let me record him or even take notes. It was no doubt his way of trying to provide deniability for whatever I would write. (I can hear him now: "Jon Wells? Never heard of him. Knew a Wells in the Bay Area once but that's another story …") When I left each of our interview sessions I immediately turned on my tape recorder and dictated. While Kopp rambled on many tangents, much of what he said stuck with me—indeed, probably for longer than I would have liked. Eventually Kopp stopped contacting me altogether, just as he told me he would one day without warning, and just as he vowed to others he knew over the years. As the story illustrates, this was at his core. Unpredictability, deception—what he called "*Romanita*"—even towards his friends and family, was by his reckoning essential for everyone's own good, and the good of a movement for which he ultimately deemed it a moral necessity to shoot doctors under cover of darkness.

The letters he did mail my way were unusual to say the least, peppered with code phrases and references that were difficult to decipher. He listed names of friends for me to try and visit. I was, he assured me, all along being "vetted" by allies of his. There were times when Kopp's friends were less than anxious to admit their affiliation with him, however. I found a priest at a hermitage high atop breathtaking Big Sur who would have nothing to do with me when I told him the story I was writing, and an elderly woman named Beatrice in San Francisco shut the door in my face when I mentioned Jim Kopp's name. As for the emails he forwarded through a third party when I was in Ireland and France, some of the tips were so cryptic I never did figure them out while others panned out quite nicely—like the one I quoted in that early draft, when a writer hungrily retrieved a message in Dublin containing advice on where to go and who to meet, all while warning of traps lying in wait.

Subject: From Jim
Be careful. Interpol could retrace your steps ... Please do not ask first or last names. Do not ask or write down first names. Do not attribute. These are my close friends. They saved my life. They know nothing. I am Timothy.

As this book relates, the sniper himself did not sufficiently heed his own warnings.

CHAPTER 1—A BURNING CROSS

Amherst, N.Y.
October 23, 1998
9:55 p.m.

A gray-blue eye boring through the rifle scope into the window of the doctor's home 100 feet away, meeting a turquoise electric glow in the white kitchen. Must be the microwave, he thought. The target standing, raising his left arm, the mass of the shoulder in the crosshairs—and disappearing. The sniper waiting, bracing himself against a tree in the woods. The doctor—*the abortionist*—must have pressed the numbers on the microwave, he thought, and left the room. The sniper calculated that the abortionist would return, to that very spot, in 35, maybe 40 seconds. *You can cut a few holes in the fences around the death camps. Derail some trains. Let a few babies crawl to freedom. A mere trickle of relief in the abortion Holocaust. But you do it. It is your duty to do it.*

An orange flash in the darkness, the full metal jacket exploding out of the barrel, spiraling like a football, spinning, stabilizing, 2,300 feet per second, popping through double-pane glass and wire screen as though puncturing tissue paper. The hot copper-coated lead knifing into the doctor's back and, by design, the soft tip of the round mushrooming on contact, ripping through cartilage, vertebrae, right lung, two ribs, exiting out the armpit, blood bursting onto the clean white floor. How severe were the doctor's injuries? The sniper was certain of just one thing: he would not be killing any babies tomorrow, perhaps not for a very long time.

The smell of smoke from the Russian-made SKS rifle lingering in the air, leaves and branches cracking outside, he was on the move, disappearing into the night. Martyrdom was definitely not part of the plan. What, he mused, you think a soldier engages the enemy under cover of darkness and sticks around? Puts out his hands for cuffing, awaits his appointment with a firing squad? Does the CIA ask its agents to embark upon a mission—correction, a morally licit mission—and suggest they undertake *some kind of quixotic gesture, some act of schoolboy chivalry?* A difficult way to spend one's life, shooting abortionists, he reflected, but as it happened he was good at it.

Police in Amherst, near Buffalo, arrived in minutes at the home of Dr. Barnett Slepian, a gynecologist who provided abortions as part of his practice. But they had nothing. The shooter was gone. No weapon. No suspects. The FBI was alerted—this was no typical shooting in a nation of shootings. What the sniper had done was as conspicuous as a burning cross. Within hours a statement

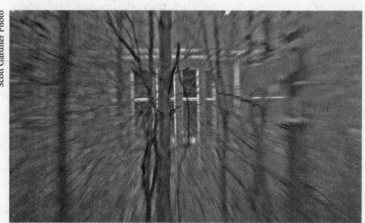

The view of Dr. Barnett Slepian's home from the wooded area behind his house.

Scott Gardner Photo

was issued from Washington. The attempt on Dr. Slepian's life was called "an act of brutal terrorism." Two visitors came to Buffalo to meet the Slepians in person. The visitors are Bill and Hillary Clinton.

* * *

Ancaster, Ontario
November 1995

It had been the wettest fall anyone could remember. Rain came hard, every day it seemed. But the season had also been unusually warm, and so the smell of damp leaves and grass and bark hung in the

Scott Gardner Photo

Sulphur Springs Road, near Dr. Hugh Short's home in Ancaster, Ontario.

air, masking the reality that, any day, any hour now, the air would turn cold with winter's first gasp. The days grew shorter, darkness closed in.

While the caricature is not entirely accurate, Ancaster is known as the well-heeled, leafy suburb of rugged Hamilton—a steel town and port city on Lake Ontario, an hour west from where the Peace Bridge crosses the Canada–U.S. border at Buffalo. On Sulphur Springs Road in Ancaster, large homes intrude on the forested parkland of the Dundas Valley Conservation Area that dominates the area. You can park your car along the road, take one of the trails and lose yourself among the sugar maples and red oaks, maybe spot an endangered Louisiana waterthrush or hooded warbler overhead. No sound except dead leaves dancing precariously in the fall wind.

Dr. Hugh Alexander Short. Sixty-two years old. Practised at

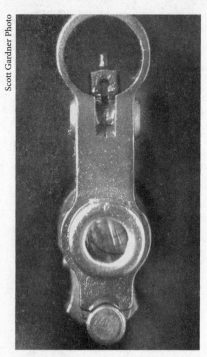

The view looking into the barrel of an SKS rifle.

Hamilton's Henderson Hospital. His house on Sulphur Springs backed onto the woods. Inside his den on the second floor, his favorite chair was turned on a 45-degree angle facing the television and positioned near the low-slung window, exposing both the right side of the chair, and the doctor. From outside, in the dark, the light shining through the window silhouetted the target perfectly.

What was the sniper's mission? To kill the doctor—or wound him? "Just War" theory outlined by theologians from Augustine to Thomas Aquinas says: The cause must be just, force must be a last resort, and the level of force must be proportionate to the goal. Stopping a doctor from killing babies snug in a mother's womb. That certainly justified a war. Didn't it? Wounding would keep the doctor away from work for quite some time.

But if wounding was the sniper's goal, there was the practical matter of actions matching intent. Hitting the center mass of a human target, aiming for the torso, was difficult enough. But hitting an extremity? The sniper knew the variables. He would be at relatively close range, but it would be under pressure, in the dark. Quite a challenge.

Even for police officers, "shooting for the knees" is a fiction. Most cops aren't expert shots. They take target practice maybe two or three times a year. Compare that to someone who spends day after day at a rifle range, clustering rounds in a tight circle, wearing earmuffs to block the echo of rifle shots bouncing off steel-plated walls—Pop! Pop! Pop!

Then again, he would be employing a military-style assault rifle, not a high-precision sniper's weapon. Of course, an Italian army Mannlicher-Carcano rifle isn't a high-precision weapon either, but it took out JFK, didn't it? Oswald was shooting to kill, though. An experienced marksman would say that shooting to wound with a high-powered rifle simply isn't a rational proposition. Even if you manage to hit an extremity, the victim can quickly bleed out and die. But who needs the proposition to be rational? Maybe all you need is someone who truly believes he can pull it off. Or someone who has, in fact, pulled it off before.

* * *

Ancaster, Ontario
November 3, 1995
9:50 p.m.

The Ontario Provincial Police officer watched a car merge onto Highway 403 from Mohawk Road. Old beater. Vermont plate. The cop was 25-year-old Dwayne Frook. He lived in nearby Burlington. Had been a cop four years but just joined the OPP the year before, and was posted to the local detachment. Once the car left Ancaster and merged onto the highway, the driver had left Hamilton city police jurisdiction and entered the OPP's. Why did Frook pull the car over? Slight weaving of the car in its lane? Maybe the beater was also moving too cautiously, as though driven by someone with a few drinks. Or maybe the cop felt a vibe in the rapidly cooling air, a presence, something that didn't belong.

His eyes lingered on the vehicle. Wet snow continued to fall. Frook walked slowly up alongside the Vermont beater, shoes clicking on wet pavement. The driver rolled down his window. He wore glasses. Pale skin, pronounced jaw. Light blue eyes. Frook examined the driver's I.D. Kopp, James Charles.

Jim was soft-spoken, respectful when speaking with police, lawyers. Others might ridicule the notion, given his record as a hard-core pro-lifer. But he liked to think he respected authority, really he did. It was part of who he was. It came from his father, he mused. Hey, he was a law and order guy—so long as the law and order didn't fall on the side of people who favored killing babies. Now, on the other hand, authority didn't always respect *him*. Not unless you consider arm locks—*arm locks that felt like your bones would snap*—from cops at protests to be signs of respect.

* * *

For years he had taken part in anti-abortion rescues at women's health clinics in the United States. It started in the 1980s, activists showing up early in the morning outside clinics "rescuing" the fetuses to be aborted that day. The operations grew bolder, resulting in arrests, protesters getting dragged away by police. Jim Kopp was at the center of it. His expertise was well known in pro-life circles. He took a welding course and designed intricate, kryptonite-style locks that enabled rescuers to blockade a clinic for hours, forcing police to cut them loose. He had it down to a science. First he would twist pieces of cardboard, wrapping them together in a Gordian knot, then copy the design in steel, heating it, bending it, molding it with his blowtorch. The locks meant you didn't need an army of people on-site, just enough to lock down the door.

There was one rescue in Pittsburgh back in the late eighties that really pushed the envelope, a great scene. A Friday morning, and as usual the group gathered before dawn, about 20 of them. Jim loved the early morning, would say little at times like this. He was a planner, not the vocal leader. He let others do the talking.

He was smarter than the others. He had a knowledge of science, politics and religion that the others could not approach. He was apologetic about his intelligence, made a point of trying not to talk down to others, although his attempts not to condescend to them sometimes came off as condescension anyway. "Sorry about that. If

I sound like I'm talking down to you, please, please, just say, 'Jim, shut up, OK?'" He certainly didn't look the part of a genius, not in clothes that looked like soup kitchen rejects, an appearance that belied his upper-middle-class upbringing. He dressed down to be like the rest, people who led simple lifestyles, regular folks who were devoted to the cause, a couple of whom came down from Canada to join in the rescues. Jim Kopp made sure he looked like he belonged. But he was not one of them.

"The Dog!" Jim would smile at the sound of his nickname, and the tone that suggested his—what, celebrity?—among the activists. He wondered who started the Atomic Dog business. Was it from the 1983 George Clinton song? *Why must I feel like that/ Why must I chase the cat/ Just the dog in me/ Nothin' but the dog in me/ Just walkin' the dog. Oh, atomic dog.*

The group drove to the clinic in a van and he followed behind in the car, a junker they got for 75 bucks. The day's appointments would soon begin to arrive. The van parked first. The doors flew open, two people got out with the ramps and carried them to the clinic steps. Jim's car followed right behind, bounced up over the ramps, right in front of the door, stopped, then Jim and another man jumped out of the junker with his custom-made locks to pin themselves to the axle underneath the car, right in front of the door. It was imperative for Jim to be locked down before police arrived. Other protesters duct-taped themselves together in a semicircle around the perimeter—that's what the rescuers called it, the perimeter—to delay the cops further.

They thought of everything. Don't put too much gas in the car. If the police use blowtorches to try and break the locks the whole thing will blow up. The clinic workers, the cops, so angry, it was amazing. Shut the place down the entire day. Beautiful stuff. There he was, pinned under the car, fire from the police torches laboring to destroy what he, Jim Kopp, had created, heat thrown against his face as preborn babies slumbered in the warmth of their mothers' wombs, safe, for one more day.

* * *

This police officer looking him in the eye, was he RCMP? Like the Mountie on that TV show. What was it called again? Later Jim Kopp tried to jog his memory. Saw the show on TV in Chicago once. Due North? Due South? Yes, *Due South*. Tall handsome actor, very Canadian. Paul—Gross. Yes. Perfect for the part, by the way, he reflected. Not exactly a cultural icon, not like Joni, but who is?

Dwayne Frook studied the I.D. Kopp, James Charles/1977 Dodge Aspen/green/BFN595/Residence St. Albans, Vermont. When no charge is laid from a routine traffic check, an officer often thinks nothing more of the encounter, writes nothing down. But Frook made a note of the stop. It's simply a good habit. Down the road, you never know when information might come in handy. He took down the plate and the name of James Charles Kopp, then punched it into his computer, added it to thousands of others in the database. Frook let him go. There was no reason not to. The driver had done nothing wrong. Routine check. It took maybe all of five minutes. Jim Kopp rolled up the window and escaped into the darkness.

One week later, on the evening of Friday, November 10, Dr. Hugh Short and his wife, Katherine, returned to their home on Sulphur Springs. It had started to rain. Drops peppered the roof of the back-yard shed, where the sniper had lurked, waiting, preparing. In the military, infantry prepack rifle rounds in strip clips for quick and easy reloading. But the sniper would likely have opportunity for one, maybe two shots. Rapid reloading was not required. Load the rounds, one at a time, into the slot at the top of the assault rifle. Feel the smooth, cold metal surface of each, blunt round noses, each lodging in place with a click. One down. Click. The next parallel beside it. Click. Pull on the round metal bolt, feel the stiffness of the spring, pull it all the way back, hear the faint chick of the retraction, allowing the first round to slide into the chamber, then ease the bolt back, making a harder, more violent clack, like a bone snapping. Out of the shed, on the grassy slope behind the house, the second-floor den window lighted.

A sniper must have a steady heartrate, measured breathing, a clarity of thought and conscience that translates directly to the firearm, making the shot a mathematical certainty. If anything is off, it's a miss. In the attempted assassination of Ronald Reagan in 1981, the shot out of John Hinckley's short-barreled gun ricocheted off the armor plating of Reagan's limousine, flattened out like a dime, went through the half-inch space between the open door and the car and sliced into the president, hitting under the armpit. The bullet tumbled onward, then turned, tearing through muscles into his lung, and finally stopped one inch from his heart. That's how tenuous it all is.

At 9:25 p.m. Katherine Short sat on a couch in the den. Her husband was there watching TV, in his favorite chair up against the window, a stationary target, his right elbow visible on the armrest.

* * *

Wind gusting, temperature plunging, rain pounding in sheets on the windshield of Hamilton police constable Mike Senchyshak's parked cruiser. Terrible night. He was one of two uniform cops on patrol in the Ancaster area. Senchyshak covered area 311, was out on Trinity Church Road near Highway 53. The call came over the radio at 9:30 p.m. "Dispatch to three-eleven, over."

"Three-eleven, go ahead."

"Possible shooting. Sulphur Springs Road."

Senchyshak didn't hit the flashers. Sometimes they just slow you down. Motorists act strange when you light up the streets like that. He'd make better time without them. And he did not know if anyone had actually been hit. People hear a rifle shot and sometimes make a call. Often it's just a pellet gun going off. But he was there in minutes, turned on Sulphur Springs and missed the house. Then he drove past it again. He had been up and down that road many times, but it was pitch black and the large home was set back from the road, no house numbers visible. Finally he pulled up in front. He looked at his watch. It was 9:37 p.m. The dispatcher relayed more information.

"Confirmed shots fired. Repeat. Shots fired." Those words would bring patrol cars from all over the area. But at that moment, there was only one: Senchyshak. He pulled up the long driveway, right close to the house. A decision: stay put in the cruiser or go inside? Stay in the cruiser. Go by the book. If you're alone at a shooting scene that might be still hot, wait at a safe distance for backup. You make your own rules, go Lone Ranger and stick your head in without knowing what's there, you might be handed your brain in pieces. No. Someone could be hurt, the shooter could be inside, might fire again. Senchyshak opened the door of his cruiser, stepped into the cold rain, towards the scene, alone. He spoke quietly and evenly into his radio. "This is three-eleven. I'm approaching the premises."

Senchyshak, who stood six feet and weighed nearly 200 pounds, felt the even weight of the Glock hanging at his hip. It had been just a few months since cops had switched from the .38 revolvers to the automatic Glocks, after a couple of shootouts in Ontario where the criminals had the upper hand in firepower. He stood on the front step of the large home. Could be a domestic, he reflected. Husband could have a gun, waiting to blow a hole in the next person to come inside. He knocked on the door, his senses on high alert. A woman answered the door. It was Katherine Short. A male voice yelling frantically from upstairs.

"Help! Help!"

Katherine rushed up the stairs and Senchyshak followed cautiously behind. He knew nothing about the Shorts, didn't know who else was in the house, who had taken a shot, and he had no backup. He made quick mental notes of the layout on the main floor as he climbed, planning an escape route in case he needed one. He spoke quietly into his radio again, offering a live play-by-play of the consequences of his decision. "Three-eleven going upstairs." He entered the den and saw Katherine's husband on the floor, his clothes soaked with blood. He was alive.

"Three-eleven. Three-eleven with the victim. Victim conscious. Arm wound. Bleeding. Tell the ambulance to step on it."

The bullet had blown through Dr. Hugh Short's elbow. The doctor and his wife were hysterical now, yelling. Not in pain so much as fear, terror. Short would have felt unworldly pain when the shot hit but then the adrenaline blasted through his system, shock, fear—survival. Stop the bleeding. Stop it, or you're dead in minutes. Wrap the wound, wrap it now, or bleed out. He had one belt tied in a tourniquet just above the wound on the right elbow, and he was trying, with help from his wife, to wrap a second belt. His eyes met Senchyshak's. "I'm a doctor."

The cop put his hands into the fray, helping tighten the second belt, soaking his bare hands in blood. "What happened?" asked Senchyshak, trying to get more information, mindful that the shooter could be somewhere near.

"Two shots through the window," replied Short. "Heard the first. Hit by the second."

The paramedics arrived, several police cars, the dark street now ablaze with flashing lights. Short continued giving directions, the combination of his survival and healing instincts in overdrive. "OK, doctor," said the paramedic. "Just let us do what we do."

Senchyshak rode with Short in the ambulance to Hamilton General Hospital. As his shift came to an end at dawn, he kept going over it in his head, replaying the possibilities. Where had the shooter gone? Back into the woods? Probably not. Driven right past Senchyshak the other way on Sulphur Springs? Unlikely. Shots fired at about 9:25 p.m. Arrival at scene at 9:37 p.m. The sniper would have already hit the road before police arrived, would have his escape planned in advance. A getaway car? And why shoot Dr. Short? So many questions. But the detectives had the case now. In a bathroom, Mike Senchyshak scrubbed his hands. Hugh Short's dried blood turned to liquid and flowed down the drain.

CHAPTER 2—ATOMIC DOG

Jim Kopp heard the news. He read voraciously, made a point of knowing everything that was happening in the abortion wars, was always connecting the dots. The Canadian doctor had been severely wounded, his elbow smashed to a pulp, but he was going to live. And Dr. Hugh Short might never be able to practise medicine again. Kopp enjoyed reflecting upon moral considerations in the abortion war, debating them. By wounding the doctor, the shooter had prevented the doctor from aborting fetuses for some time. Thus the doctor could no longer violate the physician's oath to do no harm.

The Hippocratic Oath? Yes, it was true, the Hippocratic Oath actually mentioned abortion. True. You didn't hear much about it, the oath was revised over the years. But the original version said that a physician shall not "give a woman a pessary to procure abortion." Harm? A bullet to the elbow is painful indeed, a nasty piece of business, but what of the unborn child, thought Jim, what of the child *no bigger than a field mouse*, helpless when facing the suction equipment, *the equivalent of being tossed into the inside of a jet engine? You want to talk about a victim?* Harm! He saw in his mind's eye the baby in the safety of the uterus fighting off the forceps gripping its leg, feel the abortionist grab the femur and twist it, *snap it off like a turkey leg, and yes, even still, he fights back*, tries to get away, but doesn't stand a chance.

Oh yes, no doubt there would be much hand-wringing over the

shooting of the doctor. But Jim Kopp, for one, felt there were already people being hurt in the war—preborn babies. *In the blink of an eye as God measures time everyone will be called to task—what did we do when the world feasted on the blood of our children?*

* * *

Ancaster, Ontario
November 11, 1995

The morning after, the air cold and dry, sunshine peeking through thick layers of cloud. The detective walked up the stairs of the house. Mike Campbell entered a room filled with light and looked at the chair where Dr. Hugh Short had been sitting. Campbell was a plain-clothes detective with the Major Crimes division of Hamilton police. He had sandy blond hair, friendly eyes, and spoke with a classic just-the-facts-ma'am cop inflection. And he was a Roman Catholic. Considered himself pro-life.

He moved closer to the window. Outside, the forensic detectives were gathering evidence. The shooting had clearly been well planned, the home cased out, the Shorts' schedule monitored in advance. He had planned his escape. Detectives are trained to keep an open mind, even when most clues point to one motive. But Campbell had a feeling. He saw the splinters on the floor. The two rounds had not punctured the window glass, but rather the wooden frame. He noted the two holes were close together. It all spoke to him. Planning. Intent. Accuracy. Abortion.

Campbell's father was the late Jimmy Campbell, one of Hamilton's legendary old school detectives. Crime in Hamilton was not as colorful as it once was, or as it was remembered. Steeltown's past was filled with the stuff of movies, gangsters with tommy guns, tough cops manning the thin blue line against organized crime, the force's "morality squad" sweeping the streets clean. Godfathers like the infamous Johnny (Pops) Papalia, bombs in bakeries, paid hits, blood justice meted out in alleyways with two-by-fours, and underworld kingpins, some believed, encased in concrete at the bottom of murky Hamilton Harbor, granted for eternity an up-close view of freighters coming into port loaded with iron ore.

The nature of the crimes, focused as they were on money, liquor, drugs, sex and power, was not difficult to comprehend. Black and white, good guys and bad guys. But the maiming of Hugh Short by a rifle one dark night in a wealthy suburb was a first, opening up a world of gray, streaked with blood.

Back in the old days, when Jimmy Campbell worked the streets, a detective assigned to a violent crime might have jumped in the car, headed for a run-down bar, trolled the ranks of the disenfranchised, shone a light into dark corners and watched where the roaches scurried. His son hit the modern, high-tech version of that bar. He surfed the Internet, in 1995 a relatively new tool for investigators. Campbell typed key words into a search engine, words like "abortion," "violence," "radical." The home page of the Army of God appeared on Mike Campbell's screen. It was a hardcore anti-abortion group in the United States, of unknown strength and numbers.

Blood flowing, photos of aborted fetuses, limbs severed, torn reddish-brown flesh, photos that were pornographic in their stark presentation. A related website called The Nuremberg Files listed doctors providing abortion services in the United States, Canada, the United Kingdom. Some of the names had strokes through them. Well, Campbell thought, I'm getting the flavor of the movement. Clearly there were people in cyberspace for whom the abortion war was literal. But who were they, where were they, and what were their names? Would one of them bring the war to a suburb of Hamilton? And why?

Campbell sensed the enormity of the case. The person who shot Dr. Short might be American, he thought. The number of potential suspects was unknown, and they were spread across the continent. He would need to go through American authorities, tap federal, state and city law enforcement agencies to look for pro-life activists with violent histories. It boggled the mind. There was, on the Internet, a document called the Army of God Manual. It was a manifesto offering direction for those anxious to take the gloves off in the abortion debate. "This is a manual for those who have come to understand that the battle against abortion is a battle not against flesh and blood, but against the devil and all the evil he can muster." There was advice on how to battle in court, and tactics for vandalizing clinics. ("By simply walking by the doors of the abortuary and squirting super glue into the locks you have effectively stopped the opening of the killing center.") There were philosophical musings on submitting your life completely and totally to the cause:

Some single covert activists will be counted as wise for at least considering, prayerfully, the possibility of a life of single-minded covert activism. Practically speaking, a covert activist with no ties could save thousands of children and their mothers in a lifetime. Once an activist is married, and especially after having children, the constraints of parenthood are profound.

Compassion for one's own brood will curtail the level of covert activity—and a lot of other activity as well! Most termites are going to be busy making the next generation of warriors. But for those few exceptions, carry on proudly with unbridled and righteous fury. *Ut in omnibus glorificetur Deus!* All of our options have expired. Our most Dread Sovereign Lord God requires that whosoever sheds man's blood, by man shall his blood be shed. Not out of hatred for you, but out of the love for the persons you exterminate, we are forced to take up arms against you. Our life for yours, a simple equation. Dreadful. Sad. Reality nonetheless. You shall be tortured at our hands. Vengeance belongs to God only. However, execution is rarely gentle.

Charles Leo "Chuck" Kopp

Mike Campbell saw only nicknames listed for the activists: Baby Huey, Intimidator, Mad Gluer, Cannonball, Daisy, Road Warrior, Scruffy South, Iron Maiden. The Army of God Manual also contained a cryptic dedication: "Special thanks to Atomic Dog, you nuclear canine."

* * *

San Francisco, California
1967

Chuck Kopp rose from bed, stepped on the floor and ambled to the bathroom. His limp was not helped by the weight he had been putting on. At 45, the husband, father of five, corporate lawyer, could see in the mirror his graying, receding hair and thick face. Only the green eyes had not changed. Perhaps he also saw a flash of the young man who had been a wiry and slender six feet tall, a young Marine in khaki uniform serving in the Second world war. He put on the pressed white shirt, blue tie, gray suit. Old school dress, as always, because that's what Chuck Kopp was, a man's man. He got into his company car, backed carefully out of the steeply sloping driveway, and then down the hill, out to Sir Francis Drake Boulevard to Highway 101 and out of Marin County. In 10 minutes he'd emerge from the early-morning sunshine and perhaps hit the fog rolling in to San Francisco Bay as he crossed the Golden Gate Bridge. He worked as chief legal counsel for West Coast Life.

He worked with friends like Anne, Harry and Joan. They would often lunch at Sam's Grill, a fashionable spot in the financial district on Bush Street, their preferred seats being the dark brown wooden booths—real booths, with walls extending up nearly to the ceiling and a curtain in the doorway for privacy. (Some lawyers chose them to do private business, but still checked the neighboring booths to ensure no one was eavesdropping.) They talked business over some Napa Valley wine, Sam's legendary sand dabs and creamed spinach. Chuck Kopp was polite, held doors for women. He spoke in a deep baritone, mannered, intelligent. There was something just below the surface, a toughness that those who spent time with him could sense. When angered, though, Chuck would not let it out.

* * *

Charles Leo "Chuck" Kopp was born in 1922 in Los Angeles, named after his father, Charles Sr., who had emigrated from Austria. Chuck's parents were Christian Scientists and the story went that he quit the group in his late teens when he was told to have his appendix removed and his mother opposed the operation, urging him to let God take care of it.

Also in 1922, on April 13, Nancy Leonard was born in Los Angeles to Walter Leonard, a physician, and Kathryn Leonard. Both Chuck and Nancy attended John Marshall High, a school named for America's most famous Supreme Court justice. Alphabetic fate brought them together. The class was seated that way: Kopp, then Leonard. Chuck was tall and lean, Nancy had sandy-blond hair. Back then, a couple could be called high school sweethearts without a trace of irony. And Chuck and Nancy were just that, sweethearts, destined to one day be married.

By the summer of 1941 they had graduated. Nancy went to Berkeley for nursing, Chuck to Los Angeles City College before attending College of the Redlands. The war against the Nazis had raged in Europe for almost two years. What cause is just enough to go to war? So far, the war against Hitler was not a struggle for which Americans were ready to fight, die, and kill. On Sunday, December 7, 1941, America's dreamy isolation exploded at Pearl

Harbor. Monday morning, Chuck Kopp enlisted in the Marines. He scored high enough on his entrance exam that he was sent for officer's training in Virginia, and became a lieutenant.

The training center was in Quantico, which later became the home of the FBI's behavioral science unit—a place where, one day in the distant future, Chuck's son would be the subject of concerted attention. Nancy, meanwhile, earned her nursing diploma at St. Mary's Hospital in Minnesota. In 1944, she took a train cross-country to visit Chuck in Quantico. They got married that year. They were both 22 years old.

Early in 1945, Chuck was shipped out to California, en route to Hawaii, where he stayed for about six months awaiting orders for the anticipated invasion of Japan. The invasion never happened, and Chuck never saw combat. On August 6, an 8,000-pound atomic bomb was dropped on Hiroshima, killing about 70,000 people. A second bomb was dropped on Nagasaki on August 9, killing 40,000. An American invasion of the main island of Japan would have produced massive casualties for both sides. The bomb perhaps saved lives. But it killed, over time, perhaps as many as 350,000 people, some instantly, some slowly, rotting bodies from the inside out. When does the end justify the means? When is it just to kill an innocent? In the autumn of 1945, American forces landed to mop up and occupy the country, and Chuck was among those in the occupational force, based in Osaka.

After the war Chuck and Nancy Kopp lived in San Gabriel, and then settled in nearby South Pasadena. Chuck entered law school at the University of Southern California. On July 20, 1948, before Chuck had finished law school, Nancy Kopp gave birth to their first child, Anne. In 1949, Chuck graduated with his doctorate in jurisprudence—finishing in the top third of his class. At the end of that year, December 17, 1949, Martha—"Marty"—was born. The Kopps lived in a roomy two-storey home at 1947 Oak Street in South Pasadena, a city located along historic Route 66, just ten miles from downtown Los Angeles. It was an idyllic place, although the neighborhood was still haunted by the "Monday Massacre," which occurred less than a kilometer from Chuck and Nancy's home.

On May 6, 1940, Verlin Spencer, the thin, bespectacled vice-principal of South Pasadena junior high school called a meeting of school district officials. "Good morning, Spence," one of them said, and not long after that, Spencer shot five of his colleagues dead with his Colt Woodsman automatic .22-caliber pistol and crippled another before wounding himself with the gun. He was found lying in a pool of blood on the floor of the cafeteria.

There was no apparent motive, and Spencer swore for the rest of his life he did not remember any events of the day. A psychologist theorized that Spencer, a man of considerable intelligence working towards his doctorate in education, was a clinical paranoiac who wanted to improve the education system, and in doing so, elevated himself to the position of a "benevolent deity." His suicide was intentionally, though subconsciously botched, went the theory, so he could "remain the center of attention, commanding that position in a grisly triumph over imaginary enemies."

On August 14, 1952, Chuck and Nancy had a daughter, Mary. They now had three girls. Perhaps Chuck Kopp, being old school, wanted to have a boy. In any event, Nancy became pregnant again. On August 2, 1954, at age 32, she gave birth to twin boys at Pasadena Memorial Hospital. There were complications. The babies had to be delivered by Caesarian section. The first son they named Walter Charles. The second, James Charles—Jim, the baby of the family. The boys were born two minutes apart—a period of time in history, Jim always joked, that Walter would never let his fraternal twin forget.

Jim would always look lovingly upon his days growing up in South Pasadena. See dad rousting the family well before dawn, New Year's Day, 1965. The two 10-year-old boys and three teenage girls and mom and dad get on their bicycles and ride to Pasadena to secure a good spot for the Rose Parade. They are there, front row, to see the Spanish horses, the St. Bernards from Sierra Madre search and rescue team, marching bands.

Jim was like any other kid. He took six stitches in his eyebrow playing baseball. In his teens he hummed the melodies of the Beach Boys and Jan and Dean while body surfing at Huntington Beach— the future site of the *Baywatch* TV series, as he would later enjoy pointing out.

By the end of the 1960s Los Angeles was booming but California's financial capital was still in San Francisco, where all the insurance head offices were located. For Chuck Kopp, an insurance lawyer, the Bay Area was a step up. When Jim and Walt were 13 years old, Chuck and Nancy moved the family just as protest and revolution reached their climax in the Bay Area. In 1967 Chuck bought a house that sat across the bay from the chaos in San Francisco proper, a modest house on Via Lerida in a suburb called Greenbrae in Marin County. Their home, like others in the neighborhood, was built into the side of a steep hill, a natural skateboard park for young Jim and his friends. From his living room window Chuck could see the land unfold like a carpet at his feet. In the distance, just barely visible, was the bay. He had a successful legal career, a family man who had fought for his country. He was a member of what would, in more nostalgic times to come, be called the Greatest Generation.

CHAPTER 3—DON QUIXOTE

In the late 1960s Bart Slepian yearned to be a doctor but there was still the matter of earning a medical degree. As he entered his mid-20s, Bart had not reached his goal. He attended a community college in Rochester, New York, then enrolled at the University of Denver, majoring in zoology. But he was not a star student. He couldn't get into medical schools in the United States. He wasn't the only one—if your academic record was less than sterling, you didn't stand a chance. Two out of three applicants were denied entry in the late sixties.

Barnett Slepian was born in 1946 into a family where expectations were high long before he entered the world. He was the youngest of four kids. Bart's grandfather was a Russian Jewish immigrant who sold shoelaces from a pushcart in Cambridge, Massachusetts Bart's father, Philip, attended Harvard, but following his graduation the family company failed, and Philip never recovered financially, struggling to make a living. He moved his wife and their four kids out of Boston to his in-laws' apartment in McKeesport, in southwest Pennsylvania, then to Pittsburgh, and then to Rochester. He set himself up as a freelance writer, driving across the country in a Studebaker to research the origins of prominent citizens and writing their stories for small-town newspapers.

In spite of his personal struggles, or perhaps because of them,

Philip, like his father, insisted on the best education for his children, pushing them hard. That was part of the family tradition, and part of his Jewish heritage as well. You do well in school. End of discussion. Bart perhaps felt the pressure differently. He was so much younger than his siblings, and he was tremendously shy. When his sister Serena chided him saying, "Look at you, Bart, the handsome boy." Bart would look away with embarrassment, or cry.

As he got older Bart saw one of his brothers earn a doctorate in mathematics. Another became an ear-nose-and-throat specialist, Serena an educator. He eventually overcame his boyhood shyness, grew to enjoy putting people on, joking. With his failure to get into med school in the United States, Bart considered other avenues for earning a medical degree—and one of those was in Belgium, at the University of Louvain. Among other Americans he met there was a guy named Rick Schwarz, who grew up in the Bronx and could not get into New York University. Getting into the overseas school wasn't the hard part—staying in was. The standards were high. Moreover, he had to study medicine in French. Bart often spent all-nighters studying with a friend named Carole Lieberman. His irreverent humor made her laugh. She saw him as this guy fighting the odds to become a doctor. He had no French, and barely enough money for food. She saw him as a Don Quixote figure, this guy armed for battle in life with little more than dry quips and an invincible will. He did not finish the program, and neither did Rick Schwarz, who in 1970 returned to New York to consider his options.

That November Bart visited his sister Serena in Reno, Nevada. Serena had been left a widow the previous July with a four-year-old daughter named Amanda. She was also eight months pregnant, struggling to pay for ballet and piano lessons and summer camp by, among other things, dealing cards at the blackjack table at Harrah's. In her adult life, daughter Amanda would eventually grow to become a talented writer, and author an article for *George* magazine about her uncle in the days when he was struggling to make it:

November 1970. Dark, stringy Bart parked his rusting '65 Chevy crammed with his every possession in front of my paternal grandparents' white-trimmed house in Reno, Nevada. They were still ashen from my father's death four months earlier; still ashen from my father's elopement with my Jewish mother five years earlier. My eight months pregnant mother hugged her baby brother with a fervor that enraged me. My grandfather took a long time to say, "Come in. Come in." In the den, conversation spluttered.

"So you missed the funeral because you were in Belgium?" my grandfather asked.

"Yes," Bart answered.

"Medical school?"

Nod.

"Shouldn't you be in classes right now?"

"I flunked out."

"Cocktail?"

"No, thank you ... It was my French. I didn't spend enough time on my French."

"Maybe you should make it easier on yourself and go to an American school?"

"They all rejected me."

"Boy you must really want to be a doctor."

Low, sardonic laugh.

Bart Slepian may have been a wilting flower as a young boy but he had, by 1970, at age 24, hardened himself to take whatever came at him with dark humor and a stubborn, take-no-crap attitude that went beyond conventional notions of determination. In the absence of a med school that he could both enter and finish, he drove a taxi for a time. Serena used to watch the faces of Amanda and her friends light up when Bart arrived in the cab and told the girls to hop in. He shoveled manure at a friend's farm near his sister's place in Reno. He would not let go of his dream of becoming a doctor. Backing down was not an option.

* * *

Greenbrae, California
Redwood High School
1971

Inside the high school auditorium the bass creeps in, *boom-boom-ba-boom-boom*, the hi-hat clicks in smartly, *tish-tish-tish*, melting into hot licks from the trumpets, *bam-bam-BAM*, as Sammy Nestico's The Blues Machine cooks on stage. School bandleader Syd Gordon stands off in the wings, lets the kids swing, then counts them in on the next number—"Here we go now!"—into the most famous swing song of all time, Glen Miller's "In The Mood," a throwback to the jitterbugging forties. In the old days, Syd remembered the kids in the band looked pretty sharp, wore red blazers. This being the 1970s, though, the players are dressed casual, no uniforms. In the front row, the jazz band features the saxes, in the middle the trombones, and the back row four trumpets. Off to the side are the piano, drums, guitar. In back, his lips working the brass trumpet mouthpiece, is a skinny, 16-year-old boy with dark-rimmed glasses, rust-brown hair and pale blue eyes. Jim Kopp.

Redwood High was a big school, 2,500 students. The building was pure Bauhaus architecture, several blocks joined together. Teachers joked that they taught at "San Quentin west," a reference to the maximum security prison, not too far along the highway from the school, that had replaced Alcatraz. But Redwood was a mostly staid, upper-middle-class place. Teachers wanted to be there. The San Francisco Bay Area was at the center of America's cultural tug of war, but the struggle was not in much evidence at Redwood, ten minutes north of the Golden Gate Bridge in prosperous Marin County. Still, there was "respectable" activism—the teachers were proudly liberal and most of the students were, too.

Young Jim Kopp (second from right)

Jim Kopp was not immune to the idealistic vibes of his time, or at least the music that grew from it. One artist in particular struck a chord—the Canadian painter-turned-folksinger Joni Mitchell. Once he heard her, that was it, he forever held the music, and Joni, close to his heart. It gave him a kind of spiritual connection with Canada, a place he had visited in 1965 when he was 11, when he saw picturesque Bouchard Gardens in Victoria, British Columbia. Joni Mitchell was not just a folksinger to him. She was a poet. An angel poet.

Jim did not bond with music teacher Syd Gordon like students often did. Gordon stayed in touch with some of them long after graduation, but years later he had little recollection of Jim Kopp, other than that he was not an exceptional talent. Jim played trumpet in the school orchestra, marching band, jazz band, went on the school trip to Anaheim and Disneyland, where the marching band appeared in a parade. Good enough to play in the bands, but that was it. In general his personality was understated, years later students would have only a vague recollection of him. Those who did recall him remembered his intelligence, a sardonic sense of humour, an ability to see the absurd, irony. He disdained the conventional, what he called

Teenage Jim Kopp

"boilerplate" even though he did not stand out in any way as being unconventional.

During the school day, with Mt. Tamalpais in the background, students talked and hung out on the side lawn. There were the normal cliques, the freaks, artsies, jocks. Jim didn't belong to any one particular group. After school, or at lunch, some students went on hikes, visited each other's homes. Jim was not one of them. He was not exactly a loner, he had friends, maybe even a girlfriend. It was easy to blend into the woodwork at the school, especially when you were a twin, and Jim's brother, Walter, also attended Redwood, a member of the United Nations club, a more personable guy than he was.

So many students, many from privileged backgrounds with considerable expectations for their future. One who cut a popular figure in the class of 1969 was Robin Williams, who was voted Most Humorous and Most Likely To Succeed by his classmates.

Yearbook photos of Jim Kopp, far left, and sister Mary, middle, and brother Walt.

Jim's final full year at Redwood was 1971. His yearbook
photo showed him in heavy,
black-rimmed glasses, his
neatly trimmed, rust-colored
hair brushed across his forehead, wearing a striped tie and
a restrained confident smile. A
conservative exterior, but then
there were other boys with a
similar look. He took summer school in order to graduate early. It was as though
he didn't need the glorious
trappings of his senior year, he
was smart enough to graduate
early, and so he did.

Grave marker for Jim Kopp's sister, Mary, in
Novato, California.

During his last year, Jim
made what amounted to, for
him, a political statement. Syd Gordon had an idea. The Redwood
Giants football team had a game that Friday night. Time, thought
Syd, to shake things up a bit, to make a statement. Syd asked the
kids: why not do something different at halftime, make a statement
against the Vietnam war? They would form a peace sign at the center
of the field. A couple of the students spoke out against doing it. One
of them was Jim Kopp. When it came time to do it, he and the other
dissenters stood off to one side in silence. Vietnam would soon
cease to be an abstraction for him. According to his own account,
in 1973 he and Walt had their names drawn as "high probability"
numbers in the U.S. draft lottery. But the war ended before their
numbers were called.

* * *

Life for Mary Kopp, the youngest of Chuck and Nancy's three daughters, was never easy. To the neighborhood boys living near the Kopp house on Via Lerida, Mary seemed odd. She was a heavy girl with a round face, who wore dark-rimmed glasses. She resembled her mother, Nancy, who also struggled to keep her weight down. It was Marty, the middle sister, who had the looks, the personality.

Jim believed Mary was tormented by other students. They were shallow and cruel. He knew she was a gentle soul who taught everyone how to love. She was the one who first taught him to read when he was four. *Jack and the Beanstalk*. He still could see sunlight pouring in the window back in South Pasadena, the room with walls covered in knotty pine and painted a garish pink. Mary had been diagnosed with schizophrenia in 1965, when she was 13. Not uncommon for those suffering mental illness at the time, she underwent electric shock therapy. She was diagnosed with leukemia six years later, when she was 19. Even as she fought the disease, Mary managed to graduate from Redwood high in 1972. She became a born-again Christian.

On May 2 1974, she died. Three months away from his 20th birthday, it was the first time Jim could say that death had truly affected him. The family gathered for the burial in a town just north of Greenbrae called Novato, where Nancy's Lutheran Church was located. It is a beautiful spot, lush green grass of the cemetery set against the parched foothills in the background. On top of the main stone is a concrete cast of her small hands, with "Mary" written freehand with a finger above it. She was buried next to her grandmother, Kathryn Leonard. Jim wept along with Mary's friends from the neighborhood, the ones who had understood her and had cared about her.

* * *

Guadalajara, Mexico
1974

"OK, so I ask to borrow the book. *Borrow*, you understand."

Bart was at it again, holding court. Could anyone tell an anecdote better? He had that delivery, that Bill Cosby thing going. He picked out things in everyday life, little absurdities, ironies. It was a Sunday night, and Bart was hanging out with the guys, Rick, Lawson, John. None of the others could match his jokes, his knack for telling a story, apocryphal or not, to highlight an absurdity, and just be damn funny. Maybe it was the setting that gave him so much material. What he and the others were engaged in was a serious enterprise, to be sure, but here they were, in their mid-20s, studying medicine in Mexico for Chrissakes. They were attending med school at Universidad Autonoma de Guadalajara (UAG) with its more liberal admission standards.

"Borrow. A book. Just—a book. From Brian," continued Bart. "I needed to borrow it, you understand. It was mainly for this one chapter."

The guys grinned and listened. Bart Slepian shared an apartment with a married couple who were also in the med school. The husband's name was Brian. He was pleasant enough, but Bart did not get along at all with Brian's wife.

"And so Brian says, 'I don't see why not,' and he turns to his wife. 'Can Bart borrow the book?' And she says, 'Well, you know, we, ah, paid for that book.'"

Pause.

"And the husband said, 'Well, he's just going to read it. He's just going to read a chapter. Just the one chapter.'" Pause. "And she says, 'Well what if he reads the whole thing?'"

The guys roared.

UAG was a strange place to be back then. Most of the students were local, but there were also about 2,500 Americans down there. The Americans didn't really associate with the Mexicans, who were mostly kids, right out of high school. Bart made the most of life there. He always caught the Sunday American movie carried on a local TV station. Sometimes it was a classic western, like *High Noon* with Gary Cooper. His favorite was *The Man Who Shot Liberty Vallance*.

Rick became the mouthpiece for their group, because Bart's Spanish was, to put it charitably, a work in progress. Bart was 28, not quite six feet tall, maybe 170 pounds. He wore big round glasses, had unruly hair that was receding, and did not yet have the beard he would grow in his thirties. Jogging kept him slim, but he did not have a particularly athletic build. Still, Bart had a sharp mind, the sense of humor. He could be very charming with women and he dated American students here and there. Bart also used his modest appearance to his own benefit, turned it into a strength, a game. His exterior masked sinewy strength.

He was also a bit of a con. Actually, a lot of a con. A hustler. He took his act to a local pool hall. Bart did not look especially hip or cool. He wore schleppy T-shirts, jeans. He'd linger around the tables until challenged to a game.

"Well, O.K. I guess."

Bart would toy with the opponent, just hold his own, let the bets grow, and grow—then run the table and send the other guy home with an empty wallet. His buddies took it all in, stifling their laughter. He played backgammon with friends like Lee and Brian, for high stakes. For a time, arm wrestling, of all things, became his best con of all. Early days at the school, he challenged Rick to a match. They set up at the table, locked hands.

"You ready?" said Bart.

"Yep." Someone yelled, "Go!"

It was over. Bart's first move was lightning, so quick and sneaky that Rick had barely felt his arm tense with anticipation before the back of his right hand was flat on the table. They tried again, and again Bart won. He was the best arm wrestler any of them had ever seen. He beat all comers, took some money in side bets, too. In second year, after beating some of the local Mexican students, national pride came into play. A hulking guy was brought forward by the Mexicans, his arm the size of a man's leg. Even cocky Bart looked taken aback by the ringer.

"Uh, Bart," said Rick. "Sure you want to do this?"

"Not a problem," said Bart.

"Bart, this guy's gonna break your friggin' arm."

It was a raucous scene in the cafeteria, the air of a championship fight, gringos lined up behind their unlikely-looking-but-undefeated champion, Mexicans behind their mountainous local boy (who may or may not have been an actual student). Bets were down. John, Lawson and Rick all knew that Bart surely didn't stand a chance. But they bet on him anyway. The two combatants locked hands, Bart's hand swallowed by his opponent's, the roar from the spectators grew. At "go," Bart was already on top, accelerating as he always did. This time, he was overmatched, even the quick start wasn't enough. He lost.

CHAPTER 4—SILENT SCREAM

Walter Kopp attended Berkeley after graduating from Redwood, en route to the University of Colorado for his master's in hospital administration. What would Jim do? His roots required that it be something special. His father had once told him that one day Jim would be a small part of something very big.

Jim was convinced that his forefathers' experiences were indicators of his own destiny. A great-grandmother on his mother's side was a full-blooded Cherokee Indian, "a strikingly beautiful woman." His maternal grandfather, Walter Leonard, was a physician who counted Hollywood stars such as John Wayne among his patients.

He believed his was a family of survivors in a country founded by survivors—the disenfranchised, mavericks who had either fled or been kicked out of the Old World. His mother, Nancy, had Irish heritage—but Jim liked to stress that her background was "Black Irish" (Irish who had dark hair and eyes as descendants, according to legend, of Spaniards who landed on the Western seaboard of Ireland in 1588, after surviving the defeat of the Spanish Armada.). He would talk of how a grandmother on his mother's side survived the great earthquake of 1906 as an eight-year-old. His paternal grandfather, Charles Sr., survived a gas attack in France during the First World War. He had come to America from Austria to escape anti-Semitic pogroms and, upon arrival at Ellis Island in New York Harbor, he shortened the family name from Koppensteiner to Kopp. Jim liked to claim that his grandfather spoke "every continental language" and worked as a translator in Alsace-Lorraine interrogating POWs for the allies during the war. He died young, at 42, from chronic health defects due to the gas attack.

Jim admired his father greatly—the doctor of laws, corporate lawyer, former Marine. Chuck Kopp had won the Award of Merit from the San Francisco Bar Association, was a leader of the Boy Scouts of America. With his political connections and influence, Jim believed his dad to be a "maker of kings."

Politically he had conservative roots. His parents were solid Nixon people. Jim said that his father had worked to help put Richard Nixon in the White House and, later, helped Ronald Reagan get elected governor of California. In the living room hung a photo of Chuck Kopp with Reagan at a reception. Jim said his dad was offered a post as a cabinet aide in the first Nixon administration, but turned down the offer because moving the family from California to Washington was too big a move. Later in his life Jim believed that he could contact former Nixon administration officials for advice, or to vet potential enemies.

It was a fact that in December 1969 Nixon appointed a man named Jesse Steinfeld as his surgeon general, and that Steinfeld had lived across the street from the Kopps back in South Pasadena when Jim was a boy. Jim told the story that his dad helped smooth the way for Jesse to land the surgeon general's position by putting in a good word for his old neighbor. Many years later, reached on the telephone, 76-year-old Jesse Steinfeld said that the story was possible, but he could not remember it specifically.

Jim's mother was active in her church and also with work, a home care service she founded called Nancy's Nurses, running it out of the house on Via Lerida. She was also active in politics, working for local Republicans, and a member of the John Birch Society, a fiercely anticommunist organization led by Robert Welch, inaugurated in 1958. It became known as a looney-right movement, most often cited for its contention that Dwight Eisenhower, five-star American general, D-Day commander, and two-term president, was himself a communist.

The John Birch Society became, one of the most powerful post-war groups in America, with 100,000 members. One-quarter of those members lived in California. Charitably, Birchers were mostly conservatives holding Washington accountable for defending freedom in the face of Soviet expansion. Less charitably, the society capitalized on a McCarthyist ethos of conspiracy, grand schemes and secret government plots that appealed to base paranoia. This sense of mission, fighting a moral battle against a powerful, ubiquitous, left-wing enemy allied to the federal government, harmonized well with Jim Kopp's sense of personal destiny.

* * *

Given his background it was an odd choice for Jim to enroll at the ultra-liberal University of California at Santa Cruz, which was just 10 years old, an invention of the sixties. The campus was gorgeous but unconventional. UC Santa Cruz sprawled, laid out over farmland and forests of redwoods. It looked more like a nature retreat than a university. There were courses like "The Chicken in History," which critics relished invoking as representative of all you needed to know about UC Santa Cruz and its brand of pop-intellectualism. It represented everything Jim Kopp would ultimately disdain: left wing orthodoxy, a godless peace-and-love doctrine that was morally blind to the real world—an anything-goes ethos.

He could have gone to any school. His family had the resources and he was intelligent, especially in science. The reason he went to this school was because he followed his heart. Her name was Jenny. His girlfriend. They lived together for a time, he said, in an off-campus apartment. He could focus on Jenny at school, and study a world you could fit on the head of a pin, the microscopic world of biology, and embryology. They lived together his senior year.

At that time, he was not actively engaged in the abortion debate, although he did hold a position. It had been in January 1973 when the verdict was issued in the case of *Roe* v. *Wade*, in which the United States Supreme Court essentially legalized abortion, ruling that the termination of an unwanted pregnancy is up to a woman and her doctor. The court ruled that state criminal abortion laws violate a constitutional "right of privacy" and must therefore be struck down. The issue had made its way to the dinner table debate in the Kopp household. Jim was instinctively opposed to the decision, following his mother's lead.

Did Jenny really get pregnant? Accounts got muddy over the years. He told some friends that Jenny had had an abortion and did not tell him about it. He said that her abortion crushed him, brought him to tears. A transforming experience. Later he denied the story. He admitted that he had offered to drive her to an abortion clinic, but said it turned out she was not pregnant. The fact he had found himself willing to help her get an abortion upset him.

In 1976, he graduated from Santa Cruz with an honors degree in biology. "By and large," wrote his college evaluator, Jim's work "has been superior from the outset, particularly in the sciences." Jim succeeded academically, and failed in his personal life. Jenny left him to pursue studies at the University of Texas. Broke Jim's heart, some said. He didn't want to give up on her, though. The story went that he followed her to Texas for a time, spent a semester there working at the University of Texas in a laboratory. He returned to California and the Bay Area, moved south to pursue postgraduate studies in embryology at Cal State Fullerton.

As for abortion, the young Jim questioned it, but it was still an intellectual exercise; the act itself did not yet register with him as something singularly evil.

* * *

Lewisburg, Tennessee

Joan Andrews was raised on a farm in Lewisburg. Her family claimed to be the first Catholics to settle in that part of the state and she grew up feeling part of an embattled religious minority. The Ku Klux Klan was founded in the neighboring town of Pulaski. The KKK, haters of blacks and many others, including Catholics, burned a cross right in the front yard of her Catholic girls' school.

Young Joan had a particularly inquisitive mind. She was unafraid, even at a young age, to reflect upon darkness. She heard about the Holocaust, and, not long after she was first able to read, she went to the library and read books about it. She felt it inside, not just sympathy or intellectual curiosity, but a burning need to protect the weak. It can't be left to the law, the politicians, the democratic process. Leave it to the establishment, trust the state, the wisdom of the people, and you end up with Auschwitz. Her older brother served in Vietnam. As a teenager, Joan begged her parents: "Let me go, let me just volunteer to go over." It's not that she was hungry for combat. Her family had a pacifist bent. But you must protect the victimized. And sometimes that requires force. Gandhi was a pacifist, the kids were told, but far worse than engaging in violence when faced with a moral crisis is to do nothing at all.

Picture Joan Andrews one afternoon around Christmastime 1958. She is all of nine years old, holding the lifeless body of the newborn baby boy:

> *The baby limp, a pale, broken doll. The pain in Joan's small face, the tears, as she cuts off a piece of her hair to bury with little Joel. Mom had delivered the baby at home. Joel had lived, but briefly. Mom had phoned dad at the school where he was principal, and Joan came right home. They immerse the baby in baptismal water. The family speaks in whispers. He was perfect, so perfect. They put him in a small box, then each of them cuts a lock from their hair to make a bed for him inside.*

The vigil complete, they bury him in the backyard. Stillborn?
Fetus? No. Joel is a baby. A child of God. Joan's brother.

Fast-forward to 1973, and a 24-year-old woman from Tennessee stands on a sidewalk outside a women's health clinic in Chicago. Joan Andrews is at the abortion clinic—the mill, the death camp itself. That's where they were killing the babies, she thought. She could all but feel the devil's presence. She was a meek-looking woman, her eyes didn't look directly at you when she spoke, but angled away, as though avoiding any hint of confrontation, as if she were staring at images that only she could see. What should she do? She wasn't exactly sure. Disarm them? In 1973 there was no active anti-abortion counterrevolution to speak of. She felt alone. Joan turned and walked away from the clinic. She would start with some little things, small protests, until she heard a louder calling from God.

* * *

Science did much to fuel the growing pro-life movement in the 1970s. The field of fetology was a new frontier, unveiling some of the mystery of what was developing inside a woman's uterus, using new technologies like electronic fetal heart monitoring, hysteroscopy, radio-immuno chemistry, and, most of all, ultrasound, in 1976.

The visual, and emotional, impact of ultrasound was enormous. Not only was it a revolutionary technology for monitoring the fetus from a medical standpoint, it was also a new weapon for the pro-life side of the debate. The ultrasound used sound waves to outline and project the image of the fetus. Now doctors and patients could watch the movements of the fetus, consider its shape, size, gender, watch it swallow, urinate. The ultrasound humanized the fetus. In 1984, a movie called *The Silent Scream* radicalized some who watched the grainy images of a fetus being terminated.

"The child is extremely agitated," intoned the narrator. "Even though the suction tip has not touched it. We see the child's mouth open in a silent scream, a child threatened with extinction. The heart rate has sped up, it does sense aggression in its sanctuary. It is moving away, in a pathetic attempt to escape. The body is now being torn, systematically, from the head."

The figurative slap in the face for Jim Kopp on abortion came in 1980. As part of his research at Cal State Fullerton, he worked on a project at Stanford Hospital involving nerve reconnection for Vietnam veterans with spinal-cord injuries. He would one day tell a court of law how the incident had been the turning point for him. He said he knew a doctor:

> She takes him down to visit the morgue, in the bowels of the hospital. Jim stands by a long metal table with a paper bucket at one end. He looks inside the bucket at the aborted fetus. Birth defects, six fingers on one hand, genitalia not properly developed. Sees the doctor, instrument in hand, flipping this fetus—this baby—back and forth. She's doing it so casually, like a rag doll. This nice, intelligent woman probably feels she's doing nothing wrong, seems proud, because she has detected some of these defects. Recommended the abortion.
>
> "Glad we found the defects in time, in-utero," the doctor observes. "When you see stuff like this it reminds you why you believe in abortion."
>
> His gray-blue eyes focus, Jim's face freezes in an intense stare, taking it all in, processing the information.

The scientist in him—and that's how he thought of himself, as a scientist—could look at it dispassionately, perhaps, but something else was speaking to him. He had never seen a baby that had been—killed—before. His mind spun. He was stunned. At conception, 23 chromosomes from the sperm meet 23 chromosomes from the egg. A blueprint of a unique individual is formed, right there. And, now, destroyed. It was coming together for him, had been for some time. His research on embryos helped support what he was feeling in his heart, that abortion killed an innocent human life. And if this is so, what is the abortionist engaged in? Murder? How could it be otherwise?

"Show me a counterargument, based on science, or faith, or something, anything," he thought. "I'm from Missouri, so show me!"

He had seen the mind of God in his research, felt a love and compassion he had never felt before for anyone or anything. He was connecting with the unborn child.

In 1981 Jim's sister Marty died of cancer at just 32 years old. Marty, attractive, rebellious against her father's discipline had gone north to Oregon, "the commune scene," as Jim called it, and never returned. First Mary, now Marty, had died from the disease. Jim felt powerless to stop the death of his sisters, just as he felt powerless facing another painful development in his family. His father had begun an affair with another woman.

Jim completed his thesis in embryology and had an article published in the *International Journal of Invertebrate Reproduction and Development*. It was titled, "A Preliminary Ultrastructural Study of Phragmatopoma Gametes." ("The mature sperm morphology most strongly resembles that of certain mussel sperm, with weaker resemblance to other polychaete and mollusk sperms ...?) He had enveloped himself in a microscopic world, a separate dimension, studying the science of conception itself.

In 1983, he graduated with his master's degree in biology from Cal State Fullerton, with a 3.84 on a 4.0 scale—an "A" average. Biology backed up his conviction about the illegitimacy of abortion, from a clinical scientific perspective. But what to do about that? What action does one take, in a tangible way, but also spiritually?

He traveled to L'Abri, Switzerland, lived at a study center founded by Protestant theologian Francis Schaeffer. He heard about the center from a friend who had spent time with Schaeffer and returned transformed by the experience. Schaeffer was an influential man leading something of a Christian revival movement. He was pro-life and encouraged activism, even civil disobedience, to oppose abortion. "At a certain point it is the duty of the Christian to disobey the government," he had said in a speech in Fort Lauderdale in 1982.

Jim took to quoting Schaeffer to others. "If you are a Christian," Schaeffer had said, "then act like it." Jim phoned his mother from Switzerland. He had an announcement to make. He had converted to Presbyterianism.

A man named Michael Bray was also at L'Abri. Bray was the 30-year-old son of an American naval officer. He was a former Maryland state wrestling champ, champion diver and football player. Mike Bray had followed his father's path, becoming a midshipman. But he dropped out of the Naval Academy at Annapolis, hit the road, traveled. Bray met and spoke with Jim in Switzerland. Years later, Bray declined to get too specific about how well they knew each other. Jim Kopp, he said, was simply a young man searching for truth and trying to walk in it.

Bray had led a charmed life, but he felt a yearning to pursue something more enduring. He would become an American Lutheran lay minister, and later co-pastor of the independent Reformation Lutheran Church in Bowie, Maryland. He had long been pro-life. His search for spiritual fulfillment ultimately put dynamite in his hands.

In 1985 Bray and two other men were charged with eight abortion clinic bombings in Virginia, Maryland, and Washington, D.C. He was sentenced to ten years in prison. At the time of his arrest, Bray had publicly argued against violence. He even belonged to a chapter of the Pro-Life Non-Violent Action League.

But Bray's thinking, or at least the public expression of his thought, was changing, particularly regarding "use of force" in the abortion war. Thomas Aquinas set it out in his *Summa Theologiae* in the 14th century, defending violence for a defensive purpose: stopping an act of aggression in defense of oneself or another must be done with the moral certitude that great harm will be inflicted upon that individual if force is not used, and that the force will indeed stop it. And there was, in modern American law, something called "justifiable homicide," or defensive killing. The state of Colorado even put a name to the type of vigilante-justice made famous in Clint Eastwood's *Dirty Harry* movies. Colorado's law of self-defense for victims of violent crime is called the "Make My Day" defense. That law means, for example, that an occupant of a dwelling is justified in using any degree of physical force against a person who has unlawfully entered the dwelling, "if the occupant reasonably believes that the intruder has committed, is committing or is about to commit a crime in addition to the unlawful entry and also reasonably believes that the intruder might use any physical force against any occupant."

The logic, for some in the pro-life movement, was inescapable. If one starts from the notion that the unborn child is a life in bloom, then what of the attack by the doctor? What is the proper defensive response, given that the unborn baby is unable to respond? Bray was a dynamic speaker and became an influential voice for those gravitating to the fringe of the movement. Those who called themselves pro-life, but opposed "defensive action"—violence—in the abortion war, were, in Bray's view, simply fearful of the truth, that there was no contradiction between a pro-life ethic and "supporting force." He began working on a book that would outline his beliefs more completely. He called it *A Time To Kill*.

* * *

Jim Kopp worked in a mission in South America with the Wycliffe Bible Translators, and also in Africa. Back in California, he went to hear firsthand accounts from mothers who had fled from China, and who spoke of forced abortions in that country. It made perfect sense, a logical progression: free states sanction abortion, encourage it, then a totalitarian state forces it on its population. Jim was convinced he was the first westerner to hear from these women who were driven into hiding to have their babies, he was getting a unique perspective on all of it.

He returned to the house on Via Lerida for dinners with his family, from whom he increasingly felt estranged. Chuck Kopp didn't understand why his youngest son wasn't using his masters' degree to build a career in biology. Bible translation? Where was Jim going with that? On occasions when the family was together the conversation would sometimes venture into abortion. Arguing against abortion were Nancy, Jim and Anne, who were devout Christians. Chuck and Walt were in favor of a woman's right to choose. Jim expected nothing less from Walt, certainly. As someone in the hospital administration business, he was by definition, to Jim, a member of the Abortion Industry. Eventually the issue was kept off the table. Abortion was, thought Jim with a grin, rather like the proverbial Ol' Uncle Harry showing up for Christmas dinner: you let him go and get drunk on the porch, you just leave his drinking be, you don't go there.

There were larger problems than political issues threatening the family foundations. In the summer of 1981, Chuck, who was 59 years old, flew to Dallas for an insurance case trial. One August night, he attended a dinner party held for some of the principles. A legal secretary named Lynn Willhoite Hightower was there. She was 44, and four months removed from the divorce from her husband of 24 years. She saw Chuck Kopp walk in the door, and instantly wanted to learn more about him. Chuck had put on weight, was balding. But he had a presence.

Lynn was five-foot-three, with short dark hair. Some would later tell her that she looked like a younger version of Nancy Kopp. She had a Texas accent, a funny, gregarious manner, and six kids. Both were feeling their age, getting a little plump, was how Lynn thought of it. Chuck was feeling old in his marriage, was ripe for a change. Lynn, younger, feisty, funny, was it. They talked and hit it off. Chuck loved to talk, about any subject, and Lynn could hold her own, too. The verdict in the insurance trial was appealed. The case kept Chuck returning to Dallas for work, and to Lynn. They phoned regularly, wrote letters. He told Lynn that he had been divorced from Nancy for several years. Nancy found one of the letters and learned about the affair, filed for divorce, changed her mind, filed again. Lynn confronted Chuck, he admitted to her that he lied because he knew he'd lose her if he didn't.

Some said Jim was unaware of his father's affair and was shocked when it came to light. Jim claimed he knew exactly what was going on. Heck, his mother showed him the letters. It made him angry. Very angry. He had a bone to pick with that woman. Always would. Everyone felt they knew the gentle, bookish, prayerful Jim Kopp. They didn't see what burned inside, the red glare that could, when provoked, film over his eyes, turn his pronounced jaw to stone:

> *Phone rings at Lynn Willhoite Hightower's home in Texas. She picks up.*
>> *"Hello?"*
>> *"This is Jim Kopp speaking," he said. "You stay the f—k away from my father."*

CHAPTER 5—VICTIM SOUL

Guadalajara, Mexico
1979

Bart Slepian neared completion of his medical degree from Universidad Autonoma de Guadalajara. He still had little cons on the go, even after ending his career as an arm-wrestling hustler. Maybe it was because, during his early life, Bart saw his dad scrape for every penny he made. Maybe it was a matter of necessity, given his own financial needs and those of his sister, Serena, in Nevada. Or maybe Bart Slepian simply liked the game, liked to challenge authority and figured there's no harm being done. Whatever it was, Bart took to smuggling goods back and forth across the border. He drove what the guys had dubbed "the family car," a boat of a Chevy, navy blue, his pride and joy, put a huge sound system in it. He'd buy items cheap in Mexico, lamps, home fixtures, sell them out of the trunk when he got to Reno.

Bart's instinct to never back down got him in trouble. One night he got into it with a group of teens. He came home from school and found a group of them in front of his driveway. He asked them to move, an argument started, one of the teens threw a rock through Bart's window. The police got involved and Bart spent the night at the police station—along with buddy Rick Schwarz, who had been dragged into it since Rick spoke Spanish.

Rick always said that Bart never started anything, but he would not walk away when he felt somebody was being unreasonable. Typically he would confront situations on his own, for better or worse. In that respect he admired the Israelis tremendously. Bart Slepian, like Rick, held great respect for the Jewish culture, but rarely set foot inside a synagogue. Bart admired the way the Israelis got things done in the face of the terrorist threat, speaking softly and carrying a very big stick.

Rick, an unabashed liberal, disagreed with him on the Middle East, but Bart would never soften his view.

"Israel," he told Rick, "doesn't sit around wringing its hands. They take care of things."

"Bart—"

"You might not like how they take care of it, but they take care of it, end of story."

"But—"

"No sitting around, 'woe is us.' They do something."

Bart voted Republican, while Rick, a proud liberal, voted for Jimmy Carter in 1976.

"That's not principled, Rick," Bart cracked, "that's plain stupid voting for that dopey peanut farmer."

In 1979, Bart left Mexico and returned to New York State to complete his fifth year of meds. It was called the Fifth Pathway system to becoming a doctor. It was for Americans who had completed medical school abroad. They had to spend a year working in the States under supervision, something between a fourth-year medical student and intern. If you did OK, you could take the licensing exam, which Bart did, and passed, qualifying him for a normal internship and residency. He applied to specialize in obstetrics and gynecology. During his residency in 1979, he met a nurse at Buffalo General Hospital named Lynne Breitbart. At the time, he was doing what he could to get by, did physicals at the hospital for five dollars an hour. She was 23 years old, ten years Bart's junior. They soon got married.

Bart Slepian had no burning desire to deliver babies or help women. But he had solid technical skills, was good with his hands. He wanted to get a mix of surgery and general medicine. With the 1980s dawning, a conservative Republican and staunch ally of Israel, Ronald Reagan, soundly beat the liberal peanut farmer for the presidency. And Bart Slepian was, finally, a doctor. He was 34 years old and an OB, never mind the setbacks and the people who said he couldn't do it.

* * *

For the pro-life movement, the 1980s promised an era of revolutionary change. Ronald Reagan was a hero to conservatives who opposed abortion. "Regrettably," Reagan said, "we live at a time when some persons do not value all human life. They want to pick and choose which individuals have value. We cannot diminish the value of one category of human life—the unborn—without diminishing the value of all human life."

At the same time, the pro-life rescue movement interfering with abortion services at women's health clinics grew. The rescues had several elements to them: picket signs and chanting, but also "sidewalk counseling." That meant cornering a patient outside the clinic, lobbying the woman to reconsider her choice. Activists felt that one in five prospective patients would not make it to a subsequent appointment if deterred from attending her first appointment to abort. Other times, pro-lifers blockaded the entrance. Police got involved.

Others took the violence up several notches. On August 12, 1982, an Illinois doctor and his wife were kidnapped by three pro-life radicals and held at gunpoint for eight days. The trio, headed by Don Benny Anderson, claimed to be with a group called the Army of God. In 1984, clinics were being targeted more frequently for firebombs, arson, vandalism. There were 18 incidents in all, a couple of dozen death threats called in. Three men went to jail: Thomas Spinks, Kenneth Shields, and Michael Bray—the man who had met Jim Kopp in Switzerland. The bombings illustrated the double-edged sword of abortion procedures being confined to clinics instead of hospitals. Clinics offered women preferred service, argued pro-choice advocates, but also, in contrast to hospitals, they became visible symbols in the war—"abortuaries" and "mills" where the babies were slaughtered, in the minds of radical pro-lifers. That same year, 1984, Supreme Court justice Harry Blackmun, who had written the opinion on *Roe* v. *Wade*, received a death threat in the mail. It was signed the Army of God.

* * *

Daly City, California
Spring 1984

He drove to south San Francisco, towards the airport. Daly City was in the industrial end of the city, an entirely different world from Jim Kopp's old Marin County neighborhood, far from the beauty of the waterfront, the Golden Gate Bridge, the sea lions in the harbor. Daly City sat in a valley, populated mostly by working-class people, many of them immigrants. On April 3, 1984, Jim was arrested at a protest at a clinic there, charged with trespassing, and also battery.

Battery?

In California battery is a misdemeanor, like assault, petty theft, and public drunkenness, and therefore less serious than a felony crime, like sexual offenses and drug and property violations. But battery is a violent offense: deliberately causing physical harm to another person through physical acts.

Peaceful, prayerful Jim Kopp?

Perhaps he was merely sitting there cross-legged, reciting verse, and, when he was carried away, he resisted. Or maybe he felt a current running through him, physical, angry, one that inspired more potent action than peaceful resistance. Most everyone who met Jim was struck by what they considered his soulful, gentle nature: the boyish grin, the soft voice. Jim knew his friends felt he was incapable of violence. He also knew they were mistaken. Those who caught him in moments of candor, who looked square into his eyes, waited long enough for his self-effacing "who me?" routine to pass, could see flashes of the intensity and seriousness of purpose that went well beyond that of a conscientious objector.

Jim continued to read voraciously, and fell in love with a book called *Story of a Soul*, the autobiography of Saint Thérèse d'Lisieux, a woman who entered a convent at the age of 15 and died in obscurity at age 24. "At last I have found my calling," she wrote in her journals. "My calling is love." The core of her spiritual message was the "little way," that any act, no matter how trivial, is infinitely valuable if done out of love. He studied the history of birth control, sterilization law. He started drawing connections between the Holocaust and abortion. It was all becoming so clear to him. Everything happens for a reason, and every event influences another.

Through the fall of 1984 he attended protests outside abortion clinics in the Bay Area. In September Jim was arrested for trespassing and battery. A month later, the same thing. Early December, assault with a deadly weapon. He relished the courtroom atmosphere. The strategy, the use of language, nuance. He knew how to play the game. Down the road, he would offer advice to other pro-lifers on how to navigate the judicial system. He was, he frequently reminded others, a lawyer's son. In the fall of 1984, he formally received his master's degree from Cal State Fullerton. He founded a group in San Francisco called the Lourdes Foundation, which opened a "Free Pregnancy Center," and named himself its president. Jim billed it as a birth control referral and information center. The center gave pregnancy tests, educated women on the dangers of abortion and assisted pregnant women. It also showed graphic photos of aborted fetuses to patients, who were then also referred to doctors who opposed abortion.

On Good Friday, 1985, he marched in a pro-life procession that went nine miles from St. Martin Church in San Jose to Our Lady of Peace in Santa Clara. Then he drove to south San Francisco to Juvenile Hall detention center. Officials only knew that this pleasant, bookish man was president of the Lourdes Foundation. They learned later, to their horror, that he was an anti-abortion radical—but not before he had an opportunity to take the stage before a group of female inmates and present his pro-life stump speech. Here was Jim, the missionary bestowing wisdom, saving women from so much pain that they did not understand—they had been brainwashed by the media, the liberal culture, the feminists. The young women were, he said, mostly young prostitutes, and three of them were pregnant. You do not have to get an abortion, he told them. You do not. God bless.

* * *

For some time, Jim had considered converting to Catholicism, perhaps even pursuing the priesthood. One day he hopped in his car and drove south down the coast, Highway 1, past windswept beaches, Monterey, Carmel. Four hours later he was negotiating cliffs along the coastline known as Big Sur. He gained elevation, where the water is metallic against the sun, its texture dimpled by the wind. Then off the highway along a dirt road, steeper still, straight up, a harrowing ride, he had never experienced anything like it. Finally, at the top, he found the humble monastery called New Camaldoli Hermitage.

The hermitage was a place where aspiring monks came to study and learn. You could smell the flowers and pine in the air, hear nothing but silence. He met Father Isaiah Teichert, talked for many hours with the priest. Father Isaiah, Jim reflected, came to know him better than anyone in the Bay Area. That included, sadly, he thought, his family, who had never really known him. His fellow pro-lifers never quite figured him out either.

What, exactly, did Father Isaiah advise? Years later, his relationship with Jim Kopp was not something the priest was willing to discuss. Whatever Father Isaiah's advice, Jim now wondered if his mission might be to embrace the world of the Benedictine monk. He had been called to pray but action was necessary, too. So much violence, so much blood shed by innocent babies. Jim knew what his mission could ultimately mean—that he was destined to die a drawn-out, painful death. So be it.

The notion of the "victim soul" came from Jesus, who redeemed mankind by dying for their sins. It also derived from the Old Testament and the ancient Jewish custom of letting a goat loose in the wilderness on Yom Kippur, after the high priest had symbolically laid upon the goat all the sins of the people. The unborn babies were victim souls. Jim decided he would be one as well.

Later that year he went east, to New York, joining the Missionaries of Charity, founded by Mother Teresa, housed in a convent in the Bronx not far from Yankee Stadium. He was there several months, rising before dawn each day to feed the homeless and drug addicts who came to the order's soup kitchen. He prayed, meditated and studied. He had few possessions and didn't talk much to others. He owned three sets of clothes, washed them in a bucket.

Mother Teresa had said that "I feel that the greatest destroyer of peace today is abortion, because it is a war against the child, murder by the mother herself." Jim would tell friends for years that he had once met Mother Teresa face-to-face, he told her about his calling from God, and she suggested he become a priest. Jim then told her that he was conflicted on the priesthood, because he felt a separate calling from Jesus to devote his life to stopping abortion.

About six months after joining the Bronx mission, he left, returning to California. He never stayed in one place for long. On May 21, 1986, in Redwood City, south of San Francisco, he was arrested at a protest outside a clinic and charged with obstruction and resisting arrest. On July 19 he was arrested in San Francisco for using force. He headed east.

On August 5, 1986 he was in Pensacola, Florida. He was anxious to show his support for the woman whose reputation within the anti-abortion movement was reaching heroic proportions. Her name was Joan Andrews. It was back in March 1986, in Pensacola, that Andrews cemented her status as "patron saint of the rescue movement" at the Pensacola Ladies Center. Along with another protester, Reverend John Burt, and his two daughters, Andrews walked inside the clinic and, with police in pursuit, tried to unplug a suction abortion machine. Police cuffed her, then arrested the others. Andrews grabbed the edge of the machine behind her cuffed hands, yanked and toppled it over, disabling it. There were no abortions that day. The trial made her a star within the movement, she was sentenced to five years at the Broward Correctional Institute, Florida's toughest maximum-security prison for women.

Jim Kopp and 300 others from far and wide made the trip to Pensacola, stood outside the clinic to protest the outrageous injustice done to Joan Andrews. It was heavenly for Jim to be among so many like-minded souls. He decided that, from that moment on, he would no longer go to jail angry, but with a cheerful heart. Among the group in Pensacola was a 58-year-old professor of philosophy from Fordham University in New York. His name was William Marra.

"We're not eccentric, or extremist, but we're here to see Joan Andrews free," Marra told a reporter.

William Marra had a daughter named Loretta. She had just turned 23, studied philosophy at Fordham, and had, like her father, embraced the pro-life cause. Jim Kopp instantly felt great respect for William Marra, who had, like Jim's father, served in the military. As for Loretta, Jim would, in time, make a connection with her that would grow stronger and stronger and ultimately, change his life.

Kopp headed back to California, and more protests and charges. September 6, in Richmond, trespassing. October 25, in San Jose, he invaded a clinic with another man and chained themselves to an examination table as 15 others protested outside. November 22 in Alameda, trespassing, causing injury, damaging property. He again headed for Florida. On Friday, November 28, the day after Thanksgiving, he was arrested for disorderly conduct and resisting arrest at the same Pensacola clinic where Joan Andrews had been arrested. Jim and others blocked the clinic doors with a truck. That same weekend a meeting was held at the Western Sizzlin' steakhouse in town. One of the organizers was a man named Randall Terry. Terry unveiled his vision for a new, national, direct action campaign inspired by the impromptu assaults on clinics that had taken place. Terry called it "Operation Rescue."

Among pro-lifers there were differences of opinion on tactics, on means and ends. Save the preborn, but how? What was the time frame for political change? What kind of action? Jim Kopp was part of the movement, had found a group to connect with—but how long could it conceivably last? He joined Randall Terry's staff, but he would last only six months. His thinking was evolving on the utility of violence in the cause, and the distinction between man's law and God's law. Was history not replete with examples where man's law required trumping by those willing to carry the torch, and weapons, for God's law? Slavery was one example that pro-lifers most frequently cited. Jim listened to mainstream pro-life leaders take great pains to denounce violence in the cause. He felt they were not practicing Gandhi's true *satyagraha*—civil resistance —which Jim thought should be active, outcome based, and sacrificial. He had a name for people who abused the concept: cowards.

CHAPTER 6—*ROMANITA*

On December 16, 1986, smoke filled the Manhattan Planned Parenthood headquarters at Second Avenue and 22nd Street in New York City. One of the bombs was relatively small. No major damage, the carpet caught fire. But police found a larger bomb as well with a detonator designed to be triggered by the smaller explosion—it had not gone off. It was made of 15 sticks of dynamite, powerful enough to collapse the entire building and break windows blocks away. Bomb squad officers examined the blasting cap, timer and battery. Pro job. And there was something else stuck among the sticks of dynamite. It was a medal of St. Benedict, with the likeness of a monk on it, and the phrase *Eius in obitu nostro praesentia muniamur* (may we be strengthened by his presence in the hour of our death). A bomb squad officer gingerly defused it. No one was caught.

In February, Cardinal John O'Connor appeared on TV urging the bomber to turn himself in. A 37-year-old ex-Vietnam Marine named Dennis John Malvasi surrendered. Malvasi was also involved in a bombing in Queens in November 1985. "If the Cardinal says something and you don't listen," he told a newspaper, "then when you stand before the magistrate in the celestial court, you got problems. And I got enough problems without God being mad at me."

Malvasi had fought in the bloody aftermath of the Tet Offensive, serving as a field radio operator. He later told the *New York Times* that he never felt more alive than when under fire. After the war, he trained as an actor at workshops on the Lower East Side, worked as an entertainer on cruise ships. He was reportedly arrested in September 1972 for stabbing a man in a traffic altercation and sentenced to five years' probation. In 1975, two months after early release from probation, he was arrested for carrying a .25-caliber pistol and jailed for two years. He went underground upon his release, using at least five aliases. In 1984, he was thrown in jail again for two years in Florida after attempting to buy firearms in that state.

Malvasi pled guilty to the Manhattan Planned Parenthood bombing. He was sentenced to seven years in prison and five years' probation. Two other men received jail terms as well, including his brother-in-law. Malvasi told authorities where he had stored his explosives, and police found 78 dynamite sticks, black powder, and electric detonating plastic caps. Malvasi had a sharp, angular nose and dark eyes. He was a small man, perhaps a generous five-foot-seven, but an angry intensity radiated from him. Upon his release from prison he began dating a woman he met in the pro-life movement. She too was Catholic, and not only shared his pro-life beliefs, but also his belief in taking action to further the cause. She was 13 years his junior, and her name was Loretta Marra.

* * *

On January 5, 1987, Jim Kopp was arrested in San Francisco for unlawful entry, obstruction, resist arrest, trespass. As was now routine with pro-life agitators, he was released. The next day, he was arrested again. February 25 he was arrested in Oakland, and two days later, in Woodbridge, New Jersey, for criminal trespassing and burglary. March 11, he was tried in Florida for breach of the peace. July 25, Manchester, Missouri, and later in Houston, charged with criminal trespass, fined $500 and jailed for two weeks. On August 22, 10,000 pro-lifers rallied at the Washington Monument, and nine people who entered a clinic in the city were arrested. Jim was among them.

During lulls in protests and rescues, Jim did odd jobs, construction and welding work. He had by the late 1980s made friends in the movement across the country, there was a light in the window for him when he needed a place to stay. In Pittsburgh, that light was at Doris Grady's place. Doris was active back then. On more than one occasion, she and her pro-life friends raided trash cans behind a health clinic in the city. Some clinics had spotty privacy protocols in place back in those days. It was a typical tactic of hardcore pro-life activists to gather up piles of garbage and see what the abortionists were up to. Doris stuffed several bags to take home. Sometimes the city garbage guys would be there, and would let them rob the trash in exchange for a case of beer, you know? So Doris got home, sorted through the stuff. The golden items were billing records, they had the phone numbers on them. Doris made some calls.

"Yes, hello, Barb," Doris would say to the patient whose number was on a form, feigning her best soft, caring, nurse voice. "Just checking in, Barb, to make sure you know your appointment time. Uh-huh. That's right. And we'd also like to talk to you about the procedure."

"Procedure?" This was the payoff. You tried to talk the woman out of it. Subtly at first, then hit them with the graphic stuff. Pretty slick, Doris thought.

"Did anyone talk to you about the procedure, and what it entails?"

"Not really." They always said that. So first you just mention that they aren't supposed to eat before the abortion, stuff like that. And then Doris would launch into a list of the risks of having the abortion, risks to the patient's health and mental well-being. If the listener still hadn't caught on to the ruse, Doris went for the jugular.

"And Barb, can you please tell us what you'd like us to do with the body?"

Silence.

"Barb?" Sometimes they got angry at this point. Doris would continue—calmly, clinically. "Well, there is a baby in there, Barb. We've got to do something with it. What do you want us to do? Flush it, or into the incinerator, or …?"

Click. Yes, Doris was a player. But then again, she had a life. Young children. Devoted husband. She could not be a warrior, could not pay the full price. Doris knew it, too, and felt guilt about it—guilt, and fear that one day she'd be called on the carpet by the Lord for her half measures.

Jim Kopp and Doris sat in front of the TV like old friends, although that was not quite true. Not old friends, but rather acquaintances who shared a passion for the cause. Jim would also chat with her husband, Pat, a Vietnam veteran, a former Marine, wounded in action. Jim respected that greatly. Jim and Doris watched rented movies. He enjoyed classics like *Gone With the Wind*, *Wuthering Heights*. Had the occasional beer, a Stroh's perhaps. He was a "temperate" drinker, as he put it. To Doris, Jim was a prayerful, spiritual man, someone with no personal effects, and seemingly no passion beyond his faith in God and the cause. It made him more endearing. Doris mentioned his girlfriend. Well, she wasn't really a girlfriend, but Jim did profess to being in love, grinning in that shy way of his. Jim led a monastic life in many ways, owning few clothes and washing them by hand, embracing celibacy, or at least monogamy. But he wanted to get married some day, have kids.

"C'mon, Jim, what's her name, anyway?" asked Doris.

Jim kept smiling. Don't go there. Pro-life women, thought Jim with a grin, they can't keep quiet. Give them a chance, they'll tell all. Doris enjoyed chatting with him. He was so well read, could talk about anything, with anyone. You started talking, and before you knew it, three hours had passed in the blink of an eye. She enjoyed feeling as though she was exploring philosophy and politics with him. She felt a connection and a respect for his convictions and quiet intelligence. But Jim Kopp wasn't connecting, not in the same way as Doris. He adjusted his conversation to whoever he was with, playing whatever role was necessary, trying to make his audience feel good about their relationship. He was always playing.

Late in the evening Jim would rise from his chair and go outside for a long slow walk, gathering his thoughts, a solitary thin figure disappearing into the gloom. Was there anyone with whom Jim could truly connect, who could appreciate his intellect and reciprocate—and who could even look into the bloody abyss and not blink like the others? That was not the case with Doris Grady, sweet as she was, and as committed, on a certain level, as she was to the cause, the mission. No, Jim could not lower the mask for her.

For a time Jim lived in Binghamton, New York, where the headquarters of Operation Rescue was located, to do further work for Randall Terry. Jim was also affiliated with a militant group called The Lambs of Christ. But he didn't last long with any one group. God love all pro-lifers, but did any of them feel the cause in the pit of their soul like he did? Ultimately, Terry, the public face of the movement for years, would go mainstream, even run for Congress, foreswear violence in the fight. He proudly proclaimed that he led the "largest civil disobedience movement in American history ... Operation Rescue's peaceful sit-ins resulted in over 70,000 arrests."

Years later, Terry would say he remembered little about James Charles Kopp, other than he had been on his staff, and that he was devout. No, Operation Rescue did not suit Jim's needs. Terry and the rescuers were, thank the Lord, engaged in the same cause. But there wasn't extra room in Jim Kopp's personal spiritual foxhole. He was disappearing, turning within himself, and to God, for direction. Before long, Randall Terry heard little of Kopp, and then not at all.

* * *

Amherst, N.Y.
Hanukkah, December 1988

The pro-life activists set up in front of Bart Slepian's home in Amherst. Usually they wielded signs outside the clinic called Womenservices, where he worked in Buffalo. As an OB, he delivered babies and performed abortions at the clinic. But now they had taken the fight right in front of his home. They sang and jeered, called him a pig, a baby killer. Inside the house, Bart, his wife Lynne, and his young sons, Andrew, who was about five, Brian, three, were opening presents. Bart couldn't take it anymore. He grabbed a baseball bat and came out and smashed the window of a protester's van. He was charged by police. He spoke to his old friend Rick on the phone later. Rick knew it would come to this, the harassment would escalate. They had talked about it before. It could get worse. Bart had to keep his cool.

"A baseball bat, Bart?" Rick said.

"This guy was on my property."

"Bart, I totally understand why you did it. I don't really blame you, but still, it's stupid. You are the guy who got charged."

"He was scaring my kids. It's not going to happen."

"Couldn't you have found a little less dramatic way of dealing with it?"

"It's not like I spent a lot of time thinking about it. It's the only way I know how."

The campaign against him reached bizarre proportions. Early one morning before dawn a white car with its lights off rolled down the Slepians' street. Someone got out of the car, stole their garbage, and sped away. They were looking for billing records, phone numbers of women considering having an abortion. It turned out the trash thief in this case had been arrested four times for anti-abortion activities. He did it another morning. And another. Bart called the police, but he didn't leave it at that. He waited inside the door one morning. At 6:15 a.m., he saw the car pull up. He sprinted towards it and got the licence number as it squealed away.

He talked to the media about it. "It's kind of bizarre," he said. "They must be looking for anything they can use against me. Hopefully they got the bag full of dirty diapers."

* * *

In July 1988, the Democratic Party held its convention in Atlanta. Pro-life activists showed up to grab a share of the media attention. There were more than 350 people arrested and many spent several weeks in jail. Pro-lifers dubbed it "the siege of Atlanta." Jim Kopp was among those arrested, for criminal trespassing at the Atlanta Surgi-Center. When police asked him his name, Jim, like others being arrested, repeatedly replied: "Baby Doe."

While in jail, activists from around the country networked, gave themselves nicknames. Supporters of the Atlanta protests compared them to the civil rights movement in the 1960s, since pro-lifers believed they were spending time in the same jail where Martin Luther King was once held. It was here that the early pages of the Army of God Manual were drafted. The manual would become a bible for the radical fringe of the movement. It was never clear who authored the document, which underwent revisions after Atlanta. Some of the passages sounded like Jim's voice: "Once an activist is married, and especially after having children, the constraints of parenthood are profound. Compassion for one's own brood will curtail the level of covert activity—and a lot of other activity, as well!"

The manual offered advice on wreaking violence on clinics, blockading, acid attacks, arson, bomb making. When the siege ended, most protesters returned to their homes, and lives. Jim? The cause was his life, and he had no home. His lists of aliases continued to grow, a tactical move, but also, perhaps, a sign that his identity had ceased to rest on firm ground even in his own mind. He was a chameleon. He was John Doe, James Charles Copp, John Kapp, Clyde Swenson, Clyde Swanson, Jack Cotty, Jack Crotty, John Kopp, Jacob Koch, Charles Cooper, John Capp, Jim Cobb, James Cobb, Samuel E. Weinstein, Jacob I. Croninger, Enoch A. Guettler, Jonathan H. Henderson, Samuel E. Blanton, Soloman E. Aranburg, Aaron A. Bernstein, Eli A. Hochenleit, Dwight Hanson, K. Jawes Gavin, P. Anastation, and B. James Milton.

* * *

On January 28, 1989, Jim was arrested at a protest in Woodbridge, New Jersey. Later that year, he attempted to realize the destiny he had long pondered, converting to Catholicism. He turned to a priest, who was based at a reputable university, to oversee the process. But first Jim had some views he wanted to air with the priest. He wanted to talk about the notion of unjust laws in the eyes of God, and what the committed Catholic should do when an unjust law is forced upon the people. The priest listened and was concerned. He already knew that Jim Kopp had been rejected for conversion by another priest, due to his views on fighting abortion. This man, Kopp, was sounding like someone who wanted to be an avenger for the pro-life cause, perhaps use extreme violence towards that end.

"Jim," said the priest, "the Catholic Church does not tolerate, nor does it condone, in any way, shape or form, deadly violence."

Of course not. Jim knew that was the official position. The priest was obligated to tell him that. Jim understood perfectly. There was a concept that he thought about often. He called it "*Romanita.*" To him it meant a way of talking to another person strategically, using ambiguity, even deception, to further a just cause. A way to tell someone what they need to hear, for their own good, and for the good of the unborn. Jim used it himself all the time.

Yes, yes, *certainly*, the Catholic Church does not condone violence, ever. *Romanita*. And the U.S. government has a law forbidding foreign assassinations. There is the official position, and the practical necessities that flow beneath it. International law says you don't injure or kill civilians in wartime, either. *Right*. Jim Kopp's father had seen, firsthand, how that precept was applied when he was based in Hiroshima for the occupation after the atomic bombs were dropped. "Thou shalt not kill?" An official position of God, if you will, but if you could roll back history, and give a good Christian the opportunity to shoot and kill Hitler, and thus prevent the Holocaust, that Christian would in fact have been honoring the spirit of the Sixth Commandment by pulling the trigger—he would be saving lives, preventing murder. But no, *of course*, a Christian must never hurt, or kill, another person.

Romanita. The priest supervised and oversaw James Charles Kopp's conversion. He was now a Roman Catholic. Today, the priest asks that his name not be made public.

* * *

Rome, Italy
September 19, 1989

"Hail Mary, full of grace ..." The group of pro-lifers sat outside the hospital singing the rosary as Italian police looked on. Jim Kopp knew the Latin version. *"Ave Maria, gratia plena ..."* It was a big crowd, activists from 19 countries had made the trip. There was a group from Canada, including two men from British Columbia named Maurice Lewis and Barrie Norman. Barrie was 41 years old, from Vancouver. He noticed that Jimmy Kopp was there. The Dog! The next day the Italian papers ran with the news: "American anti-abortionist commandos invaded San Camillo Hospital with the precision of a military operation." Commandos! Really? It hadn't gone down quite like that, Barrie Norman reflected, nobody swung down on ropes and took machine guns to anybody. The Italians had quite a flair for embellishment!

The protesters had arrived at six in the morning. San Camillo was the closest abortion-performing hospital to the Vatican, so why not start there? Jim, Barrie and several others walked into the clinic without incident. A nurse came by. One of the protesters spoke Italian. *"Dove effettuate gli aborti?"* (Where do you do the abortions?) The nurse pointed down the hall. Wonderful, thought Barrie. The rescuers said thank you very much. They went down the hall. A few of them sat in the killing room, others in the hallway. Not exactly the Green Berets swinging into action, eh?

Four or five hours passed. The abortions were put on hold. There were four priests among the rescuers. As everyone waited for the police to be given authority to act, one of the priests went for pizza. Barrie loved telling the tale: Father gets back, everyone grabs a slice, and that included a few of the police officers! Great stuff. The police started making arrests but refused to arrest the priests, simply taking them outside and letting them go, much to the priests' disappointment. The others were taken to the local police station.

Later in the European pro-life tour, there was a big rescue in Manchester, England. Barrie, Jim and the rest ended up in old Strangways Prison, along with Maurice Lewis and others. Barrie was in cell 20, Jim was across the hall. The protests in Europe and the Philippines were a bonding experience, and jail was where some of the most interesting conversations took place. They sat in their cells, chatted back and forth with each other, prayed. Barrie thought Jimmy Kopp had a dry sense of humor.

There were a couple of times the idea came up. Nothing serious, mind you. Someone would start it, playing a bit, a little black humor. "You could always just shoot the bloody abortionists," someone would say, maybe even one of the inmates with no allegiance to the rescuers at all. Barrie laughed. So did everyone else. Most everyone. Barrie couldn't really tell, actually. Couldn't see everyone in their cells. "You can't just go around killing people," Barrie said. "God's not going to like that a whole heck of a lot. It's against the Sixth Commandment. Although there's nothing in there that says you can't wound them." Joking—Barrie was joking. Much later, Barrie Norman wondered if perhaps The Dog had taken the joke somewhat differently than the others.

CHAPTER 7—LORETTA

Jim Kopp's string of arrests continued into the new year. January 6, 1990, in Charleston, West Virginia. January 19, in Toledo. Two days after that, in Pittsburgh. And then he was on the move again, in New Jersey. The phone rang at the home of James Gannon, in Whiting, New Jersey.

"Jay?"

"Hey, Jim, how are you?" replied James Gannon jovially. "And where are you?"

"Just a couple hours away. Mind if I come by?"

"Of course not."

"Sure?"

"Jim, you know the door is always open, and so is my heart—and for your sake, so is the fridge!"

James Gannon hung up the phone. That was the way he spoke, the kindest, sweetest elderly man you could imagine. If you were nice and polite to Jim Gannon, he would instantly reciprocate, embrace you like a son or daughter. He was in his seventies, white hair, blue eyes, soft hands and a face that was so fair it seemed pink. He enjoyed wearing his University of Michigan ball cap, the navy one with the yellow "M" on the front. "M" for the Virgin Mary, he liked to joke. He was a devout Catholic, lived in the Crestwood Village retirement community.

The previous year, in 1989, Gannon had still just been curious about the workings of Operation Rescue and the pro-life movement. A friend told him there was a rescue about to take place nearby. He told Gannon: you'll see a yellow ribbon around the clinic. Stay outside of the line, and you won't be arrested. Go inside, you'll be arrested. Gannon had just retired. He was looking for a new focus in his life and, perhaps, new friends. Raised on Staten Island, he worked in administration for an engineering firm for 40 years, the last few on the 89th floor of the World Trade Center. His beloved wife had been dead more than 20 years.

Gannon showed up at the rescue. Should he take part, or not? He saw that his friends stood inside the ribbon. He figured that's where he belonged, too. He joined them. Got arrested. His new life was under way. Gannon took part in 14 rescues, went to jail each time. They were exciting days. The night before, they'd all gather at an agreed location, plan, pray. Some of them slept on the floor. No food or drink in the morning, so they could stay locked down at a clinic for as long as possible without needing to use a bathroom. Great memories, great people, he reflected.

It was at a rescue later that year, in West Hartford, where he met Jim Kopp. He would never tell Gannon where he had been or where he was going. But Gannon's door was always open. Eventually Jim had his mail forwarded to Gannon's box. When he stayed at the house the two of them went to mass at St. Elizabeth Church every day at 8 a.m., protested at the abortion center on Wednesdays and Saturdays. Gannon didn't dress fancy for church, but Jim, he stood out. Just wore whatever was on his back. They could all tell he was a visitor. Gannon joined the Lambs of Christ pro-life group. Jim called his elderly friend "Jay" for short, an old nickname from their time in jail.

They didn't watch TV together, or talk all that much. Jim did his own thing, went for his walks in the nearby wooded area. His quiet time, he called it. Gannon thought the solitude was good for his friend. Gannon did the cooking. Not that Jim put much emphasis on food, or drink. He was always thinking. Food didn't seem to mean much to him. Ate what was put before him. He had other things on his mind. One night, when Jim was out walking, Gannon heard a knock on the door. The local police who patrolled the retirement community had seen a lanky, bearded man walking slowly by himself not far away and had picked him up.

"He says he's with you," the cop told Gannon.

"Oh yes—he's one of us," Gannon said cheerfully. Kopp's bearded face lit up with a grin.

Days later, Jim was gone, again. It was imperative he remain in the field. He lived for longer stretches in St. Albans, Vermont, with a man named Anthony Kenny and his wife, in a dusty wooden farmhouse with a view of the mountains. Vermont was the setting for a story that Jim was telling. It was an abortion mill in Burlington, Vermont. The operators of the mill were using the drained blood from aborted babies in a Black Mass satanic ritual. Jim had heard the story. Or read about it. Or maybe it surfaced from somewhere else entirely, from a red-black dimension of his mind's eye where abortion lurked as pure evil.

* * *

On March 20, 1990, he was arrested outside the Vermont Women's Health Center in Burlington. Jim was now 36. It was a big protest, 95 arrests. It was a pretty diverse crowd, including his old friend Jay Gannon, as well as young activists new to the cause, women like Jennifer Rock and Amy Boissonneault. Amy was 23, from Fairfax, Vermont. Jim had great affection for her, everyone did. But for Jim there was another—a 27-year-old woman with dark hair and pale green eyes: Loretta Claire Marra, daughter of William Marra, the Fordham professor whom Jim greatly admired. Loretta studied graduate philosophy, was intellectually charged, a spirited conver-sationalist. Jim had connected with few people, if anyone. Loretta was different.

Her father was a prominent Catholic apologist who founded

a radio program in the 1970s called "Where Catholics Meet." In 1988, William Marra ran for the U.S. presidency for the Right To Life Party, winning 20,504 votes—in the middle of the pack among several fringe candidates. Loretta's mother, Marcelle Haricot Marra, had served with the French resistance during the Second World War. The story went that in Normandy, when paratroopers landed far afield of their intended target, she helped lead them back to their destination, and saved many lives. Loretta told her friends that her mother had even received the Croix de Guerre medal from General Charles de Gaulle, and that Rue Marcelle Haricot in Paris was named after her mother. Loretta Marra had much to live up to.

Pro-lifers were mesmerized when she spoke. Loretta was five-foot-six, 130 pounds, an unremarkable appearance at first glance, but up close she drew people in, a passionate light flaring in her eyes, always speaking from a place deep in her soul. James Gannon was transfixed, and Jim Kopp as well. Loretta and Jim had an instant rapport, so much in common. Gannon watched the two of them interact, banter, jumping from politics and history to pop culture. It was as though Loretta could hum the first few notes to a song and Jim could pick it right up and continue, he reflected.

In January 1991, Jim and Loretta were arrested together at a protest outside a clinic in Levittown, Long Island. He had invented a new steel, donut-shaped locking device. They used it to lock their feet together to block the door of the clinic. Saving babies, connecting in body and soul. Police needed power tools to separate them.

* * *

Back out west, Chuck Kopp had retired at 69. He had been living with his second wife, Lynn, in San Rafael, not far from where Jim's mother, Nancy, still lived in the family house in Marin County. Mid-life and beyond had been a rocky road for Chuck. He nearly lost his job, had problems with drinking, all of it surely exacerbated by the stress created by his affair with Lynn and the divorce from

Nancy. He had a stroke. Friends couldn't believe how much he had changed. Chuck, the ex-Marine, who used to be so sharp, seemed gone. One day Jim returned home to visit his father at the hospital, and sat with Lynn in the cafeteria. Jim had not spoken to her for a couple of years. He never warmed to her.

"That last time we talked you said you weren't going to see him any more," Jim said.

"That's how I felt at the time," Lynn told him. "But it reached the point of no return." Jim put his head in his hands, elbows on the table, staring at her, incredulous, and then glowered at her, saying nothing.

Chuck slowly bounced back from the stroke. He kicked his drinking habit. Things were improving, but there remained the problem with his youngest son, and his antics in the anti-abortion movement. Lynn told the story how one night, she and Chuck were out for dinner with Jim's twin brother, Walt, and Chuck's brother, James, from Los Angeles.

"So did you see Jim on TV last night?" asked Walt. The TV news had carried a story about a violent protest at a clinic in the Bay Area. The footage showed Jim arrested after chaining himself to an examining table.

Chuck's lips narrowed. "Damn fool," he said.

Was it possible that on some level, while shaking his head at his son's behavior, Chuck appreciated Jim's passion? If that sentiment did exist, Chuck did not express it to anyone. Jim believed he knew. He looked into his dad's eyes on the occasions when they were together and was certain he saw pride.

In 1991, Chuck picked up and moved with Lynn to her home state of Texas. In September 1992, Lynn persuaded him to go on an Alaskan cruise. Their first port was Juneau. Chuck had a heart attack on board. Just over a week later, he suffered another heart attack, and died at 2:30 a.m. on September 26.

The funeral was held at Trinity Baptist Church in Sherman, Texas. Walter Kopp gave the eulogy, spoke of his dad's military service and legal career. Jim, who was listed as "James C. Kopp of New York City" in the official obituary, was at the service. Outside, at the burial at West Hill Cemetery, Lynn Kopp arranged for the release of colorful balloons. She thought it was a nice touch, there were grandkids there who had never been at a funeral before. Lynn told the story later that Jim turned away, as though angry, refusing to look at the balloons. Maybe he felt it was sacrilegious, she thought. Despite his longtime antipathy towards her, Jim stayed at Lynn's house for ten days. She urged him to start fresh.

"You should do something with your life," she said.

"But I am. And Dad was proud of me," Jim said.

"No, he was distressed by what you were doing."

Jim did not, ever, put stock in Lynn's words. She had broken up his parents' marriage, hurt his mother, and his father. He also did not care for Lynn's recollection of events years later, when she was sought after by journalists for opinions on Jim and the Kopp family. Lynn told stories of how, among other things, Chuck Kopp hit his kids. Lynn claimed she saw a letter that Marty had written about Chuck, recalling a blow she took to her back when she was a girl, saying she had never forgiven him. Hanging out the family's dirty laundry, true or not, only deepened the anger for Lynn that Jim already felt to his core.

* * *

Gyn Womenservices Clinic
Buffalo, N.Y.
September 28, 1991

"Slepian! You pig!"

Pro-life protesters blocked the clinic's driveway off Main Street as Bart Slepian tried to come to work. A man named Paul Schenck stepped in front of the car, lay down on the pavement. Bart and others at the clinic filed charges. Six of the protesters were ordered to pay more than $100,000 in legal fees incurred by Bart and other doctors and clinic workers. The protesters had been, wrote a federal judge, in contempt of a previous court ruling governing the nature of the protests. U.S. District judge Richard J. Arcara ordered that key Buffalo-area pro-life leaders stay at least 100 yards away from any health clinic.

Bart Slepian did not shrink into the background, he did not have it in him. He gave a speech to health care officials called "It's Not Over Yet: The Rising Tide of Anti-Choice Violence and What You Can Do About It." Bart was a physician, he had no intention of becoming a pro-choice activist. But, intentionally or not, he had become a visible personality in the pro-choice camp.

At the end of the year, in December, for the first time a doctor who provided abortions was shot. Dr. Douglas Karpen was wounded in a parking garage in Houston. Two weeks before that attack, two clinic staffers in Springfield, Missouri, had been wounded by a man wearing a ski mask and wielding a sawed-off shotgun. The shooter in both incidents was never caught.

Fifteen months later marked the first time a physician who provided abortion services was murdered. It happened on March 10, 1993, outside a Pensacola, Florida, clinic. Dr. David Gunn was shot three times in the back and killed by a man named Michael Griffin. Most pro-lifers decried the violence. One man, a Presbyterian minister named Paul Hill, went on the Donahue talk show and defended the shooting, comparing it to killing a Nazi concentration camp doctor. Two weeks after the shooting, Massachusetts senator Ted Kennedy introduced a bill to enforce protection of abortion clinics.

On August 19, in Wichita, Kansas, a 38-year-old woman named Rachelle "Shelley" Shannon walked up to Dr. George Tiller—a physician reviled by pro-lifers as "killer Tiller"—and shot him outside his office. The .25-caliber handgun she fired was never recovered. Shannon was arrested when returning her rental car. Investigators found the Army of God handbook buried in her backyard. Federal agents hooked her up to a lie detector and asked her about the manual.

"Who is The Mad Gluer?"

"I don't know."

"Who is The Mad Gluer?"

"I don't know."

"Who is Atomic Dog?"

"I don't know. His first name is Steve."

"Is Reverend Michael Bray teaching people how to blow up clinics?"

"I don't know."

Shannon failed the polygraph test and was later convicted of attempted murder and sentenced to 11 years in prison.

The day before the Tiller shooting, meanwhile, Jim Kopp was arrested in San Jose for trespassing and damaging property, then went north to be with old friends, spent some time in Delaware with his sister, Anne. He would sometimes drop in like that, usually in desperate need of a shower, with just the clothes on his back. On occasion he took Anne's son, Jeff, to a local shooting range for target practice. "I'm thinking about writing a book about my experiences in pro-life," Jim told Anne.

On February 22, 1994, Nancy Kopp, at 72, died from cancer, the same disease that had claimed Jim's sisters Mary and Marty at a young age. Jim had always revered his mother. He compared her capacity for love and healing others to that of Mother Teresa. Her death severed whatever emotional ties that remained for Jim with his boyhood home in the Bay Area. He helped clean out the family home in Marin, but kept little for himself. One of the others (probably Walt, he figured) took the photo of Chuck Kopp with Governor Ronald Reagan. Nancy was buried in Marin Memorial Gardens, in Novato, north of San Francisco, where one of the churches she attended was located. A beautiful spot, the flat stone that covered Nancy's grave lay not far from the markers for Mary and Nancy's mother.

The gravestone for Jim Kopp's mother, Nancy.

The day before Nancy Kopp died, the trial of doctor-killer Michael Griffin began in Pensacola. Pro-lifers demonstrated on a street corner near the courthouse. Among them was Paul Hill, an apologist for Griffin, struggling to keep aloft his sign which read: "Execute Abortionists." Beside him stood Michael Bray, whose profile in the radical pro-life fringe continued to grow. An activist walked up to Hill and chastised him for the violent message on the sign. Hill was "spewing false teaching."

Bray chided Hill's detractor. "So why aren't you out blocking doors?" he said.

Paul Hill drafted and circulated a document pledging support for Griffin and the philosophy of justifiable homicide against abortion providers. It was called the Defensive Action Statement: "We, the undersigned, declare the justice of taking all Godly action necessary to defend innocent human life including the use of force. We proclaim that whatever force is legitimate to defend the life of a born child is legitimate to defend the life of an unborn child."

The list of 31 signatures included Bray and his wife, several other clergy and evangelists, a lawyer, a priest who was at the time in prison. The name of James Charles Kopp did not appear on the petition. *Romanita.*

* * *

The White House
Washington, D.C.
May 26, 1994

President Bill Clinton took his seat at the long table in the Roosevelt Room. Media and politicians gathered for the announcement that he had signed a bill into law.

"I'd like to acknowledge the presence here today of David and Wendy Gunn, the children of Dr. David Gunn, from Florida."

He had taken office 16 months earlier, the first pro-choice president since Jimmy Carter, although, as with many things, Bill Clinton took a "nuanced" position on the issue. Abortion, he said, should be "safe, legal and rare."

The new bill was called the Freedom of Access to Clinic Entrances Act, and was intended to bring federal law enforcement into play to stop the "rescues" and intimidation at clinics where women obtained abortion services.

Two months later, on Friday morning, July 22, Paul Hill joined protesters in front of the Pensacola Ladies Center, as he usually did. No rescuing anymore, Clinton had made the stakes too high for most pro-lifers, effectively killing the tactic.

Hill had a lot on his mind. Michael Griffin had apologized for shooting and killing the abortionist. Hill found that morally inconsistent. If given the opportunity, he would not make the same error. There was a new doctor named John Britton replacing Gunn at the clinic.

The next day, Saturday afternoon, Paul Hill, his wife Karen, and their three young children went to the beach. He played in the surf with the kids, his thoughts swirling, heart pounding, his eyes nearly tearing up. He prayed for strength. He held each child in the deep water, over their heads, briefly, as they clung to him. "Here, Lord," he thought. "I offer you my children, as Abraham offered you his son."

His inaction to date gnawed at him. Here he had defended use of force on TV, but never taken action himself. On Wednesday he bought a 12-gauge Mosberg pump-action shotgun from Mike's Gun Shop. The firearm was called The Defender, used for close-range shooting. At another gun shop, Hill bought 12-gauge, 2¾-inch shells containing buckshot. Later that day he signed in at a shooting range and practiced, and returned the next day as well.

On Friday, Hill planted white crosses in the grass just outside the Ladies Center clinic. He was ordered by police to pull them out. He obeyed. At 7:20 a.m. a Nissan pickup carrying Dr. Britton and a security guard pulled up. Paul Hill pulled out The Defender, which had been hidden in a rolled-up pro-life sign he was carrying. Aim, fire. Reload. Aim, fire. In seconds he pumped out seven shells, spraying the truck with 90 buckshot pellets, shattering windows, killing the doctor and security guard. Then he set the shotgun down on the ground, walked over to the policemen at the scene who were running toward him.

"One thing's for sure," Hill said aloud as he was cuffed. "No babies will be killed here today."

Radical pro-lifers who supported any means to stop abortion admired Hill for taking action. But Paul—Lord keep and nurture his soul—got caught, didn't he? Just like Griffin. The shootings had sent a chill through the abortion industry, but were clumsy, executed in broad daylight. No chance the pro-lifer could get away. Neither Hill nor Griffin had been a soldier. The soldier trains and plans in order to fight, escape, and engage the enemy another day. It would take someone with a razor-sharp mind, a tactician, someone smarter than the police and the FBI, with a military mind-set and a secret agent's discretion, to operate ruthlessly yet in the shadows, to take the battle to a new level.

CHAPTER 8—REMEMBRANCE DAY

The most visible and violent fronts in the abortion war were in the United States. Across the border in Canada, doctors were not being shot. The most serious act of anti-abortion violence in the country had been the 1992 firebombing of the Morgentaler clinic in Toronto. To the extent the pro-life fringe existed in Canada, Vancouver, British Columbia, was the most fertile ground for it. The roots of that lay in peculiarities of the "Left Coast" political culture. It was a province where politics was a contact sport, passions running high, as though those arriving from back east took one whiff of the cedar in the air and suddenly became high on it. This extreme political climate gave the province a hardcore religious right that was a Canadian anomaly.

Gynecologists and obstetricians generally are not high-profile physicians. But in Vancouver, Dr. Gary Romalis was becoming known, at least in some circles. He provided abortion services as part of his practice, and had been quoted in the press speaking on medical issues related to abortion. To a few pro-life activists in B.C. who looked out for such things—such as Betty Green, known as the godmother of all things pro-life in the province—an article in a scholarly journal was proof that Dr. Romalis was a busy terminator of preborn babies:

"Abortion Experience At The Vancouver General Hospital"
By Garson Romalis, MD, FRCSC
Journal of the Society of Obstetricians and Gynecologists of Canada

The article noted that Vancouver General Hospital performed about 5,000 abortions a year. Of those, 89 percent were at 13 weeks or less. But the remaining 11 percent was the key to pro-lifers—550 abortions were performed in the second trimester. Bottom line to the activists was that Dr. Romalis was doing late-term abortions.

The pro-life movement flowered in B.C. but so too did the pro-choice response, which came back just as hard, working with police, taking videotapes of demonstrations. One of the regulars seen on those videos was a man named Gordon Watson. Gord had worked at a sawmill at one time. His father had fought in Korea as a Provost captain, his grandfather had been gassed at Ypres in the First World War. And Gord Watson?

"A full-tilt Bible-thumper," he said. "That's me. I'm it."

He was there on the street preaching the gospel of life. Mainstream pro-life types didn't do that. Gord felt they were happy just to sit around and talk about it over coffee.

He used to tag along with his father to political meetings. Dad was a bit of a hell-raiser on that front, enjoyed the battle. Gord would go further than that—he would be nastier.

It's the B.C. election of 1991 and there's Gord Watson on TV, tearing a strip off a candidate. Someone lunges at him, a full-out brawl begins, and Gord manages to get the mike, his shirt torn, yet appearing collected as can be—this is great stuff—and he politely asks, "Can I address the chair, please?" The TV journalists there take to him like moths to a flame, cameras rolling, and: "Abortion is murder, and I think British Columbians deserve the right to have a referendum on it."

The pro-lifers loved it, this 42-year-old firecracker who stood up and said what they all believed, fearless.

"Betty," he later said to veteran pro-lifer Betty Green, "I'll make you look like sweetness and light."

Others in the movement couldn't quite figure him out. He ended up in and out of jail, alternately the darling and pariah of the movement, constantly writing letters, getting in a war with a *Vancouver Sun* reporter whom he called an "abortion promoter." Once, Gord Watson went south to attend a pro-life conference in San Antonio, a big event. Joe Scheidler, the Chicago pro-life leader, put it on. Great guy, thought Gord. At one of the big sessions, a fellow stood up and spoke about pro-lifers being condemned for violent acts. "We are moderates, the speaker insisted. We don't lynch abortionists, we don't blow up abortion mills." Pause. Grin. "Not that we have any moral problem with that!"

Gord thought about it. If you have a belief, don't you have to back it up? What is the line between belief and action? He could feel the tension between pro-life camps on the issue. One night he was pulled aside and asked to attend a private meeting at a motel off the freeway. Why not? The motel had its own steakhouse. My kinda place, he said to himself.

He went to the assigned room. A man asked him questions. How long you been active? Where you from? Family? Gord told him about his dad's service in Korea.

"You know anything about firearms?"

Gord looked at his interrogator, puzzled. Bit of an odd question, wasn't it?

"Ever had any sort of military training?" His mind raced. This guy's assessing whether I'll take up arms for the movement, he thought. He reflected later that it was probably fifty-fifty that he was being assessed as either someone they hoped would shoot, or feared would shoot.

Gord wasn't sure where he stood on the violence option. The moral logic was unavoidable: Hey, you kill babies, you set yourself up for bad things to happen to you. But could he bring himself to hurt a doctor, attack him, shoot him, even? He wasn't against it in principle, but no. He was a loose cannon, but not stupid. He did not want to go to prison for good. The interview spooked Gordon Watson. He stopped going to the States after that.

* * *

In the summer of 1994 a man stopped at a post office-box in Maryland. He'd been living in a trailer in Delaware of late, but it was a short drive across the state line. He opened the box he had obtained under the name "Kevin James Gavin," date of birth June 8, 1951. The papers had finally arrived, from the sportsman club in Maryland. A membership application. The club had a shooting range. The man wrote on the form that he wished to join the club in order to use the range for "personal practice." The man's real name was James Charles Kopp.

On August 2, Jim Kopp turned 40. His parents were dead. The rescue movement was finished. He had no possessions, little money. He was a legend in the movement, Atomic Dog had pro-life friends across the country—but few connections of any depth. The one person Jim respected above all others was Loretta Marra. He would never talk about it with anyone, but those who knew him, and saw the two of them together, knew that Jim loved her. They had been through so much, arrested together far and wide, including in Italy ("Eleven Rescuers Blitz Abortuary in Bologna," a headline had screamed in *Life Advocate* magazine.) They connected on many levels—except one. Loretta had a boyfriend, and it wasn't Jim.

It was Dennis Malvasi. In the spring of 1994, Loretta turned 31, Malvasi was 44. Loretta married him in a ceremony performed by a Catholic priest. They did not register the marriage with the state. One of the conditions of Malvasi's parole was that he not associate with pro-life activists, and Loretta was in the hardcore of the movement. In choosing Dennis, she had married a man with a fiercer reputation within the radical fringe than Jim's, a former Marine who bombed abortion clinics.

On October 17, 1994, just before 10 p.m., an old tan-colored Datsun bearing the license plate 330JLL crossed the American-Canadian border at the Peace Arch crossing at Blaine, Washington, into from British Columbia. The car was legally registered to Lorretta Marra.

* * *

Vancouver, B.C.
Monday, November 7, 1994

Early morning, cold and damp, raining, like just about every November day in Vancouver. Phone ringing at the house on West 46th Avenue.

"Hello?"

Silence.

Sheila had picked up the phone. She hung up. A short time passed. Breakfast time. It rang again. Again the caller hung up. And shortly after that, Sheila's husband, Dr. Gary Romalis, finished his breakfast and went to work. He had a serious, reserved demeanor, spoke in a deliberate, scholarly manner. He lived with Sheila and their daughter, Lisa, in a residential area, a ten-minute drive in good traffic across the Granville Street bridge to downtown Vancouver. The house was Tudor style but not nearly as palatial as some of the newer ones on the street.

Dr. Garson Romalis was one of about 25 physicians in the Vancouver area who performed abortions, although few of them let that be known. He had been a second-year medical student at the University of British Columbia in 1960 when he was asked to conduct a pathological study on a woman who had died after inducing an abortion on herself with a piece of elm bark. He learned that the bark was meant to expand upon entry and encourage infection that would abort the fetus. A postmortem revealed overwhelming sepsis—widespread infection—causing multiple abscesses in the patient's brain, lungs, liver and abdominal cavity. He never forgot her, nor did he forget his experiences on the front line in the mid-sixties, when he served his obstetrics/gynecology residency at Cook County Hospital in Chicago. Each day, he would recall in presentations and an interview with the *Canadian Medical Association Journal* years later, there were patients admitted with infections from self-performed abortion.

Chicago became legendary in pro-choice circles in the years before *Roe* v. *Wade* made abortion legal. It was the home of "The Jane Collective," or simply "Jane," an underground abortion service. Women were quietly referred to Jane nurses by police, social workers, clergy and hospital staff. Operating out of apartments in the city, Jane provided abortions for an estimated 11,000 women. When Dr. Romalis returned to Vancouver in the 1970s, abortions became a part of his practice—even though the operation still bore a stigma to many people, even among his colleagues. Some would leave the doctor's lounge when he entered. Ultimately, while Romalis said he did not plan to be a crusader on the issue, and did not intend to become a poster boy of the pro-choice movement, that's what he became. Pro-life protesters scattered nails on his driveway, picketed his house, passed flyers to his neighbors with the message "Do you know who your neighbor is?"

The night of Monday, November 7, it had rained steadily, and continued off and on overnight. Just past 6:30 a.m. Tuesday morning, Dr, Romalis rose. By 7 a.m. he was downstairs in his bathrobe in the kitchen making breakfast, alone. As he did every morning, he walked over to the counter, placed bread in the toaster, and sat at the table. He opened some mail. Quiet. Waiting for the toast to pop. He leaned forward, just slightly, perhaps to reach for something or to look more closely at a letter, or for no reason at all.

An explosion, glass breaking. The kitchen chair jerked out from underneath him as the bullet tore through the back of it. The round had missed him. He jumped to his feet, and then he felt a blow to his leg, his thigh, the impact of the second shot like a cannonball, his body falling, crashing to the floor, facedown. 7:10 a.m. The time on his watch glared at him as he lay there, the numbers burning into his memory. He looked down at his left leg. He saw a hole the size of a grapefruit, and a geyser of blood as thick as his finger pouring out. I am—going to die, he thought. Blood everywhere, coating the floor. Where did the shot come from? He didn't know. He felt at his left leg, the wound. "I've been shot, bleeding heavily call 911!" he shouted. He knew there wasn't much time. His thighbone was shattered, a major artery, the femoral artery severed. Stop the blood flow, or die, he would bleed out in minutes. "Stay upstairs!" he shouted to his wife and daughter. The shooter might come into the house to finish him off. The shooter was an abortion sniper, he had felt it instantly. He reached for his bathrobe belt, yanked it out, began tying it tight around the thigh above the gushing wound. He dragged himself across the floor to get out of the room, blood painting the tiles. His daughter called 911. "Someone's shot at my house and my dad. Can you please come?"

"What?" asked the operator.

"I think someone's been shot in my house!" the young woman repeated.

"Possible shot fired," relayed a dispatcher. "Victim just yelled that he's been shot."

Dr. Romalis felt his consciousness fading, his tight grip on the tourniquet weakening. Outside the house, the shooter was on the move. He had been there in a laneway behind West 46th Street, a narrow, hidden roadway where the garbage was collected. The rain started falling again. The wind picked up. Two hours and 45 minutes after the shooting, 72 kilometers from Vancouver, just before 10 p.m., the tan Datsun, license plate 330JLL, crossed back into the United States at the Peace Arch Crossing.

* * *

The ambulance and police reached the Romalis house within five minutes. The doctor was placed on the stretcher, unconscious, his skin gray. The attendants were doing all they could to keep him alive. A nine-hour operation followed. Eight units of blood. The lead story on local TV news that night: gynecologist Dr. Garson Romalis in critical condition, unconscious, images of his daughter, Lisa, pacing the ER.

Local pro-choice activists and clinic workers were shocked. They had thought of the pro-lifers as noisy and pushy and obnoxious. But shooting someone? By the time the evening news rolled around, the media were already reflecting on the abortion battle:

TV Anchorwoman (*wearing a Remembrance Day poppy*): No one knows for sure what provoked the attack on Dr. Romalis, but tonight police throughout the Lower Mainland are stepping up protection for people who work in Vancouver's abortion clinics. If this shooting is related, it's the most serious act of anti-abortion violence in Canada.
(*Visual: A woman, face darkened.*)
Narrator: We can't identify her. She's afraid she and her family are in danger, too.
Woman: I've frequently said that in Canada we are safe. We have crazy people after us, but they don't carry guns.
Narrator: Today she realizes she may have been wrong.
(*Quick cut to pro-life firebrand Gord Watson's bearded face, a camcorder date on the screen reading August 3, 1994, 11:44 a.m. He's shown lecturing a woman about to enter an abortion clinic in Vancouver.*)
Watson: If you kill this baby, you will be murdering your own child … Do you believe there is a God? (*He glowers into the lens.*) Get that stupid camera out of my face. (*Picture scrambles as he shoves the camera away.*) You get out of my way, lady, or you're going to get it.
(*Cut to mainstream, nonviolent pro-lifer Will Johnston, a member of Physicians for Life.*)

Johnston: We feel revulsion at this cowardly and murderous attack on Dr. Romalis.
(*Cut back to Gord Watson.*)
Watson: This country has perpetrated violence for a generation against unborn children and that violence is now coming against the people who perpetrated it.

Police searched in the laneway behind the Romalis home, piecing together what happened. It had been dark when the shooter crept silently up the alley, past one backyard, two, three, four, five—about 110 paces to the spot. He would have seen the top quarter of the house over the fence, the upstairs windows. There was a Beware of Dog sign, but no dog. The Romalis family had just returned from a week-long vacation. The dog was still in a kennel in Langley. There were two battered silver-gray metal garbage cans in the square cubby.

The sniper had taped the lids down with silver duct tape—better stability, less noise when taking up a position. He rested the rifle on top of the cans and cleared dead leaves from inside the cubby, which was elevated off the ground a few inches. It was big enough for him to kneel inside on his right knee, left elbow steady on the lids, hand cradling the forestock of the AK rifle, his right hand and trigger finger free. He pointed through a missing panel in the fence, toward the sliding glass door of the kitchen. And waited.

It was a well-planned attack. The first bullet neatly punctured the glass of the sliding door, creating a spiders web of cracks; the second shot, the one that shattered the doctor's thigh, hit lower, splitting the glass above it in a V-shape, shards of glass flying from the impact.

The two bullets were mangled—the one from Romalis's thigh and the one that went through his chair and lodged in a closet door in the kitchen. Difficult to get a make on their type. Bullets only hold their shape in the movies. But these could still be useful in determining what kind of firearm had been used. When a round is fired, the barrel makes identifiable markings on the bullet. Those markings tie the bullet to a particular firearm. Under a microscope the bullets from the Romalis shooting seemed to have rifling marks known in ballistics terminology as "four barrel markings with a right-handed twist"—four "lands" and "grooves" with a right-hand twist to them. The marks were characteristic of an assault rifle such as an AK-47.

Police searched up and down the laneway, looking in composters and other garbage cans for clues.

"Got one."

The uniformed cop bent over a wooden enclosure. He reached into a composter several houses down and picked out the object with his gloved hand. It was a cartridge, a live round. And another. And another—20 unused cartridges in all, all of them AK-47 military hard-points. An important clue. Or was it? It didn't add up. Why would the sniper have carried so much ammunition? Surely he had no intention of showering the house with bullets? And having fired and fled, why leave the cartridges? Another question: was the sniper trying to kill? A Vancouver detective named George Kristensen was assigned to the case. He heard a theory making the rounds that the sniper was trying to wound the doctor, end a medical career but not a life. Not a chance, thought the detective. It was just his opinion, but there was no way on God's green earth you could tell where a bullet would end up after it was fired through a window like that.

CHAPTER 9—SNEAKY BASTARD

Jim Kopp spent Christmas in Delaware with his sister Anne. Jim would just show up unannounced with his dirty laundry, unshaven, looking like he'd been living in the woods for months. Then he'd be gone again.

On December 30, 1994, John Salvi, a 24-year-old drifter, sprayed two Boston-area abortion clinics with gunfire, killing two women who worked there and wounding several other people. Anne was pro-life, but never took part in protests.

"So is this what's happening to the movement?" she asked Jim about the violence.

"No-no," he said. "It's not good for the movement."

Early in the new year, Pope John Paul II released an encyclical letter, *Evangelium Vitae*. Jim always followed the Pontiff's words carefully. It was in the encyclical that he used the phrase "culture of death" to describe the combination of laws, political and social institutions that undermined the value of life. Abortion, he said, is "deliberate and direct killing … We are dealing with murder."

In the summer of 1995 Jim Kopp bought a car—although bought is probably the wrong word. He filed no income tax forms from 1994 through 1997. In 1995, his official earnings totaled less than $4,000. He worked odd jobs here and there, handyman work. He got the old beater from Loretta Marra, a green 1977 Dodge Aspen registered with the Vermont Department of Motor Vehicles under a new license plate number, BFN 595. In the fall he spent time in Vermont, lived in a farmhouse in Swanton, a town of 6,000 near St. Albans, about ten minutes from the Canadian border. He stayed with Anthony and Anne Kenny. Anthony Kenny was among the 95 anti-abortion protesters, including Kopp, arrested and charged with trespassing outside one of the two women's clinics in Burlington, Vermont, a few years earlier. Jim also spent time in Fairfax, Vermont. He had met a young woman named Jennifer Rock through the movement and for a time he lived at Rock's parents' home on Buck Hollow Road. Just passing through, he told them.

He got in the green Aspen and headed north. On the evening of November 3, near Ancaster, Ontario, he was pulled over and released by a police officer on a routine traffic stop. One week later, Ancaster physician Hugh Short was shot and wounded by a high-powered rifle fired through his den window.

* * *

Ancaster, Ontario
Friday, November 10, 1995

Hamilton Major Crime Unit detective Mike Holk squinted through the windshield into the blackness, the wipers battling a cold hard rain. Where the hell was the house on Sulphur Springs Road? For the Hamilton detectives charged with cracking the mystery of the shooting earlier that night, finding the crime scene was a chore in itself. It was an appropriate start to a case which, from the word go, would be like nothing they had ever experienced.

The 911 "shots fired" call had come in at 9:30 p.m. Dr. Short had wrapped his elbow wound and was taken to Hamilton General Hospital. Mike Holk was the senior ranking officer, 48 years old, a 24-year veteran on the force. It was an ugly night, cold and wet. He found the Short house, got out of his unmarked car and stepped into the downpour, walking towards the flashing police lights. A uniformed officer approached. The detective identified himself. "Staff Sergeant Holk," he said, and flashed his badge. "Who's in charge?"

The cop took Holk to meet John Bronson. Bronson, himself a veteran cop and detective, was the duty officer assigned to evaluate the scene before handing it off to Holk. Bronson said there had been shots from the rear of the home. Blew through the den window— window frame, actually. Two holes visible.

Hamilton Police stake out the crime scene at Dr. Hugh Short's home.

Orders were given to expand the official crime scene area, to include the front and back yards, swaths of the wooded area. About ten acres in all. They used so much yellow tape they almost ran out. All officers entering the crime scene had to record their movements to minimize contamination of any evidence. Holk stood in the driveway, rain pelting his trench coat, water streaming down his face and mustache.

It didn't take long for him to see it, the cardboard box on the upper part of the driveway.

"What do we have?" Holk asked.

It was a ski mask. Black. One of the officers covered it with the box to keep the evidence dry. Was it the sniper's? And why would he have left it there? Dropped it? In a hurry? Frightened by something? A plant, by either the shooter or another party, to confuse police? It all raced through Mike Holk's mind—all questions, no answers. Even though he was a veteran cop, the whole scene left him feeling ill at ease, his head spinning. It was all so—big. The crime scene. The questions. Who comes to a place like this, he thought, on a miserable night like tonight, waits in the shadows and takes a shot at a physician?

At the hospital, Detective Mike Campbell met with Short's wife, Katherine, her husband's blood still fresh on her clothes. Dr. Short, meanwhile, was awake when Detective Peter Abi-Rashed came to his bedside in the trauma suite. He had been treated, was in stable condition and could talk. Abi-Rashed was broad shouldered, with dark hair, olive skin, dark eyes. He was a sharp investigator who had a playfully brusque manner. He followed the book on investigating. You put the biggest umbrella possible over the investigation, consider all angles.

"Is my family all right?" asked Short.

"They're fine, Dr. Short."

It's not something a homicide detective telegraphs to a victim, but the cold fact is, the first suspect who needs to be eliminated in an attempted-murder investigation is—the victim himself. Suicide. But Abi-Rashed was satisfied, after conversations with medical staff, that Short's wound from a high-powered rifle could not have been self-inflicted. He needed to start fishing for suspects.

"Dr. Short, can you think of any reason someone would want to do this to you?"

"I can't think of any reason for the shooting," he replied.

A doctor, any doctor, can have disgruntled patients, patients who might not be entirely mentally stable. Hugh Short was an OB. Delivered babies, performed standard gynecological services. Like most doctors, he had a couple of patients who had been unhappy about something—but there was nothing to suggest they'd want to shoot him.

Dr. Short mentioned one call that was a bit different, though. About ten years earlier a man named Randy Dyer had called Short's office. Dyer had been bitter towards the doctor for a long time because his girlfriend had had an abortion against his wishes, and he was certain Short had performed the procedure and terminated his unborn son. There were days when the darker instincts inside Dyer urged him to hurt Dr. Short for what he had done.

Scott Gardner Photo

Randy Dyer

But in fact by the time Dyer actually phoned Short, in 1985, the bitterness was gone. He wanted the doctor to know he no longer felt ill will towards him. Hugh Short's receptionist had put the call through. Short picked up.

"Hello?" Dr. Short had said.

"I want to say, as a Christian man, I forgive you for taking the life of my child in 1982." A disquieting experience, but certainly no threat.

Peter Abi-Rashed met with the other detectives, then drove out to the house to take a look. He ducked under the police tape, went upstairs and saw the chair where Short had been sitting, saw the splinters on the floor from where the two rounds had punctured the wooden window frame. Camera flashes popped in the dark backyard. Ident was out there—forensic identification officers.

Detective Larry Penfold was out in the rain with his partner, Bill Cook. Time was short to gather evidence and take photos. The forecast was not good, snow on the way. It would cover the scene, transform it. The scientific ballistic work needed to be done to determine where the shots had come from, the bullet trajectory. In the critical early hours, Penfold and Cook tried to reconstruct what had happened. "Tell me a story," Penfold beseeched his surroundings.

The bullets were easy enough to find. Inside the house, Penfold and Cook had already collected the rounds that had splintered the window frame—7.62 x 39 ammunition. They examined the inside of a tool shed in the backyard. Bingo. Someone had definitely been inside, and very recently, for an extended period. Items had been moved around, space made. Whoever was here had made himself at home, prepared. Eaten some food. They found earmuffs, the type worn by shooters at gun clubs. They collected the black ski mask from the driveway. A key piece of evidence, perhaps, there might be hairs on it.

Back at the station, Penfold walked through the main doors, past the desk, and turned left into the ident department. Then a quick right, into the storage section, his shoes clicking on the gray-blue concrete floor, to the biohazard locker and the glass-doored cabinet

Scott Gardner Photo

Hamilton detective Abi-Rashed appears on TV talking about the case.

for blood samples and other materials that would need drying out. Penfold stored the bullets, and the ski mask. He closed the door, signed in the check-in time and his case ident number, locked the door, wrote his report and went home in the early dawn. A few hours' sleep, and then back to Sulphur Springs Road.

The search of the Short property intensified the morning after the shooting, Saturday, and lasted all day. Ten auxiliary officers were brought in to comb the outer perimeter, six for the inner perimeter. The day had dawned sunny and clear. The snow hadn't materialized in the night, perhaps a good omen for the case. But the temperature had dropped and snow was still forecast. Inside the house, Detectives Mike Campbell, Frank Harild and Peter Abi-Rashed gathered, standing in a circle around the island in the kitchen, bouncing theories off each other.

The house bordered the Dundas Valley Conservation Area. Abi-Rashed wondered about a stray shot—poachers, perhaps, shooting at deer. But it could have been anything. A malicious, random act of violence in which Hugh Short happened to be in the wrong place at the wrong time? You start big, then you eliminate, eliminate. Don't pursue one path and use all your resources only to hit a dead end. Campbell knew all that. But his instincts told him there was only one possibility. It sliced through all the other noise. Deer? No.

"If it was stray shots from a hunter, the guy's misfires were awfully consistent," he said. "It's abortion. I'm sure of it."

Hamilton had had its share of violent crime, but if Campbell was right, this would be a first: a shooting for a cause, a belief. So many questions. The sniper had planned meticulously, had likely cased out the scene in advance. Yet how could he be so sloppy as to leave a ski mask there? And if he was an abortion sniper, why Ancaster, of all places?

Later that day the search party found something: spent cartridges in wet grass in the backyard, not far from the house. Larry Penfold examined the location and the empty casings. Penfold's official title was forensic identification officer. Cops called him an ident officer. In the American vernacular, he was a crime scene investigator. Penfold and Cook bounced ideas off each other. How could they determine where the shot had come from? Penfold put in a call to the Centre of Forensic Sciences in Toronto. CFS had lasers that could pinpoint such things. But CFS didn't have anyone available that day. Penfold didn't want to wait. Time to break out the tackle box.

Later, in the backyard, a nearly invisible thread stretched from the second-floor window to the ground. It was fishing line. Penfold and Cook had invented their own low-tech machinery to determine the trajectory of the shots. Penfold had once worked on the Hamilton police tactical team, knew how to use power scopes. Using the scope he estimated the line of fire from the holes in the window and frame to a spot on the ground near where the casings and footprints were found. They stretched fishing line from the holes to the spot. Between the two points, taking into account the angle of probable entry of the rounds, and other calculations, Penfold and Cook established where the shot had probably come from on the grass. When CFS did show up with their laser beams and other special equipment, technicians took their measurements. Penfold's fishing expedition had come within inches of the CFS finding.

* * *

Central Station
Hamilton, Ontario
Saturday, November 11, 1995

The detectives were soon made aware of a similar case from the year before in Vancouver—the sniper attack on Dr. Garson Romalis. Romalis performed abortions, too. In spite of the similarities, the link did not seem conclusive to a few of the Hamilton cops. What did a shooting on the west coast have to do with a shooting in Ancaster? The bizarre nature of the case raised so many questions. If the sniper in both cases was the same person, what was the intent?

Murder? Detective Frank Harild thought that, in hitting Short's arm, the sniper had simply missed. He had wanted to put a hole through Short that would kill. The sniper's lousy aim saved the doctor's life.

"It's not a hard shot, hitting centre mass from 123 feet," he said. "I mean, you can just about throw a baseball with accuracy from that distance." Moreover, the sniper had put one bullet in the window frame. "If you're such a great shot, so great that you are specifically intending to wound the doctor, trying to be that particular, wouldn't you at least hit the windowpane? But the shot hits the frame."

On the other hand, if anti-abortion was the motive, clearly the sniper did not have the mind-set of a typical criminal. Someone with a grandiose, ideologically driven mission could have all kinds of notions in his head. Also, military-style firearms like those used in the two attacks are designed to propel rounds through metal, wood, without losing much accuracy. The path of the bullet is unlikely to change dramatically. So maybe he had intended to hit the doctors in an extremity. It was an interesting debate. But the task at hand was not proving intent, it was building a list of suspects and finding the shooter.

Mike Campbell explored the abortion angle. There were no previous examples of anti-abortion violence in Hamilton. The city did have a vigorous pro-life movement, however, and that fact was common knowledge to pro-lifers in other parts of Canada. Hamilton typically had big turnouts for events such as the annual "Life Chain," which drew 5,000 people a year in the early 1990s. Those silent protests were, however, a far cry from the abortion clinic rescues in the United States, or the raucous protests and arrests in Toronto in the late 1980s, or in nearby Buffalo. Hamilton Right to Life, its officials always stressed, was the "educational arm" of the movement. It wasn't political, and confrontation wasn't their game, they said. Out west, in Winnipeg, pro-lifers had drafted a list of doctors who provided abortions. Was it so activists could harass them? Or to let the public at large know what was going on? There was no evidence of any similar list in Hamilton.

Campbell started to make a list of local pro-lifers, activists, those who picketed at local hospitals. But once police identify a name in their investigation, the name has to be pursued completely. "Calm down with all the goddam anti-abortion suspects," one cop warned Campbell. "You throw your net too wide, and we'll have to clear them all."

There was one name that needed to be checked—Randy Dyer, the man who had been angry at Dr. Short for performing an abortion on his girlfriend. Dyer had even cut a CD of his own songs soon before the Short shooting, and they included one number called "Daniel's Song," named for his aborted child. The doctor was referred to in the song as the executioner. Dyer was sorting through boxes of the new CD the day a police cruiser pulled in front of the house on Highcliffe Avenue in central Hamilton. It was about two weeks after the attack on Dr. Short.

Dyer lived alone in the basement apartment., used to drive a truck for a living but, after being injured in a traffic accident, had lived on a pension and was taking courses at Redeemer College in social work and religion. He was not surprised to see the police at his door. Surely he was a suspect. The detectives invited him to join them in the cruiser for a chat. Ever own firearms? No. Ever belong to a gun club? No. "Where were you, the night of Friday, November 10?" Much to his relief, Dyer had an alibi.

He didn't drink, didn't go out much. Most nights he would have been at home, alone, with no witness to corroborate his whereabouts. But as it happened, that night he had been in church, at Flamborough Christian Fellowship in nearby Millgrove. He worked the sound board that night for the pastor's microphone and the musical instruments. In theory Dyer could have popped out, gone to Hugh Short's place, shot him and returned to the church—except there was a woman at the church who could put Randy in the building, at nearly the exact time of the shooting.

Funny how things work out. That night, the woman had gone into labor right in the church. She had walked gingerly down the aisle, helped by someone else, and she had recalled seeing Randy at the back of the room, at the sound board. Then, after church that night, Dyer had gone to Tim Hortons, met a buddy there for coffee. He made a call on his cell phone. The police checked out phone records to confirm the story. After he talked to police, he went back to Hortons and saw the waitress who had served him. She remembered getting his order wrong.

"Hey, if the police come and talk to you, make sure you tell them I was here," he said to her with a smile. Dyer got the feeling, though, that the detectives knew pretty quickly that he was a dead end. Although, as it happened, it was not the last he would hear from Hamilton police about the case.

* * *

The black balaclava that Hamilton police recovered from Dr. Hugh Short's driveway was delivered to the Centre of Forensic Sciences in Toronto. Technicians found fibers from a carpet, and from an animal, perhaps a cat or a dog. And there was human hair. They also tested for saliva and mucus around the mouth and nose hole of the mask. November 10 had been a cold and wet night, and the shooter was under pressure. Perhaps he drooled, or maybe his nose ran. Testing for saliva and mucus was relatively straightforward. In order to find nuclear DNA on human hair fibers, however, the hair root must be present. Hair is essentially dead material, but the root contains the blueprint of life.

In the final test results, the balaclava produced a DNA profile for an individual. But it meant little at that point. A DNA profile, in isolation, means nothing when there is nothing to compare it to. Whoever wore the balaclava was still merely a chart of color-coded numbers.

Detectives Mike Campbell and Frank Harild chased the ballistics angle. No rifle was recovered. But there were the bullets and casings. The two rounds fired at Dr. Short had been found—the one that shattered the doctor's arm, and the one that had landed in the den. Both were taken to CFS. Bullets from a shooting scene are often crushed, looking like fillings that have been knocked out of someone's mouth. Empty shells, however, indicate the type of weapon used. Two shell casings had been found behind Short's house on the small slope down towards the woods. Curious that the shooter wouldn't have used a brass-catcher to prevent the casings from ending up in police hands. They were from ammunition for an M-14 rifle.

Even though the bullets had been mangled, it still was useful to examine them. The police had caught a break. Even though the bullets had passed through a wooden window frame, they were sufficiently intact to be examined. Under a microscope, scratches and grooves were visible; the bullets were a four-groove with a right-hand twist. A technician got on the phone to Harild. The barrel markings suggested that the bullets were fired from either an AK-47 or SKS rifle, he said.

"What?!" Harild exclaimed. It didn't add up. What about the casings from an M-14? They didn't match the bullets. It was a nice little diversion, getting police to look for the wrong weapon. "The sneaky bastard left different casings on purpose—he's dropping phony ammunition."

Harild phoned Detective George Kristenson in Vancouver for a comparison with the live ammunition Vancouver police found in the composter behind Dr. Garson Romalis's house the day he was shot. "You better double-check the rounds you found in the house against the unused live rounds you found in the alley," Harild advised Kristenson. Sure enough, the hard-point military rounds found in the composter were different from the soft-point rounds that had blown a hole in the doctor's thigh.

Detective Mike Campbell tried to use the ballistics information they had to trace the firearm. Ballistics fingerprinting was a relatively new technology, used at that time in the United States, but not Canada. He sent the bullets for testing to the U.S. Bureau of Alcohol, Tobacco and Firearms (ATF). Best-case scenario, the ballistics fingerprint would come back saying that the bullet came from a weapon within a probable serial number range, which could then be traced to one of several possible firearms purchases at specific stores. Campbell got a return call from the ATF. The round was, as CFS had said, a four-groove with a right-hand twist. Yes, but were the markings unusual, or traceable to a particular weapon? The ATF gave Campbell his answer: Those particular bullets could have come from any one of 30 to 40 million AK or SKS weapons purchased in the United States. A needle in a haystack, in a field of haystacks, Campbell reflected.

The detectives kept in close touch with the Shorts. One day Katherine Short, a small woman, with a plainspoken manner, looked up at big Frank Harild. "Honestly," she said. "Do you think you will ever identify the person who did this?" Harild paused, and looked into the eyes of the woman who had wrapped her husband's bloody wounds.

"The fact is," he said, "he may well act again, and the more times he does this, with every shot, there are more clues."

"But will you catch him?"

"Not unless we get international resources behind this."

CHAPTER 10—"I'M HEMORRHAGING HERE"

Old Hickory, Tennessee
July 16, 1997

They sold about 50 SKS rifles a year at the A-Z Pawnshop in Old Hickory. Eventually they'd stop selling firearms altogether, too much hassle, paperwork, especially when federal laws started mandating background checks on not only handguns, but rifles and shotguns as well. But in the summer of 1997 the pawnshop sold maybe five or six guns a week. Not too many, thought Patricia Osborne, the store manager.

She did not remember much about the man who walked in that day though, Lord knows, she got asked about him enough after the fact. He came in on July 16 looking to buy a rifle. Interested in the SKS 7.62 x 39 millimeter model. His ID said his name was B. James Milton from Virginia. He filled out a firearms registration form. White male, 5'10," 180 pounds. Lived at 5674 Washington Street, Ettrick, Virginia. B. James Milton was also interested in purchasing a brass catcher and a stock extension—a brass catcher prevents expended shell casings from falling to the ground. A stock extension is often used to lengthen a rifle, making it more accurate, extending the weapon farther away from the face, particularly helpful if the shooter is tall, or wears glasses. A-Z didn't carry those accessories, however. B. James Milton paid for the rifle and left.

* * *

That summer Jim Kopp worked for Good Counsel Homes in
Hoboken, New Jersey, a group helping single mothers. Longtime
pro-life activist Joan Andrews ran the home. Another activist,
Amy Boissonneault, also worked there. She had been arrested
several times, sometimes used the alias "Emma Bossano." The
authorities had put her name on a list of 30 pro-lifers who were
considered an "ongoing threat" to a New Jersey clinic. Jim had
developed a deep affection for Amy, who was 12 years his junior. He wasn't the only one, she was popular among all the pro-
lifers. One of the other men had proposed to her once, but she
had turned him down.

Loretta Marra was still married to Dennis Malvasi and, in 1996,
at age 33, she had gone to Canada to give birth to a son, Louis. She
used the alias "Jane White" while traveling and stayed with a physician friend of her father's near a town called Beechburg, in eastern
Ontario near the Quebec border. Loretta wouldn't say precisely why
she had elected to go to Canada to have her first child.

Jim continued to take part in protests in the United States and
in rescues overseas. He traveled throughout Malaysia, the Philippines. Abortion was technically illegal in the Philippines, a strongly
Catholic nation, so the protesters were treated well by local police at
a rescue in the Manila area. He felt an "angel" helped him that day,
leading him to the right door in the clinic where the killing took
place. Jim turned to thank the angel for his help, and he was gone.
Back in the United States, on January 23, 1997, he was arrested at a
protest in Englewood, New Jersey. As was the pattern for years, he
was not held in custody long. In the spring he acquired a new car,
paying $400 for a 1987 black Cavalier.

* * *

Wawa, Northern Ontario
September 5, 1997

It wasn't long after 8 a.m. when a local trucker named Luke Amelotte came upon the tractor trailer parked alongside of Highway 17. Odd. He regularly traveled Highway 17 between Dubreuilville and Wawa and the same rig had been sitting there for almost two days. Amelotte pulled over. What was going on? It had been warm the night before. The mystery truck's engine was still running, the windows shut, doors locked. He drove to the Wawa police station to report it. A police officer drove to the scene. The officer found a dead man inside the cabin. His name was Maurice Lewis—the pro-life activist from Vancouver who had befriended Jim Kopp, protesting with him in Italy and England.

Lewis was a big name in both pro-life and pro-choice circles, the kind of guy who inspired devotion in friends and supporters, and earned the animosity of opponents. Jim and the others loved Maurice, loved his commitment, his personality. He was born in England and his activism began there. When he moved to Vancouver he became famous among pro-lifers after being arrested for violating B.C.'s "bubble zone" law that was intended to protect a perimeter around clinics. He wanted to use his case to challenge the constitutionality of the law. The case was still pending, a trial scheduled for October—and now Lewis was dead at 52. What happened on that stretch of highway?

Jim heard the news and took it hard. Murder. Had to be. Is that the game the pro-aborts were playing? Revenge on Maurice for his activism? How could it be otherwise? Lewis did have a habit of picking up hitchhikers in that part of Ontario and friends had warned him about that. Lewis's lawyer in B.C., Paul Formby, wondered about foul play, thought about traveling to Wawa to investigate for himself. What was the truth?

The police officer who answered the call that morning was Constable Scott Walker. Exhaust fumes enveloped the rig when he arrived at 9:11 a.m. He noted the interior curtains of the cabin were pulled. Walker smashed the passenger door window, opened the door. There was a strong smell. And a naked man, hanging. The body was decomposing. There was no one else in the rig. The coroner attended, the body was removed. The police constable returned to the office and wrote out his report:

INCIDENT FROM 05 SEP 97
CLASSIFICATION: SUDDEN DEATH
PRONOUNCED DEAD BY DR. GASPARELLI.
NEXT OF KIN: SISTER-IN-LAW, NOTIFIED ON 06 SEPT 97 18:00
CAUSE OF DEATH: ASPHYXIA.

Maurice's brother, Richard, flew in from England. The police told him there were rumors about the death, conspiracy theories. Maurice was an active anti-abortionist, some people were suggesting that his pending court challenge motivated someone to kill him. It wasn't true, Richard was convinced of that. He was satisfied with the job police had done. He took his brother's ashes back to England, to be buried in the town of Malvern, beside their parents. A memorial service was held for Maurice in London. Richard was amazed at the outpouring of affection from people who had worked with his brother in the pro-life movement. The case, as far as Richard was concerned, was over.

It wasn't over for Jim Kopp. He launched his own "investigation." He heard rumors that the crime scene had been "cleaned up" before police arrived. The police report, for such an unusual death, was brief. Too brief. Had there been any investigation into possible murder suspects? Later, in a letter to pro-life friends, he said Maurice had been "poisoned." He cited "the RCMP report" listing "no apparent cause" for the death. Kopp even went so far as to claim the report proved that someone had tampered with the crime scene before the arrival of police, because it made no reference to the food wrappings that would litter the cab of a pro-life driver. He said pro-lifers like

Maurice always bag their food, preferring to save money that might have been spent in diners to help support pregnant women.

The letter was wrong on several counts. The report was not an RCMP report, it was an OPP report. It contained no reference to cleaning up the scene, and the cause of death was not listed as "no apparent cause." Jim was either being fed false information, or was lying, trying to stir up a conspiracy theory. Did he really believe that Maurice Lewis was murdered and Canadian police were engaged in a cover-up, all because Lewis was a visible pro-life protester? Or was he just playing games again, pulling strings—*Romanita*—telling people what he felt they needed to hear? If he truly believed Lewis was set up, then Jim Kopp had clearly learned a lesson from his friend's death. Once you are on the radar of the FBI, RCMP, Interpol, you never turn your back. Trust no one. And do not get caught.

* * *

Just past midnight on July 5, 1997, a black 1987 Chevrolet Cavalier bearing Vermont license plate BPE 216 and registered to James Charles Kopp, crossed the Peace Bridge at Fort Erie into Canada. Back then, the Canadian side of the border was more diligent about recording plates of cars passing through than the American side. Two months later, on October 10, the same vehicle again crossed the border into Canada at 4:33 p.m.

Two and a half weeks after the second crossing, on October 28, in Perinton, N.Y., near Rochester, an obstetrician named Dr. David Gandell was in the glass-enclosed pool area of his home, toweling off his young son after a swim. At 8:35 p.m., a bullet shattered the glass. Then a second shot. Both narrowly missed the doctor and his child. The shots were fired from a wooded area behind the house. The shooter got away. The rounds were from a military assault rifle.

That same night, in Brooklyn, New York, FBI surveillance agents took photos of a dark-haired woman walking from a house. It was Loretta Marra, leaving a house belonging to a man listed in the phone book as John Howard at 2468 Lynden Avenue. His real name was Dennis Malvasi. Just after midnight, meanwhile, less than four hours after the shooting at Dr. Gandell's home, a car crossed the Rainbow Bridge in Niagara Falls into Canada. The car was a black Chevy Cavalier, Vermont plate BPE 216.

* * *

Winnipeg, Manitoba
November 1997

Manitoba's capital city had been in the eye of Canada's abortion battles ever since pro-choice standard-bearer Henry Morgentaler had opened a clinic in the city in 1983, even before he was established in Toronto, even as former Manitoba provincial cabinet minister "Holy" Joe Borowski vowed that Morgentaler's "butcher shop" would not be permitted to open. Winnipeg's police raided the clinic several times. And, in 1997, the city still had an aggressive pro-life movement. There was a document making the rounds that listed the names of all physicians in the city known to provide abortion services.

On November 4, 1997, police in Hamilton, Ontario faxed a memo across Canada. It advised all police services to issue warnings to doctors who perform abortions that they might be in danger at this time of year, around Remembrance Day—the time when doctors in Vancouver and Hamilton had been shot. The memo said doctors should be advised to take precautions in their homes, alter their routines, avoid standing in front of well-lit windows or doors at night, keep blinds drawn. In Winnipeg the warning arrived on the fax machine of the Criminal Intelligence Service of Manitoba (a provincial agency comprising city police officers) and the RCMP. The warning was filed and never circulated to the Mounties or city police.

On the night of November 11, Remembrance Day, a car drove along snow-packed streets past homes in the Winnipeg suburb of

St. Vital, stopped at a residential crescent where two streets named Salme and Lotus met. The shooter entered the woods bordering a park that ran behind homes along Victoria Crescent. He moved, cloaked in darkness, the bare thin branches nearly invisible in the blackness. It was peaceful in the woods in the late evening, the only sound the distant ambient buzz of the city. The Red River ran alongside the woods. The river floods in springtime, so residential areas in the floodplain use dikes for protection. That included Victoria Crescent, where an obstetrician lived. A mound of earth, a dike about eight meters high, ran right behind the house, some fifteen meters from his door.

The shooter walked close beside the river. There were a few clouds, but the black water shimmered in the reflected light of the moon and of the homes on the far side of the river. The shooter was now roughly parallel with the doctor's property. He stopped, scaled the riverbank, negotiating the slippery, steep hill through the trees to the chain-link fence. Up and over. And there was the dike. He climbed it, then walked along the ridge. The house was an unusual design, raised up on stilts, a carport underneath. The entire back wall of the house was glass. Winnipeg is frigid in November, on a crisp night you can feel the harsh air rip through your nostrils, your breath floating like smoke in the air. It was 8:45 p.m. Dr. Jack Fainman walked into his living room.

He had studied medicine at the University of Manitoba, further training in obstetrics and gynecology in Chicago, then moved to Emo, a town of a couple thousand in northwestern Ontario, where he set up practice. He and his wife, Fagie, eventually moved to Winnipeg. There was something of the legend about tall, handsome Jack Fainman. The story went that, when he worked as a country doctor in Emo, more than once he walked across the frozen lake in the dark, the wind whipping his face, just to get to a patient. One day, before the advent of Canada's universal health care system, a pregnant woman refused to go to hospital because she couldn't afford it. So broad-shouldered Jack Fainman went to her home, picked her off the ground and literally carried her to the hospital.

He also provided abortion services. In 1997 he was 66 years old and still working. He taught medicine at St. Boniface General Hospital. He was one of about a dozen doctors in the city who were referred patients for abortions. But Fainman didn't handle as many referrals as some of the others, nor did he tend to do later-term abortions like some. A quiet, unassuming man, he put more emphasis, people said, on prenatal care, maybe booked one or two abortions a week.

Just before 9 p.m., he sat in the living room on the other side of the yawning glass wall. To someone outside, just 15 meters away, the light of the room cast Jack Fainman in perfect silhouette.

> *The explosion, a window shatters, Jack Fainman collapses to the ground, a gusher of blood bursting from his right shoulder. His wife rushes into the room, picks up the phone, calls 911. Fainman himself takes the phone. There is urgency in his voice, but also a cool, clinical tone.*
>
> *"Hello—" he says.*
>
> *"Hello," replies the dispatcher.*
>
> *"This is Dr. Fainman. I'm hemorrhaging here. Get an ambulance quickly."*

It took nine minutes for police to arrive at the front of the Fainman house. The sniper was gone. Perhaps he drove up Salme Crescent, onto Dunkirk, past the police community kiosk in the strip mall, past the neon glow from the sign of the Dakota Motel, towards the Bishop Grandin expressway. Dr. Fainman, meanwhile, was stable in hospital, as staff debated on whether to remove the bullet embedded deep in his shoulder. Police dogs, forensic unit, detectives combed the scene. The shooter left footprints in the snow, tire tracks. Plaster casts were taken of the tracks. Ron Oliver, a city policeman, took photos of two tire impressions consistent with a General Motors car. Goodyear tire, Concorde caliber, size

195 x 75 x 14, a 5.5-inch-wide tire. Midsize GM car, consistent with model from years 1981 to 1990.

It takes an hour and half to reach the North Dakota border from Winnipeg. At night the four-lane is lonely and dark, vast stretches of farmland on either side blend into blackness, it feels as though you are in a tunnel, on a drive to nowhere. And then lights, a sign declaring you are about to cross the 49th parallel. Hard on the border is Pembina, North Dakota, population just over 600, the first opportunity for food off Route 59 is a greasy spoon called The Depot Cafe that serves lead-in-your belly cheeseburger soup. At 1:10 a.m. a car license plate was recorded crossing the border: Vermont BPE 216.

* * *

Late in 1997 the Hamilton police investigation into the maiming of Dr. Hugh Short was still open, but little was happening. A meeting was called at central station on King William Street on November 18, 1997. A detective named Aivars Jekabsons was summoned to see Acting Superintendent Dave Bowen, Steve Hrab (the senior man in the Major Crime Unit) and Detective Peter Abi-Rashed, who was one of the original detectives on the Short file. Jekabsons, who had a relaxed, irreverent air to him, entered the room, looking like an unemployed surfer. His hair hung long, past his shoulders, tied in a ponytail. Ragged clothes, beard. It was part of the uniform, working undercover on the streets. Jekabsons was a 44-year-old vice and drugs detective with 21 years on the force. His Latvian parents had wanted him to pursue accounting. Aivars had wanted to pursue criminals.

As an investigator he had come to the conclusion that everything is just a matter of time. There is always a trail. Just stay with it, good things will happen. But if ever his patience would be tried, it would be in the Hugh Short case.

Two years after the shooting, there were no suspects, and senior officers at the meeting asked Jekabsons if he would take charge of revisiting the cold case. He accepted. Soon after that, Abi-Rashed handed over boxes of evidence and background and investigator notes to the new man. "Here you go," Abi-Rashed said. "Start reading." The next step was introducing Jekabsons to Hugh and Katherine Short. Abi-Rashed and Jekabsons visited the house on Sulphur Springs.

"Detective Jekabsons will now be completely dedicated to the case," Abi-Rashed told the Shorts. "The investigation is going full bore."

Hugh Short looked over the ragged Jekabsons. "So I'm being assigned a guy who looks like this?"

Jekabsons laughed. He said he planned to get a haircut and shave. They got along just fine after that. The detective came to like the Shorts. There were good people who deserved answers.

Back at the office he started from scratch, digging through documents, forensics. Jekabsons thought the boys who first handled the case did a solid job. But sometimes a fresh set of eyes can spot something new. At least he hoped so. He visited the Shorts' backyard one night, stood inside the quiet shed where the sniper had waited, then outside, staring at the second-floor window, putting himself inside the shooter's skin, assuming the firing position, imagining the shot, checking the terrain around him. Two shots in quick succession. Where do you go? Where is the escape route? You probably don't park your car on the street. Sulphur Springs Road is narrow, in an isolated area, not many homes. A neighbor would notice a strange car parked on the street. There was probably a second person who picked him up. That needs to be co-ordinated. Not with a cell phone. Back in '95, you couldn't count on a cell in a remote area like this. You'd need a walkie-talkie, or to establish a pre-set pick-up time.

The anti-abortion motive dictated that the investigation had to stretch far and wide. Jekabsons tried to sell his superiors on the international angle. He had to take the show well beyond Hamilton. They said he was biting off too much. Let's not get too carried away here. But Aivars Jekabsons was ahead of the game. After the sniper attack on Dr. Jack Fainman, Winnipeg police chief Dave Cassels was talking privately about forming a national task force to investigate the link between the three Canadian shootings, and also the attempted shooting in Rochester, New York. On Saturday, November 29, Jekabsons flew to Winnipeg to meet with officers from Winnipeg, Vancouver, the RCMP, and the New York State Police. The task force was an unusual step. Canadian and American police did not typically combine resources. But participants in this effort would share information, hold weekly conference calls, meet in person regularly, cast the widest possible net. Detectives in each city would make up the bulk of the force and would be overseen by a joint management committee of senior officers.

In Hamilton, Detective Larry Penfold was seconded out of the forensics office to team up with Jekabsons. Penfold got the impression that his new assignment might last a couple of weeks. It turned into two years. On January 26, 1998, the task force met in Hamilton for three days, keeping the meeting a secret from the media. An officer named Jim Van Allen attended. He was a behavioral analyst with the Ontario Provincial Police, working out of Orillia. He was, in the vernacular, a criminal profiler. Van Allen was just the second behavioral profiler the OPP had ever trained, but he had been a police officer for 20 years. He was presented with the evidence to date and asked to compose a profile of the sniper—or snipers—still at large. Van Allen reviewed what had been gathered at the crime scenes. He asked the task force for more information, but there was little more to tell him. From the relatively thin evidence available, Van Allen felt that the shooter was probably Canadian, given his choice of targets, and that if he didn't strike in Quebec soon, was probably unilingual. The profiler also came to believe that, since the sniper clearly had a political goal in mind, he was not shooting to kill. He was shooting to wound.

"It's an old military tactic," Van Allen said. "If you leave the victim wounded and incapable of carrying out his skill as a physician, he is a walking, living reminder to other doctors that this can happen to them."

Van Allen also believed that another shooting was inevitable.

* * *

Jekabsons and Penfold reviewed notes, interviewed and re-interviewed those who had called in tips two years earlier. And there was a new lead. One month earlier, on December 10, a package of anonymous anti-abortion hate mail had been delivered to the *Hamilton Spectator* daily newspaper. It contained six pages of hand-written invective on photocopied newspaper articles and pictures. The package had arrived one month after the shooting of Jack Fainman. The *Spectator* notified police about the package.

Three weeks later, on December 31, a second hate letter arrived at the *Spectator*. It, too, was reported to police. Four days later, a letter containing more anti-abortion invective was hand-delivered to Vancouver General Hospital.

Was there any connection between the letters and the shooting of abortion doctors? Was it a break in the case, or did the letters throw more heat than light? Jekabsons, for one, felt they were red herrings.

At 6:50 a.m. on December 31, the same day the second hate letter arrived at the *Spectator*, a 55-year-old former taxi driver named Ron Wylie banged on the superintendent's door at his Hamilton apartment building. He wanted the storage locker opened, to get a suitcase.

"I'm going to Vancouver. Need to pack."

Ron Wylie had been arrested several times at anti-abortion protests in the United States in 1992: at Amherst, New York, during the Spring of Life in April, Milwaukee in May, Baton Rouge in July. He had taken part in the July 7, 1998, street protest in Hamilton staged by Milwaukee-based Missionaries to the PreBorn. Wylie had clearly moved in hardcore anti-abortion circles. When he first heard about the sniper shootings, his instinct was to feel sympathy for the notion of justifiable homicide, and the sniper.

But Wylie claimed that he had nothing to do with the attacks, and that he didn't know who the sniper was. Jekabsons believed him;

he was just out for attention. Hamilton police eventually charged him with five counts of threatening death and he was sentenced to 18 months in jail and three years' probation. They also took a blood sample from his fingertip. His DNA profile was compared to that retrieved from the DNA sample found on the ski mask in Hugh Short's driveway four years earlier. The two samples did not match.

Through the early weeks of 1998, Jekabsons and Penfold compiled a list of every criminal incident on record that had an anti-abortion angle. The list included everything from arson at a clinic, to a phone call to an obstetrician in which baby lullaby music was played in the background. Ultimately, they interviewed hundreds of people, most of them Canadians, some of them Americans.

One of the unanswered mysteries continued to be "Why Hugh Short?" He was not a high-profile physician before the shooting. His name had never appeared in the media. Dr. Short was no crusader. How did his name get out? Jekabsons asked Short, "Have you ever attended a medical conference on abortion?" Answer: No. Was it possible that his name was spread through the pro-life grapevine? They interviewed the few pro-life protesters who regularly marched out in front of Henderson Hospital, where Short had worked. Short was a senior physician, 62 years old, had worked enough years that his name was known in the medical community, if nowhere else. Obviously there were people who knew that he performed abortions. And anti-abortion activists travel together, talk, go to rallies. "Is it possible," Jekabsons asked one of the Henderson Hospital protesters, "that you inadvertently gave Short's name to someone, who passed it on until it was heard by the sniper?"

One who knew of Hugh Short was Dr. Carmelo Scime. He was a family physician and local coroner who regularly marched outside Henderson. Scime protested nearly every Friday on Concession Street beginning in 1986, holding high his "Justice for the Unborn" sign. He knew Short was an obstetrician and gynecologist. But then he knew most of the doctors in Hamilton. How did Scime feel when he heard that Hugh Short had been shot? "I felt sorry for the doctor," he said. "And I thought the culprit should be caught. The doctor's integrity had been attacked—just like the integrity of the unborn."

Another protester outside Henderson Hospital was Randy Dyer, who sometimes accompanied Scime. Detectives had interviewed Dyer within two weeks of the shooting in 1995. Jekabsons and Penfold listened to the CD that Dyer had recorded, in which he referred to his girlfriend having an abortion, and spoke to him again. But it was another dead end.

Aivars Jekabsons visited the shooting scenes in Rochester, Vancouver, Winnipeg. Each attack targeted a home in a suburb, maximizing the time it would take for city police to respond. As he stood in each sniper position, the similarities were eerie. They were all well planned, the ground staked out. In Winnipeg, the tracks had gone up past the house, up the riverbank, doubled back again, a route that indicated a thorough inspection of the scene prior to the shooting. The sniper had no intention of getting caught, thought Jekabsons. He planned to keep his reign of terror going.

The detective firmly believed all the shootings were connected, clearly it was the same guy. And he was convinced the shooter had not acted alone. The case haunted Jekabsons, always would. Had they done everything possible, explored every angle, 100 percent? By the fall of 1998 he had a list of names of pro-life radicals in Canada and the United States. One of them was almost certainly the sniper, or knew who the shooter was. The name of James Charles Kopp was there, but it was just one among many.

CHAPTER 11—DECIDEDLY DISTASTEFUL

On January 29, 1998, a bomb exploded at a women's clinic in Birmingham, Alabama, killing an off-duty police officer. The culprit would turn out to be domestic terrorist and Atlanta Olympics bomber Eric Rudolph. Jim Kopp was staying at Doris Grady's house in Pittsburgh, as he often did during his travels in the U.S. northeast. Jim sat with Doris and watched the news of the explosion on TV.

"What do you think about that?" Doris asked.

He said nothing.

Doris continued: "I mean, I don't know if I really have a problem with it. It's just bricks and mortar. Just a mill."

"But what if somebody gets hurt?" replied Jim. "That's the problem. What if, say, a firefighter comes in there to help, totally innocent, and he gets hurt?"

One thing was certain, the government would pin the bombing on pro-lifers. Clinton and his attorney general, Janet Reno, were out to crush the movement. "Someday, you know, they'll come for me," Jim said. "Whatever they say about me, don't believe it. Don't believe it until you talk to me."

Doris enjoyed Jim's visits. They chatted, watched rental movies. Jim enjoyed old classics, Second World War movies like *Midway*, which struck a chord in him, focusing as it did on the Pacific—an underappreciated theater, he always felt—where his father had served. Among more recent movies, he loved *The Usual Suspects*, the convoluted thriller starring Kevin Spacey. So many good lines: "One cannot be betrayed if one has no people." Lots of twists, where nothing is as it seems. Spacey had the best line in the movie, right near the end: "The greatest trick the devil ever pulled on man was to convince him that he didn't exist." A great line, although not original to the movie. The French poet Charles Baudelaire coined it in a short story in 1864, chiding the myopia of those who celebrated the triumph of the Enlightenment. Jim Kopp, who took the long view on things, understood completely.

He continued to earn money doing odd jobs, he used the alias Clyde Svenson while doing construction and carpentry work, in exchange for living in an unfurnished apartment in Jersey City. He had some small deals on the go. He and a man named Kent Richter sold a camper they owned in Kent County in Delaware. Jim gave $7,000 from the sale to young friend Jennifer Rock, for her to put in a bank account for him.

In May he was in Florida. That same month there were ten butyric acid attacks on clinics in Miami, St. Petersburg, Orlando, Daytona Beach, and Clearwater. Shortly after that he created eight false Texas driver's licenses for himself and other pro-lifers. In July there were five acid attacks in New Orleans and four in Houston.

He spent time that summer at his friend James Gannon's home in Whiting, New Jersey. Gannon always made Jim feel welcome. But a man named Alex, who shared Gannon's place at the retirement village, didn't care much for Jim just dropping in all the time, so he also stayed with Elizabeth Lewis, an elderly woman in the village. She noticed him always writing on the computer. What was he working on?

On July 17, at 2:49 p.m., Jim Kopp's black Chevy Cavalier entered Canada at the Queenston border crossing. Six days later the car returned to the United States at Niagara Falls.

* * *

"Abortion is the killing of potential life. It is not pretty. It is not easy. In a perfect world, it wouldn't be necessary." Dr. Bart Slepian had insisted on saying that part in his speech. His niece, Amanda Robb, had helped him craft the words for a presentation he made to a Buffalo group called Medical Students for Choice.

Why would Bart say those words to a pro-choice audience? He had to know pro-life activists would jump all over a quote like that, to illustrate that even abortion providers like Dr. Barnett Slepian had moral issues with the procedure. But Bart, being Bart, was simply telling it as he saw it, and damn the political optics. Quite obviously most terminated fetuses would otherwise live. But abortion was legal. Women requested them. OBs were needed to perform the surgery safely. Bart was an OB. And so he provided the service. He had a full-time private obstetrics and gynecology practice, where he provided prenatal and postnatal care. He also performed abortions at the GYN Womenservices clinic in downtown Buffalo. In one sense he was just doing his job, but Bart had become a visible player in the abortion wars in the area. Earlier in the year he was presented with a Choice Achievement Award at a rally in Buffalo marking the 25th anniversary of *Roe* v. *Wade*.

Bart was 52 years old and had made it, climbed the ladder, was a successful doctor, family man. His father, Philip, had died nine years earlier, but had lived to see the success Bart had battled to become. Bart lived with his wife Lynne, and their four sons, Andrew, 15, Brian, 13, Michael, 10, and Philip, 7, in a large house on Roxbury Park in Amherst. It was an upper-middle-class neighborhood except for a couple of streets, like Roxbury, where the homes were palatial. Some in the area dubbed Bart's home "the Taj Mahal." It was a beautiful area, mature trees, lush lawns, parkland and sprawling backyards.

As for the storm of protest surrounding his professional life, Bart joked darkly about his fate, as was his custom. Other OBs who provided abortion services were wearing bulletproof vests on the advice of police. Bart? He cracked that it wasn't necessary, they'd probably just shoot him in the head anyway. But in fact Bart bought a vest, and got in the habit of watching his back, checking under his car for explosives.

Lynne bought him a parrot once; Bart said the bird would probably outlive him—and that they should teach the parrot how to say a eulogy. He joked that, at his funeral, friends should all come in separate cars, it would make for a longer procession that way. Typical Bart. But the jokes revealed more than just his predilection for black humor. Perhaps Bart could sense that he was on a collision course that was inevitable.

* * *

Wednesday, October 14, 1998

Eyes scan the White Pages of a phone book. Residential listing for D. Slepian, 93 Garden Parkway, Grand Island, New York. Phone ringing, 7:30 p.m. A woman named Ruth Slepian answers.

"Hello?" she says.

"Is Dr. Slepian there, please?" asks a man's voice.

Doctor? Ruth has a husband named David. He is not a physician. Her father-in-law, also named Slepian, was a doctor. But he has passed on.

"Dr. Slepian—is dead," she says.

Pause.

"Right. I don't think so," the man mumbles, the words barely audible.

He hangs up.

Prepare. Plan. Remove the vagaries of the moving target. Later, near the doctor's private practice, a vanity plate on the car. "SLEPIAN." Could shoot him right here, right now. Of course, that would mean shooting across the street, can't imagine that would be appreciated, he reflected. Hard surfaces, traffic, residences, businesses, plenty of chance for ricochets.

Paradise Road, not far from the Slepians' home.

Sunday, October 18. A jogger, lanky, moving slowly, ungainly, through the leafy neighborhood, so slow that he was nearly walking, up Paradise Road in Amherst. He wore glasses, had a reddish goatee. The next day, early morning, the jogger was in the same neighborhood, where two streets named Roxbury Park and Deer Run intersected.

"Hello," said a woman passing by him. The jogger said nothing.

Friday, October 23, early morning, he shuffled through the neighborhood in his dark tracksuit. A landscaper working at a home made eye contact.

"Hello," said the worker.

"Hi," replied the jogger, before slowly disappearing around the corner.

Later, a car passed through the neighborhood. It was a black Chevy Cavalier. It glided through a boulevard stop sign. There was a police cruiser nearby. The Cavalier made a U-turn, left the area, slowly, deliberately, with the cruiser following at low speed. The cop turned away, let him go. A close call.

Kill? A thousand ways to kill someone, really, he reflected later. Blow up their car. Do a Rambo thing and empty a magazine into them. Run them over with a car. Put nicotine acid on their steering wheel.

Wounding, however, is tricky business.

* * *

The phone rang at Jim Fitzgerald's desk inside the FBI complex at Quantico, Virginia. It was early October. Fitzgerald, surrounded by stacks of papers in his office, picked up. It was the FBI's legal attaché office in Ottawa. Fitzgerald had been with the bureau 13 years, grew up in Philadelphia. His official FBI title was supervisory special agent with the Behavioral Analysis Unit. One branch, of the unit was for training and education, the other, Fitzgerald's branch was operational. In popular culture, though, Jim Fitzgerald was simply a profiler. It was too sexy a term for Hollywood and the media to resist. The psycho-thriller *Silence of the Lambs*—on which John Douglas, one of the original FBI profilers in the 1970s, served as technical consultant—ensured that. Some started to call analysts like Fitzgerald "the *Silence of the Lambs* boys."

The FBI called them "psychological profilers," as early as the 1970s, back when behavioral psychology was a relatively new tool for deconstructing criminal minds, either to identify suspects, predict violent acts, or break down suspects once they were arrested. The titles had changed, however. "Psychological profiler" left the door open to cagey defense lawyers attacking their credibility in court. "Are you, in fact, FBI Special Agent Smith, a trained psychologist? No? Then why are you called a 'psychological profiler'?" They became, instead, officially, "behavioral analysts." Jim Fitzgerald worked in Unit Number One with nine other agents.

His unit specialized in counterterrorism. The case of the abortion doctor sniper who targeted physicians in Vancouver, Ancaster, Winnipeg, and Rochester certainly qualified. The official on the phone from Ottawa briefed Fitzgerald on the latest information. He was told a profile of the sniper was being developed at the

Ontario Provincial Police's behavioral unit. Fitzgerald had dealt with the Ontario unit before—they did good work and, in fact, the FBI had trained OPP analysts. He asked to see the profile that had been developed to date. The OPP profiler was Jim Van Allen. Upon receiving the report, Fitzgerald saw that Van Allen already had a good handle on the profile.

Sniper shoots at a doctor in each of 1994, 1995, and two in 1997. All of the shootings seem well planned, no weapon ever found. There was DNA recovered at the Ancaster shooting scene. All attacks came in early November. This was a ritual. Why at this time of the year? The sniper perhaps was motivated by both symbolism and tactics.

Symbolism: He is perhaps shooting doctors to make a statement, to avenge the death of aborted fetuses. May well see himself as a soldier in the cause. November 11 is Remembrance Day, Canada's day to honor its war dead. In the United States it's Veterans' Day. The timing packs religious symbolism as well. If the sniper is Catholic, that time of year is also notable for All Saints' Day, which falls on November 1, and All Souls' Day on November 2.

Tactics: In November the nights grow long and dark. Most of the leaves have fallen from trees, making surveillance of homes in wooded areas easier.

Jim Van Allen felt there was only one shooter, and that he was not a professional. The sniper was improving his technique with each hit but, paradoxically, had left evidence at each scene, been sloppy. Van Allen said the equipment used had been primitive, from the point of view of a trained marksman. The rifle was adequate, but it was the little things—the sniper wasn't using web belts to carry his gear, he was dropping cartridges, casings. The tape he used to secure the garbage can lids in Vancouver had been silver duct tape, which was highly visible. A pro would have used black or olive-colored military tape.

Jim Fitzgerald began developing his own take on the sniper. Behaviorally there is a clear difference between a long-range sniper and the killer who shoots at close range, brandishing a .38 in an alleyway, or breaking down a door and pointing a shotgun at a victim. The close-up shooter has no issue with using violence, probably has anger-management problems. The shooter is physically secure enough to personally confront someone face-to-face, whether it's simply to tell them off or to pull a trigger. Little skill is required to shoot at close range. Target acquisition and kill zone are not relevant. The sniper mentality is much different. He lacks confrontational skills. He is more secretive, plans more, acquires lots of equipment, trains himself in weaponry and ballistics to guarantee success.

The FBI had plenty of background on close-up gun killers. That year, 1998, guns were used to murder 11,798 people in the United States. True sniper attacks, on the other hand, were rare. In 1997, there had been just four reported cases of sniper killings in the entire country. The motive of the abortion sniper seemed clear enough. Fitzgerald knew that in instances where a serial offender acts based on need or fantasy, motive is often a complicated question. This shooter, however, had a definite political-religious mission. But, even within the subgroup of moral zealots, this sniper was different. Other anti-abortion extremists who had shot doctors did so with little deliberation, and in broad daylight. This one did not intend to get caught. He was relatively intelligent. He was traveling great distances, spreading out his attacks. The sniper was probably American. If so, he was striking in Canada because he knew cross-border investigations were complicated, thought Fitzgerald.

Fitzgerald and Van Allen talked about the profile at length. One point was not included in the profile. It was one over which the two men disagreed: intent. Was the sniper shooting to kill or wound? Van Allen felt the sniper wanted to terrorize doctors. You do that by wounding them, leaving them crippled. He had certainly pulled it off so far. Fitzgerald disagreed. "You don't take all that time and effort, with all the factors that can go wrong, unless you are prepared to kill," he said. "You don't take those kinds of shots from that distance and not hope to kill someone."

"It's a dangerous game," countered Van Allen, "but if he was shooting to kill, he's even a worse shot than I give him credit for."

They agreed to keep that issue out of the profile. It wouldn't help police catch the sniper, and, if their opinions were leaked, it might just inflame the sniper, challenge him to execute better or stay long enough at the next scene to finish off his target. The profilers knew that the urgent issue for police was whether the shooter would strike again before or near Remembrance Day. On this the G-man and the OPP cop agreed. The sniper was going to hit again, and soon. Police should be on alert, and so should doctors who provide abortions in both countries.

On October 20, the joint Canada-U.S. police task force met in Winnipeg. They discussed the profile and other information and strategy. The implication of the profilers' analysis was clear. At the end of the meeting, Winnipeg detective Ron Oliver stood up and addressed the group. "We need to anticipate," he said. "There must be a sense of urgency. There may be a shooting coming up."

* * *

A fax arrived at the clinic where Bart Slepian worked. It was from the FBI. Be extra cautious at this time of year, it warned. Whoever shot obstetricians in Canada and Rochester was still out there. Clinic manager Marilyn Buckham told Bart about it.

"Be careful," she said.

"I will," he replied. The exchange had become their regular sign-off whenever Bart left the clinic for the day.

"Thanks for coming," she chirped.

"Thanks for having me."

* * *

Amherst, N.Y.
Friday, October 23, 1998
9:45 p.m.

A man gripped a rifle in the woods behind Bart Slepian's home:

> *A decidedly unpleasant thing, shooting someone. But it's*
> *not the act that answers the moral question, rather it is the*
> *desired result. Think about Dietrich Bonhoeffer: gave*
> *the Nazi salute to Hitler every day as he held the door to the*
> *staff car. Made his skin crawl. Salute the devil. Hated to do*
> *it. But he did it, to keep his cover, allow him to continue*
> *smuggling Jews to safety. Amazing, to meet the daughter of one*
> *of those survivors. She lives in Syracuse. An extreme honor.*

The clocks were to be turned back that weekend, the darkest time
of the year. How many times had Jim Kopp waited out there, late
night, early morning, anticipating the shot that had not yet come?

Twenty-four hours a day abortionists are preparing to kill more kids.
A form of serial murder. Slepian's been doing it for years. There is a
stubbornness there that requires a strong response.

He focused the binoculars on the back window. Bart and Lynne
had just pulled in the driveway, returning from synagogue, marking
the anniversary of Bart's father's death. Through the front door. The
boys were home. Into the clean white kitchen. The rear window
shade pulled halfway down.

Keys rattle on the kitchen counter. Bart puts down his pager, his
wallet. Opens the microwave door, places a bowl of soup inside. Sets
the time. Walks out of the kitchen. Lynne stays, talking with Philip
and Michael by the kitchen island. Andrew, the 15-year-old, lies
on the couch in an adjoining room. Bart back in the kitchen. Ten

feet away from Lynne and the boys. A popping sound. Bart feeling a blow to his back.

"I think I've been shot."

Lynne, incredulous. "Don't be ridiculous."

Bart falling to the floor, Lynne running to him, blood pooling on the white floor. Lynne screaming for her son to call 911. Brian dialing, Philip watching, stunned. Andrew on his knees, trying to staunch the flow of blood from both sides of his father with paper towels.

The bullet, having punctured the double-pane of the rear sun-room window and screen, had knifed through Bart, a cabinet, ricocheted off a wall between Lynne and the boys, past Andrew on the couch, hitting the marble fireplace mantel, fallen to rest on the hearth, spent.

Dispatch to Amherst police at 10:07: possible shots fired, 187 Roxbury. Police officer Ted Dinoto in the area, at the house at 10:10 p.m. Dinoto on his knees in the kitchen, ripping open Bart's shirt, seeing the hole in the left side of his back from the entrance wound, and at the right shoulder, the exit wound. Police and paramedics swarming to the street. Police search the neighborhood, the woods, finding nothing. The ambulance rushes Bart Slepian to Millard Fillmore Hospital. In the ER they declare him dead.

An FBI agent reported to the Slepian home that night. A federal crime had been committed. The sniper who murdered Dr. Barnett Slepian had joined America's most wanted list.

The phone rang early the next morning in the home of Dr. Rick Schwarz on Long Island, Bart's old friend from med school in Mexico. They hadn't seen each other for several years. The woman on the line was an old friend of Rick's.

"I'm sorry, Rick, but I can't remember—was Bart's last name Slepian?"

"Yes," Rick replied. Why?"

"I just heard on CNN he's been shot."

Shot? Wounded, thought Rick, obviously at some kind of protest. Bart. Maybe now the stubborn guy will back off.

"Aw for chrissakes, that's—goddamnit, I told him to stay away from that stuff," Rick said. "Is he OK?"

"Rick, he's—dead."

At first the information did not register. Then, suddenly, a deluge of emotion, and Rick Schwarz came unglued. He cried, and phoned Lynne. "Lynne, it's Rick, please tell me what I'm hearing is not true."

Then Rick turned on CNN and saw the news for himself. On Saturday, U.S. President Bill Clinton issued a statement. "I am outraged by the murder of Dr. Barnett Slepian in his home last night in Amherst, New York. The Department of Justice is working with state and local authorities to find the person or persons responsible and bring them to justice. While we do not have all the facts of this case, one thing is clear, this nation cannot tolerate violence directed at those providing a constitutionally protected medical service ... No matter where we stand on the issue of abortion, all Americans must stand together in condemning this tragic and brutal act. We must protect the safety and freedom of all our citizens. Hillary and I extend our thoughts and prayers to the family of Dr. Slepian."

The Amherst police and FBI agents searched for clues, checked names of anti-abortion radicals against their known locations. Bart had no shortage of pro-life enemies. Some had been charged with harassing him. Jim Kopp was not one of those people.

The gray-blue eyes looked up at the TV. He was on the road at a truck stop. The news was on. He had driven west from Amherst, into Pennsylvania, stayed overnight at a motel, then on to Cleveland. CNN was broadcasting the story over and over. The sound was turned off. Just visuals. Yellow police tape. Amherst police cruisers. Bart Slepian dead. Jim Kopp felt his body shrink, fear creeping through his bones. He left the diner and turned his car back east. He needed money. New Jersey was his next stop.

* * *

There were several hundred mourners at Bart's funeral. A letter was read from Bill and Hillary Clinton: "Bart Slepian lived to love and loved to live," it said. A few weeks later, the Clintons visited Buffalo, met with Lynne. For Bart's friends, the funeral was an awful thing—all the media attention, the surreal nature of his death. But the eulogy, read by Bart's niece, Amanda Robb, was inspired. A professional television writer, the funniest person in the family, she was eloquent, hit all the right notes. She recalled her uncle Bart back in the early seventies, the one who had the least to give to the family, and one who gave the most.

* * *

The autopsy took place early the next day, but the cause of Bart Slepian's death was no mystery. He bled to death. Erie County chief medical examiner Dr. Sung-ook Baik studied the entry and exit wounds, removed organs to examine the tissue for impact marks, traced the path the bullet traveled through the body. He recorded his findings:

- Entrance of bullet hole, left side of the back, measuring three-quarters of an inch by one-half an inch.
- No evidence of gunpowder on the skin.
- Bullet penetrated left chest wall, left eighth rib, thoracic vertebral bone, spinal cord—severing approximately two inches of the cord—right lung, right fifth and sixth ribs.
- Bullet exited body from the posterior part of the right armpit, 12 inches from the top of the head.

At the scene, police used a ballistic alignment laser to trace the trajectory of the shot. The bullet had traveled 15 feet inside the house and 31 yards outside, from the wooded area to the sunroom window. A tree was identified as the likely shooting point used by the sniper to brace himself. At this scene, unlike the Canadian shootings, there were no spent cartridges found.

Within days the FBI's Jim Fitzgerald stood out in the darkened woods, seeing what the sniper saw. What had the sniper been thinking? The focus was on execution, making the kill, thought Fitzgerald. Acquire target, squeeze trigger. This shooting—at night from the rear of the home, with a well-planned escape route—followed the MO of the other shootings to date.

A news conference was held in Buffalo by local police and the FBI. Police hold news conferences in the early hours of an investigation for two reasons. One is to protect public safety—get the killer's name and face out there. Public safety wasn't at issue here. The sniper's profile suggested that, given his cautious manner, he would stay quiet for a long time, would not risk getting caught by striking again soon. The other reason for going public is for the police to solicit help. As a police officer spoke at the podium and the cameras rolled, in the background surveying the room was a man who could pass for a young Sidney Poitier. His name was Bernard Tolbert, FBI. He was in charge and knew they were up against it. They had nothing—nothing, until the phone call.

A woman named Joan Dorn heard the plea for help in the media regarding the murder of Dr. Barnett Slepian. She was a fitness buff and lived in Bart's neighborhood, over on Paradise Road. On Wednesday, October 14, she had risen before dawn, hit the pavement for a jog in the dark at 5:30 a.m. As she ran, she saw a car parked not far from her home.

Never seen it before. Dorn was a scientist, an epidemiologist. She taught at the University of Buffalo. Noticing things, little things, patterns, things not readily apparent to the naked eye, was what she did for a living. She knew her neighborhood well, what pieces did and did not belong. She noticed the strange car. Black Cavalier. Vermont plate. Didn't belong. Who parks their car on the street at five in the morning?

A man in a dark exercise suit got out, started stretching. In the morning gloom, in the bulky clothes, he looked big. He started to jog. The stranger's gait, it was all wrong, Dorn could tell. He wasn't a jogger, not a regular, anyway. He looked slow, plodding. And he was overdressed for the mild weather they were enjoying. And why drive your car somewhere to park and then run? She watched him jog out of sight, in the direction of Roxbury.

Instead of shaking her head at the incongruity of it all and resuming her day, Joan Dorn went home and opened her personal journal, where she kept notes on her runs, how she felt, distance traveled. "Wacky car," she wrote, and the plate number: BPE 216, Vermont. Then she showed her husband the note she had written. "Honey, if I don't come home tomorrow from jogging, check this out," she quipped.

Now she heard the request from police for anyone noticing anything unusual in the area. She picked up the phone. Later she would be applauded for providing a critical tip, journalists would come knocking on her door. Dorn didn't think she had done anything remarkable—you pay attention to your neighborhood. If anything, she was hard on herself. She should have acted sooner, reported the stranger to police on the morning of her jog. Maybe, she reflected, if she had said something sooner, Lynne Slepian would still have a husband, and her sons a father.

An investigator ran the plate number she provided. It was registered to James Charles Kopp, Box 379, Highgate Road, St. Albans, Vermont, and his driving privileges had previously been suspended. The plate matched with a black Chevy Cavalier. Vehicle Identification Number 1G1JE2111H7175930. Police gathered background on the owner: arrested at least two dozen times for anti-abortion protests in the United States; 5'10," 165 pounds, blue eyes, brown hair. Date of birth 8/2/54, place of birth—California.

An Autotrak search showed four suspended or expired driver's licenses for James Charles Kopp—from New York, Rhode Island, Wisconsin and California. A nationwide alert was put out for the

Cavalier. And in Vermont, nine FBI agents showed up at the home of Anthony Kenny in Swanton. No sign of Kopp. Kenny was interviewed. Kopp had been using the Swanton address for some of his mail; he handed the agents two unopened pieces. They contained bank records for account # 644-0055964, belonging to to John C. Kopp d/b/a, JMJ Construction at PNC Bank. P.O. Box 158, Riverside, Connecticut.

"Where else does Kopp send his mail?" an agent asked Kenny.

"He called me about a month ago and gave a new forwarding address."

"Which is?"

"Box 42, Whiting, New Jersey, 08759."

CHAPTER 12—ARE YOU JAMES KOPP?

Crestwood Village Retirement Community
Whiting, N.J.

He was a pretty high-strung guy, Alex. He shared an apartment with easygoing Jim Gannon. Alex, who was not a pro-life activist, worked as a security guard. Anyone stepped onto Gannon's property, Alex heard alarms go off in his head. And so, that day when he was at the kitchen table and saw the red and blue lights flashing through the window, he leapt to his feet. What's going on? A knock. Jim Gannon, sweet old man, cool as a cucumber, stayed at his seat. Alex, his heart pumping, was at the door. He opened it. And saw the barrel pointing at the middle of his chest. The Glock was out, the FBI agent on the porch staring into Alex's eyes. Uniformed police backed up the FBI outside, guns drawn.

"Sit down." The agent motioned to a chair. Alex obeyed. "Are you James C. Kopp?"

"No," Alex said.

Five agents entered the house, Gannon stood to meet them. "Come on in!" he said, gentle blue eyes twinkling. Alex was in shock, but Gannon was not frightened. Not much rattled him. Heck, he came from a large family, six boys, six girls, he was used to commotion; Mom used to invite strangers in off the street for tea all the time. That's how worried James Gannon was about the FBI showing up at his door.

He was told the FBI was investigating the shooting of a doctor in Amherst. Special Agent Daniel McKenna asked Gannon if he knew James Charles Kopp. Sure, sure, Gannon knew Jim. Stayed there sometimes. Gannon knew there was no way Jim could be involved, although it seemed a lot of folks were entertaining a different point of view. Lordy Pete, he thought. Lordy Pete! They were acting like Jim was a terrorist or something.

The FBI interview lasted more than two hours. Gannon told agents that he forwarded Kopp's nonbanking mail to one of two addresses: Ark Sales, P.O. Box 61, Essex Junction, Vermont 05452, or Nazareth Farms, 1073 Buck Hollow Road, Fairfax, Vermont 05454, Attn: Jen—Jen, as in Jennifer Rock.

"Can I take Mr. Kopp's items?" asked Agent McKenna.

"Go right ahead." Agents gave him receipts for the items. They asked for permission to search the attic.

"Go right ahead," Gannon said. He had nothing to hide, and neither, he was certain, did Jim Kopp.

Four agents went upstairs and returned with a blue knapsack containing a toothbrush, envelopes addressed to Kopp c/o a post office box under the name "Before Dawn." The agents questioned Gannon again. What was "Before Dawn?" Jim produced the newsletter, Gannon explained, which was aimed at seeking donations for the Pro-life cause. The post office box was Gannon's mailing address, he collected donations and deposited them in an account at Sovereign Bank, gave copies of bank statements to a woman named Elizabeth Lewis, who lived in the same retirement community.

Betty had a powder-white, crinkled face, silver hair and kind eyes. She had been arrested with Kopp at a protest in Atlanta back in 1988. She was shocked to see all the police. Oh dear. The agents came into her house and looked up in her attic. "Jim was very pleasant, he just came and went," she said. "A drifter, really. Didn't talk much. He spent a lot of time on the porch, mostly reading, working on the computer. And walking, a great walker. He would be up at six, before dawn, and go walking."

When Betty heard that Jim Kopp was a suspect in the shooting of Dr. Barnett Slepian, she didn't believe it. Jim had once told her that he was as concerned for the spiritual welfare of the abortionists as he was for the babies. She believed him. Such a soft-spoken, nice man. Jim slept in the corner room and spent most of his time on the couch, on the computer, job hunting.

The FBI did not make James Charles Kopp's name public immediately. They intended to keep Kopp in the dark, wherever he was, while they gathered information, found more friends of his who wouldn't see them coming. On Sunday, October 26, three days after Bart's murder, the Bureau collected 13 videotapes of protests outside the downtown Buffalo clinic where Dr. Slepian worked.

On November 4, Amherst police continued their search in the woods behind the home. An officer found trace bits of hair and fibers on the bark of the tree the sniper had leaned against. The hair might produce a DNA profile—but that meant nothing without a match to compare it with. There was no DNA profile for James Kopp on file. But the prospect was there, at least, for Amherst police to compare their DNA sample with the one Hamilton police had retrieved three years earlier from the ski mask discovered in Dr. Hugh Short's driveway. If the two samples matched, they could make the case that the sniper was the same person in both attacks—even though the owner of the DNA profiles would still be unknown.

That same day, the FBI went public. FBI special agent Bernie Tolbert stood at the lectern at the press conference and announced there was a federal material witness warrant for apprehending James Charles Kopp. Joel Mercer, a young red-haired FBI agent, was doing the legwork, co-ordinating searches and other aspects of the investigation. He had only been with the bureau for a year; this case was a big step up. His superiors felt he could handle it. The supervisor of the investigation, and the more visible presence, was Tolbert, 55 years old, charismatic.

Bernie Tolbert had been on the job the morning after the shooting, looking over the crime scene. He lived only minutes away from

Scott Gardner Photo

Bernie Tolbert, FBI

the Slepians. The shooting got to him. He stood in the Slepians' den, saw the photos of Bart, Lynne and the boys. He had a couple of young boys himself. Bart's sons had just lost their father. So tragic. He took Lynne aside. "We'll find whoever did this, I promise you that, Lynne," he vowed. "Hey, this is my neighborhood, my town. We will find him."

"I'd just like 15 minutes alone with him," Lynne said.

Tolbert had been a star athlete in high school and university. He held high jump and triple jump records but then knee injuries slowed him down. He became a social worker. Then one day he met an aggressive recruiter from the FBI. There weren't a lot of black men in the bureau back in the mid-seventies. Most blacks only came in contact with the FBI when agents arrived to arrest someone in the neighborhood. Bernie was dubious, but he applied.

He was rejected. The examiner said the knee injuries disqualified the 30-year-old. He predicted Bernie would be in a wheelchair at 50.

That did it. Now Bernie *wanted* in. He wrote a letter to the top, to the director: "I will see any doctor, any time, at my own expense. I will pit myself against any agent." The bureau gave him another chance. This time, he made it. In the 22 years since, Tolbert had worked out of offices in New York, Philadelphia and Washington. Now he was posted back in Buffalo and standing before the TV cameras, the national media, backed by a huge Justice Department logo. He was acutely aware that the case was attracting enormous attention. It was his biggest show ever. He held up a photo of Kopp.

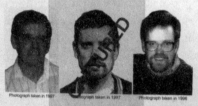

FBI TEN MOST WANTED FUGITIVE

VIOLATION OF THE FREEDOM OF ACCESS TO CLINIC ENTRANCES (FACE) ACT

JAMES CHARLES KOPP

Photograph taken in 1997   Photograph taken in 1997   Photograph taken in 1996

Aliases: James Kopp; Jim Kopp, John Doe, James Charles Copp, John Kapp, Clyde Swenson, Clyde Swanson, Jack Cotty, Jack Crotty, John Kopp, Jacob Koch, Charles Cooper, John Capp, Jim Cobb, James Cobb, Samuel E. Weinstein, Jacob I. Croninger, Enoch A. Guettler, Jonathan H. Henderson, Samuel E. Blanton, Soloman E. Aranburg, Aaron A. Bernstein, Eli A. Hochenleit, Dwight Hanson, K. Jawes Gavin, P. Anastation, B. James Milton, "Atomic Dog" and "Catfish"

"This is a picture of the individual we are looking for," he said. "We have no idea where he is. We're looking everywhere for him. "He appears to be committed to the anti-abortion movement. The problem is, I don't think you can kill someone to show your commitment."

The photo Tolbert held became the public, iconic, "most wanted" image of James Charles Kopp. The ill-trimmed goatee, the short unkempt hair, the glower he directed at the camera. He looked like a killer. Some of Jim Kopp's supporters were so struck by how different he looked, they believed the photo was a fake. But it was a mug shot from his most recent arrest, in New Jersey, on January 23, 1997. The photo did, in fact, look far different from the way Kopp appeared in person. It was as though he had affected the look on purpose, scowling, changing his look, to distort his constantly shifting identity.

On one level, Bernie Tolbert could try to think of the Slepian murder as just another case. A federal law had been broken, so the FBI was automatically involved. But he also knew there was special interest in this show that went as high as the White House. Tolbert soon found himself in conference calls with Washington, talking directly to Attorney General Janet Reno—who herself frequently talked to President Clinton about the case and about anti-abortion violence in general.

Shortly after Tolbert's announcement that James Kopp was wanted as a material witness, a $500,000 reward was offered by the Justice Department for information. The police and FBI were careful not to publicly call Kopp a suspect. They did, however, tell reporters they believed he might hold the key to the investigation.

Tolbert cursed the zeal with which reporters chased the story. Reporters didn't have to play by the same rules as agents, could talk to anyone they pleased without regard for the legalities or nuances of criminal investigation. There were times FBI agents showed up at the home of someone connected to Kopp to find journalists already there. Reporters were all over the place in Vermont. Agents were losing the element of surprise and the media attention was helping Kopp.

On the other hand, the FBI counted on media coverage to spread images of Kopp's face to encourage public tips. One of those tips came from Daniel Lenard, a Buffalo high school teacher. He told police he had seen a jogger on October 18, five days before the murder, hunched over and running slowly along a road near Dr. Slepian's house. Saw him for maybe 10, 15 seconds. He had glasses and a reddish goatee, wore a black hooded sweatshirt and black biker shorts. Ruddy complexion. Pronounced jawline. Looked stressed. And he held his hands up as though he were training for a boxing match, strange compared to other joggers you'd see around there, hardly the picture of health or fitness. Lenard later met with a detective who placed a page of head shots in front of him. There were photos of six men who had brownish-red beards or goatees. The photos were numbered 1 to 6.

"Do you recognize any of them?" the detective asked.

"Yes. Number four. That's him. No question that's the jogger, and the same guy I saw on TV."

It was a photo of James Charles Kopp. Later, FBI special agent Joel Mercer visited the home of another witness who claimed to have seen the mysterious jogger. "His beard was about the color of your hair," the witness told the redheaded Mercer. He showed the witness the same photo array that had been placed before Lenard. The witness paused.

"There—number four," he said. Kopp. Later, a third witness signed his initials beside photo number four as well.

The search in the woods behind the Slepians' house continued. On November 5, a police officer noticed a sliver of plastic sticking from the ground. It was a buried garbage bag. Contents they found inside included a green baseball cap with the inscriptions "New York" and "NY," a silver men's wristwatch, an empty rifle ammunition box, binoculars, two green earplugs, black fanny pack, flashlight, protective gun muffler earmuffs and two plastic shopping bags. Amherst police sent the evidence to the FBI's Washington lab. One latent fingerprint was eventually lifted from the evidence—but the print did not match prints on file from Kopp's criminal records. The bag was a good find, suggesting the level of planning used by the sniper. But the key piece was still missing—the weapon.

* * *

Members of the joint U.S.–Canadian police task force on the five sniper attacks continued to share information and discuss strategy. A joint management meeting was held in Hamilton. Senior Hamilton police officials discussed the investigation with task force members from the FBI, RCMP, and Winnipeg and Vancouver police forces. Amherst police chief John Askey burst into the meeting, angry. The chief had learned there had been an RCMP officer in Amherst, conducting surveillance, in the days before the murder of Bart Slepian. How could the RCMP have not told him about the suspect they were tailing? "You're following the guy, and you let him shoot one of my citizens!" he charged.

RCMP officials at the meeting said there had in fact been an agent in the Buffalo area, but it was for surveillance concerning a matter unrelated to the doctor shootings. And no one knew Kopp was a suspect prior to the shooting, so how could they be following him at the time? One man dead, three seriously injured, another barely escaping injury, and the sniper still at large. Pressure was mounting on all of the law enforcement agencies.

* * *

Phone ringing, before dawn, Wednesday morning, November 4. Jennifer Rock picks up.
   "Jen. I'm in trouble. Can you call me back?"

Jennifer Rock had an office job with IBM in Vermont. She had known Jim Kopp for several years, met him through protests several years before when she was in her early twenties, he had once stayed at her parents' home. Rock's Vermont address had been one of several to which Kopp had his mail sent, she had deposited money in banks for him. She phoned him back at 6:30 a.m.

   "Close the account, bring the money and meet me," Jim told her.

   The next day, Rock left home. She told her parents she'd be in New York for a while. Looking for some work, visiting friends. She arrived at a mall in White Plains, New York. She had the money and a false West Virginia driver's license she had made at Jim's request. She tried to look inconspicuous, browse for shoes. She stopped at the newsstand and saw the headline: "James Charles Kopp Wanted by the FBI as a Material Witness." She saw the murky photo of Jim's grimacing face. Where did they get that photo? Didn't look like him at all. The FBI had obviously pointed the finger at him. But he could never have shot someone. She spotted her friend.

   "Jim, your face is everywhere. You have to get out of here."

   They got in her car and headed for Newark, New Jersey. (Jim had changed plates again on his car, but he knew he could no longer use the wanted black Cavalier anywhere in the country.) He should get on a plane and leave the country, now, he said, until his name could be cleared. No, argued Jennifer. Had he seen the papers, the news on TV? His face was everywhere. Not to Newark airport. They should drive, in her car, south.

The FBI hit the places where Kopp had been, retracing his steps, interviewing people he had stayed with, even questioning a mailman who confirmed he had delivered mail to a "Jack Crotty," one of Kopp's aliases. They searched a Laurel Avenue residence in Newark, Delaware, and seized computer disks containing eight Texas driver's licenses under various names. They searched room 148 at the Travel Inn, 8920 Gulf Freeway, Houston, Texas, and seized a telephone book. On Thursday, November 6, agents visited TV station WOWK in Huntington, West Virginia. Kopp had once been arrested at a protest outside a clinic in nearby Charleston. The station provided video from coverage of the scene. He was on the tape. For the FBI, finding contacts of Kopp's was not the problem. He had fleeting pro-life acquaintances all over the country, people like Gannon, Betty, Anthony Kenny. But these were not the type of contacts who held the key to catching him, they knew nothing of his movements. It seemed as if he had no intimate friends, no trusted allies he would turn to at a time like this. Even his sister didn't know much about him. It was as if James Kopp had planned it that way: "One cannot be betrayed if one has no people."

* * *

From his office in Quantico, Virginia, FBI profiler James Fitzgerald advised agents in the field on what kinds of questions to ask James Kopp's friends and family, about his background, personal history. Ask the right questions, in the right order. Did he change his appearance much over the years? What about his relationships?

Fitzgerald studied the information coming in. The subject knew many people, had traveled the country, and the world, extensively.

His emerging analysis suggested James Charles Kopp was a conflicted individual. He was well educated, holding a master's degree, but had held mostly menial jobs. He was deeply religious—yet apparently a killer. Kopp clearly belonged to an extreme wing of the anti-abortion movement. But even within that wing he was a bit of a loner, marched to his own drummer, did his own thing. Nonviolent, his friends said, but Fitzgerald sensed an escalation in Kopp's thinking about how he should combat abortion. The profiler believed that Kopp had been the one who pulled the trigger in all three of the Canadian attacks, in addition to the Rochester shooting, and the Slepian murder.

Question: Would Kopp try again?

Surely not, thought Fitzgerald, now that he was a wanted man, now that his cover was blown. He would try to disappear. It would be too risky to try again in the foreseeable future. Kopp fitted the sniper mentality: calculating, careful, nonconfrontational. He would not attack again, not unless he was motivated to simply taunt the FBI. And that was highly unlikely. He was too smart for that, his mission too strictly defined.

Among the first people agents interviewed was Jim's stepmother, Lynn Kopp, in Texas. She talked about the family: Chuck Kopp, ex-Marine, disciplinarian; Nancy Kopp, devout mother; the twin brother; three sisters, two of whom had died young. Jim's past relationships? There was Jenny, the girlfriend at UC Santa Cruz. At least, that's what Lynn had heard. She had never met Jenny, had never seen Jim with any girl, actually. From what she heard, the relationship with Jenny didn't last long, and Jim went berserk when he learned she'd had an abortion.

Fitzgerald examined the interview transcripts. Interesting. Kopp had been extremely close to his mother. And over the years, on the road, protesting, he had had strong associations with women. Yet he never married, and there was no evidence of a long-term relationship with a female. Most of the relationships, if not all, appeared to have been platonic. Women were the key to James Kopp's future, Fitzgerald was convinced that if he were to communicate with anyone while on the run, either for shelter or to resume his sniper campaign, it would definitely be a woman, somewhere.

There was a list of activists who had joined Kopp at protests in Vermont. An FBI agent had titled one document, "Vermont Rescuers—February 21, 1990 to May 9, 1990," and included addresses. There were several women on the list. Agents had already located a few of them. But there was one who had not yet been found. Her name was Loretta Marra. Agents had discovered, among Kopp's possessions in James Gannon's attic, a magazine with abortion clinic bomber Dennis Malvasi's mailing address on it. Malvasi was known by the authorities to be married to Loretta. She had been photographed under surveillance at Malvasi's Brooklyn apartment back in October 1997. But she had since fallen off the radar. Perhaps Kopp would try to contact her.

CHAPTER 13—ON THE LAM

After leaving New Jersey, Jennifer Rock and Jim Kopp drove for more than 30 hours, taking turns at the wheel, sleeping in the car. Jim altered his appearance on the road, bleached his hair blond to match the photo on the fake West Virginia driver's license. There were long stretches where Jim said nothing at all to her. "The government has done this," she said. "Set you up."

Jim nodded and said nothing.

"I'll never be able to see my family again," he finally said. It is 1,986 miles from Newark to the Mexican border at Laredo, Texas. They crossed the border, parked near an airport. The thin blond man got out of the car and disappeared. On November 8, Rock drove back into the United States and headed north. When she returned to New York she dialed a pager number belonging to a "John Rizzo."

The next day, FBI special agent Walter Steffens Jr. searched a lot in a truck stop campground in Kent County, Delaware. The lot belonged to a man named Javier Hernandez, who had bought it from James Kopp. Kopp had owned the property for three years, but his name did not appear on the deed. The land included a trailer and camper top. Steffens talked to neighbors who said they recalled Kopp living in the trailer about a year and a half before. He searched the camper and found a priority mail envelope containing an updated résumé for Kopp, detailing his work history through April 1993. And he found a permit in the name of Dwight Hanson for use of the Elkneck Shooting

Range, located about an hour's drive away. There were four newsletters from another shooting range nearby, the Delmarva Sportsman Association, addressed to Kevin James Gavin at a Maryland post office box. Steffens visited the post office box and found another shooting range permit. Back at the FBI lab, the documents were dusted for fingerprints. The prints on the papers matched each other. They also matched fingerprints on file for James Charles Kopp.

That same day, agents searched the house at 1073 Buck Hollow Road, Fairfax, Vermont. It was a house belonging to a relative of Jennifer Rock. On Wednesday, November 11, agents again searched James Gannon's home in Whiting, New Jersey. They seized four boxes containing papers, maps, computer disks, books, notebooks, an address book. There was an envelope addressed to Jack Crotty, c/o Doris and Scott, Pittsburgh.

"Who owns these boxes?" an agent asked Gannon.

"I don't know," was Gannon's answer.

The contents were sealed and sent to the FBI office in Buffalo. Among the contents, an agent found a hand-drawn map. The map was dusted for prints. Also, on a torn piece of paper, the address 4990 Lebanon Road. The agent flipped the paper over, and saw on the other side a notation reading, "A to Z 883-9945." The phone number was for the 615 area code, Old Hickory, a town near Nashville.

Soon after that, a man nattily dressed in a dark suit walked through the door of the A-Z Pawn Shop in Old Hickory. He stopped at the counter and looked at Patricia Osbourne, who was working the store that day.

"I'm John Eastes. I'm a special agent with the FBI's field office in Nashville." He asked to see Osbourne's books. They went to the back of the store, and he began silently leafing through the pages.

"What are you looking for?" she asked. Eastes was the first agent to visit the store, but Osbourne would meet more in the weeks to come. They combed through the books, took materials away, brought them back. There had apparently been no gun purchase at the A-Z Pawn Shop by anyone named James C. Kopp.

* * *

Jersey City, N.J.
Thursday evening, November 12, 1998

FBI Special Agent Larry Wack learned from agents in Newark, New Jersey, of another address where Kopp had lived as late as the previous September under the alias Clyde Svenson. On the night of November 12, agents visited a three-storey, redbrick apartment on Communipaw Avenue in Jersey City. The agents moved to the back of the building, then up the stairs to a unit on the second floor, and knocked on the unfinished wooden door of number 346, the home of Seth Grodofsky. "Last time I saw Clyde was two weeks ago," said Grodofsky.

"Where is he now?"

"I think he's doing contracting work in New York."

The agents asked more questions. It seemed Clyde Svenson also kept some belongings down by the docks along the Hudson River, down on Warren Street. The agents asked to search the apartment. Grodofsky refused. They would need a warrant. One of the agents left. The others stayed overnight, making sure no potential evidence was disturbed during the wait for a court to issue the warrant.

Meanwhile, more agents headed to Warren Street, on the water, Slip No. 7. They seized three sealed cardboard boxes belonging to Clyde Svenson. One contained a computer, monitor, printer, accessories. Another held a large vinyl travel bag containing a typewriter, book, lantern. Another box had books, computer disks, software guides. Among the loose papers was a Bell Atlantic phone bill and a New York Police Department traffic ticket for New York plate number BPE 216.

Warrant in hand, agents searched Grodofsky's apartment the next afternoon. They found a padlocked maroon toolbox that had "Job Box" written on it. They cracked the lock. The box contained a hand plane, staple gun, electrical tape, heat gun and other tools.

Agents also collected clothes, bedding, a plastic mug, church news-letters, duct tape, two small flashlights, a movie stub, a bottle of sauce, a photo of the Pope, travel brochures, a toothbrush and, in the bedroom, a bottle for holy water. Special Agent Barry Lee Bush looked in the closet. He stood on a chair to check the top shelf, spotted a notebook. He opened the book and saw a notation: "716 Barnet 834-6796, Amherst." The notebook was sent to a lab for prints and analysis. The phone number was for Dr. Barnett Slepian's office in Amherst, New York.

The same day, agents searched 1073 Buckhollow Road, Fairfax, Vermont, home of Grace R. Rock. They seized one Smith & Wesson handgun, two empty magazines, two boxes of cartridges.

On Thursday, November 19, agents visited Loretta Marra's last-known address: 12 Indian Trail, West Milford, New Jersey. One of Loretta's three brothers, Nicholas Marra, answered the door. "I haven't seen Loretta. Not since the summertime," he said.

"Is that unusual?"

"No. She's like a vagabond, you know? No fixed address. I wouldn't know how to get in touch with her if I tried. But we don't talk much. Some of the family relationships are a little strained." The agents interviewed another brother, Joseph. He said he didn't get along well with his siblings—Loretta, Nick or Bill. "They have this fervent religious zeal on the abortion issue. Comes from my parents. They forced their opinions on the four kids. Loretta? No, haven't been in touch with her in a long time."

The FBI next located and interviewed Jennifer Rock, having tracked her license plate and studied her recent phone and banking records. Her calling card record indicated a call had been placed to 914-844-7355 on November 4 at 6:36 a.m. It was a pager number Kopp had given out to several people, including his sister Anne.

"Did you recently take a trip to Mexico?" the agents asked.

"Yes," she said.

"When did you come back to the United States?"

"On November 4. At Laredo."

Wrong answer. She couldn't have crossed back from Mexico that day. Phone records placed her at work, an IBM office in Vermont, on November 4.

"Did James Kopp phone you within the last two weeks?"

She said nothing.

"What about the $7,000 withdrawal you made on November 5? What was that for?"

Rock's stories did not add up. But from the phone records it was clear she had not been in touch with Kopp since Mexico. The records also showed that she had dialed pager number 917-773-3716 immediately upon arriving home. After searching the records of a pager company called Smart Beep, agents learned the pager was for a John Rizzo. On November 20, an agent called the Rizzo pager. A woman picked up the page. She went to a phone booth to return the page to avoid having her call traced, using a prepaid phone card, and unwittingly spoke to an agent on the other end. The bureau had made contact with Loretta Marra—Rizzo was one of three false pager names she used—but the agents still did not know exactly where she was living.

Gary Yokoyama/*The Hamilton Spectator*

FBI Special Agent Bernie Tolbert holds up photos of Kopp's car.

* * *

It was December 18, 56 days after the murder of Dr. Bart Slepian. A man named John Caldararo, of the Port Authority of New York and New Jersey Transit Police, conducted his routine check of the long-term parking lot at the Newark International Airport. He noticed a black Chevy Cavalier with an expired Pennsylvania registration sticker. The car had one plate on it: New Jersey, RAJ 889. He noticed the window was ajar and keys still in the ignition. The long-term parking lot was a well-known place for people to ditch cars. He recorded the car's VIN and ran a search on the number, 1G1JE2111H7175930. A notice came up on the computer screen. Amherst police and the FBI wanted that car. He got on the phone.

License plates change, but the VIN is the key. It was James Kopp's car. He had switched the Vermont license plate on it, but it was his vehicle.

Special Agent Arthur Durrant visited the airport to examine the car. He pulled out his notebook and started writing. "One 1987 Chevy Cavalier, RS Model, black in color, 2 door, hatchback, red pinstripe on the front bumper, green PA Inspection Sticker dated 4/97." The car was removed and taken to the first floor of the FBI garage at 910 Newark Avenue. Items recovered included: a Tasco binocular case on the floor in front of the passenger seat, a plastic Tops Markets grocery bag behind driver's seat, samples of hairs and fibers vacuumed up from the interior and trunk, religious medallion and hanging ribbon and flower on the front dash, service sticker on inner windshield for Autospa of North Bergen, in center console three AAA batteries, keys, fuses, bulbs, small flashlight, drill, wire, bit, chalk, token; in rear hatch knotted cord and hardware, pack of auto fuses, religious card, pine needle in engine compartment.

* * *

The jet descended over, London, the Thames River snaking through the city below. Jim Kopp had been to England several times before, primed for battle in the abortion wars. This time, he was invisible. Had to be. Indeed, he might not be staying long. Not at all. The flight touched down at Heathrow Airport. He deboarded. The connecting flight was later in the day, to Australia. Jim loved Australia. Even though he came from roots that were, he maintained, of Austrian and Irish origin, and even though he respected Canada, he identified most with the Australians. That country had the national experience that most closely resembled the American, he felt. One-time colony, a frontier mentality, fierce fighters in wartime. He sat in the airport. Something didn't feel right, though. Nothing had ever felt right since he had started running. His senses were on fire. Trust no one. The man with the $500,000 bounty on his head, the man on the FBI's Ten Most Wanted List, got up and left the airport. There would be no trip to Australia. Not today.

He thought of this time on the lam as "sleeping," as though he wasn't conscious, or was dreaming. The next several weeks were a blur. He was living hand-to-mouth, barely surviving, finding odd jobs in exchange for food and permission to sleep in a closet somewhere. On the run before long he lost 30 pounds, grew a beard, shaved it off, grew it, repeat, changing his appearance as frequently as possible. He wasn't just feeling the heat from the FBI. In his mind's eye, Scotland Yard was on his case, British intelligence, Interpol, city police—they were all looking for him. Maybe not today, maybe not tomorrow, but soon, the FBI would connect the dots, they would stomp on every person he had ever known or loved back home, he thought. That much was a no-brainer. And so they would come looking for him. But they wouldn't find him. He had to move again.

* * *

New York City
December 1998

Loretta Marra was now 35 years old, had a young son and was pregnant with a second child. She was underground. Where might she finally show her face? On December 12, her father, William Marra, was driving home to Connecticut from Birmingham, Alabama. He had spent the past two months teaching seminarians. He stopped at a friend's home in Berkeley Springs, West Virginia. After dinner he left. On Route 81 he suffered a heart attack, managed to pull over, was taken to hospital. A family friend called a priest who arrived just in time to give him last rites. The FBI learned of his death. Would Loretta surface to attend the funeral of her beloved father? Agents were among the mourners, or hidden nearby, at the service. Loretta did not attend.

On January 28, a woman named Joyce Maier took her driver's license exam in New York. The real Joyce Maier was a 31-year-old mentally disabled woman who had been unable to work for years. She was also a niece of Dennis Malvasi. The woman with dark hair and pale green eyes who passed the driver's exam was Loretta Marra. Malvasi had given Joyce's ID to Loretta. He also got his wife an ID in the name of Rosemarie Howard, who was deceased. Assuming the identity of a dead person was an easy way to get a driver's license. It was a trick that Jim Kopp himself had used many times. Officials rarely checked ID against death certificates.

Marra registered a 1988 Mazda using Joyce Maier's social security number. She listed her address as 4809 Avenue North, in Brooklyn, Apt. 148. In fact it was not a residence; 148 was a mailbox number at an American Mail Depot. In February, Marra opened a new bank account at CFS Bank in the name of Joyce Maier. She was proving to be an elusive target for the FBI. Her husband, on the other hand, had always been on the FBI's radar—he was still on probation. Agents interviewed Malvasi's probation officer, trying to determine if he was still with Marra. The probation officer told the FBI that he had recently seen a baby seat in Malvasi's Acura. The officer had also visited Malvasi at his home at 2468 Lynden Avenue, and was told through the door by a woman who remained hidden that Dennis was not home. Agents interviewed an employer of Malvasi named Anthony Castellano. He was not enthusiastic about speaking to the FBI. Castellano said that Malvasi kept company with a woman, but Castellano only knew her as "Rose." An agent pulled out a photograph.

"Is this her?"

Castellano looked at the photo of Loretta Marra. He paused. "Yes."

Malvasi was ordered to appear before a grand jury in Buffalo in connection with the search for Kopp. He testified on February 10, 1999.

"Do you know James Charles Kopp?"

"I have never met him," said Malvasi.

"Do you know Loretta Marra?"

Dennis Malvasi cited his Fifth Amendment rights and refused to answer the question. He said he lived alone.

"Has anyone used your 1990 Acura? Does anyone else drive that with your permission?"

"Not steadily, no."

"Have you ever loaned it to a friend who has a baby or has a child that requires a car seat?"

"Oh, yeah."

"And who would that be?"

"My niece."

"And her name is?"

"Joyce Maier."

On March 1, 1999, Loretta Marra signed a lease for a new apartment at 385 Chestnut Street in Brooklyn. She and Dennis were listed on the lease under the names Joyce and Ted Barnes. In April, Loretta went to Canada to give birth to her second child. She had many Canadian friends and, with her aliases, she could still easily cross the border. She gave birth that same month, near Ottawa. It was her second boy.

* * *

On March 19, 1999, Canadian law enforcement officials announced that a $547,000 reward would be offered to anyone helping lead police to "the arrest and conviction of the person or persons responsible for the shootings of the three Canadian doctors." Canadian police released a poster featuring pictures of James Charles Kopp—who was described only as a "person of interest" in the investigation. Among the groups contributing towards the reward money were the Canadian Abortion Rights Action League (CARAL), Canadian Medical Association, and provincial medical associations.

* * *

Amherst, N.Y.
April 8, 1999

No weapon had ever been found at any of the crime scenes where the sniper attacked. Amherst police had ended the search for a weapon when winter set in. With the ground now thawing, Amherst chief of detectives Joseph Scioli ordered a more thorough search of the woods behind the Slepian's home.

A detective named Donald Wright was one of those on the search that day. Wright was a former Boy Scout leader. Perhaps only someone like Wright, who was an expert in orienteering, would have noticed. As they scoured the woods, officers kept their eyes glued to the ground, searching. Wright looked up. He noticed a small paint marking, at roughly eye level, on one sapling. And then another. And a third. Triangulation? Where did the three points intersect? Wright looked closer. On two of the saplings there was a plus sign painted, and on the third, a negative sign. Painted on a small tree near the saplings were the letters N and W and the number 0. Wright slowly walked in a line due north from between the two saplings. If you did so, you would intersect with a line from the tree that was painted N,W, 0. Where the lines intersected, he noticed two cut evergreen branches crossed over each other.

"Could I have some assistance over here?" Wright said. "I think I might have something." The former Boy Scout was correct. Police started digging and, 30 centimeters down, found a tube wrapped in rubberized material. It was buried at an angle, with one end open at ground level. It was like a subterranean holster. Inside the tube was a Russian-made semiautomatic SKS rifle, with wooden stock extension. The tube also contained two pairs of gloves, one white and one brown. The location was about 160 feet away from the tree where the sniper had braced himself. He had created a guide map so he could easily find his rifle in the dark, take his shot at Dr. Slepian, slip the gun back in its holster and escape. The cops would never figure it out, and the SKS would remain buried forever, or someone could return some day and retrieve it. The serial number was GYUT10251.

Two days later, the FBI made a return visit to the A-Z Pawn Shop in Old Hickory, Tennessee. This time, Bureau of Alcohol, Tobacco and Firearms agent Mark Hoback wasn't looking for a name, but rather a serial number. The store records showed the gun buried on Bart Slepian's property had indeed been sold by A-Z. The man who purchased it on July 16, 1997 was a B. James Milton, of Virginia. The FBI checked Virginia records. B. James Milton did not exist.

CHAPTER 14—WANTED

FBI agents continued searching and gathering anything related to Kopp. On April 15, FBI agents searched the Raymond P. Betit Agency, at 439 Main St., Room Seven, Bennington, Vt. and seized Kopp's insurance file. April 19, agents searched 4112 Pleasure Ave., Sea Isle City, N.J. and seized an arc welder. That same day they searched the grounds at 148 Deep Grass Lane, Greenwood, Del. In an abandoned building on the property they found a passport in the name of Nancy Kopp, some papers, rope and a ceramic cup. On May 5 and 6 they searched Seth Grodofsky's apartment in Jersey City again, seized a pad of tracing paper, a piece of wire with pink plastic insulation, and a piece of armored three-wire electrical conduit. On May 11, agents searched CVS Pharmacy, 1099 Route. 33, Hamilton, New Jersey, and collected one videotape labeled "Thursday."

Forensics agents sifted through reams of DNA and fiber evidence. Hair found in a green hat at the scene behind the Slepians' home did not contain roots, and thus no DNA. Instead a mitochondrial DNA analysis was performed. The profile was compared to DNA evidence obtained from a toothbrush found in James Gannon's attic. The two samples matched, and excluded 99.35 percent of the general Caucasian population. The guy who had been in the woods behind Dr. Slepian's house had also stayed at Gannon's. Was it James Kopp? They needed to capture Kopp and retrieve his DNA to prove that.

Meanwhile, Karen Lanning, an FBI lab scientist, studied the blue-green acrylic fibers discovered on the wooden stock extension attached to the rifle. There were similar fibers on the pair of white gloves and a belted fanny pack—much like the fibers found on the tree where the sniper had positioned himself, which in turn resembled those found on clothing and bedding in Seth Grodofsky's Jersey City apartment, and those vacuumed from James Kopp's Chevy Cavalier in Newark.

Ballistics focused on the SKS rifle. FBI firearms expert James Cadigan determined that the full metal jacket 7.42 x 39-millimeter bullet recovered inside the house was of a caliber consistent with the rifle found in the woods. But there was a snag. When Cadigan test fired the SKS at an FBI range to confirm it was operable, he could not conclusively link the Slepian bullet to the rifle. The rifling marks on the bullet he fired did not match those on the evidence. Had the bullet that killed Dr. Slepian been fired from another rifle? Not necessarily, Cadigan argued. It was not uncommon for the internal characteristics of the barrel of a high-powered rifle to change with each shot, which meant rifling marks would change as well.

A second issue was the rifle's accuracy. If the case ever went to trial, they would have to reconstruct the shooting scene and the sniper's position in meticulous detail. That included test firing the weapon. But the rifle's scope had been removed to test the eyepiece glass for DNA. When the scope was remounted, the alignment was off. An FBI marksman later had to align it properly. Those were issues that FBI investigators knew could come back to bite them in court, if they ever made an arrest in the case.

The evidence collected so far was sufficient. An arrest warrant was issued for James Charles Kopp in the murder of Dr. Barnett Slepian. The federal warrant, signed by Judge Hugh B. Scott, referred to Kopp using "force, intentionally injuring, intimidating and interfering with Dr. Barnett Slepian because he was and had been providing reproductive health services."

* * *

Bernie Tolbert watched his son take to the baseball diamond with the other kids. Springtime in Amherst. His youngest boy played in the Lou Gehrig Little League. Tolbert walked over to the bleachers. There was Lynne Slepian. She had a son playing ball, too. She was playing the role of both mother and father now. It had been seven months since the murder, seven months since Bart's boys had been there, kneeling on the floor, watching their father bleed to death. She stayed in touch with Bernie, quizzing him for updates on the investigation. What are you doing? What is going on? Bernie told her the FBI put Kopp on its Ten Most Wanted Fugitives List. "But will that help, Bernie, have a tangible effect?"

"It's an important, maybe critical, step, Lynne," he said in his deep, deliberate baritone. "The success rate is something like 94 percent captured," he said. It was hard for Bernie to look into Lynne's face when she watched her fatherless sons. It was a reminder that they had to get Kopp. Had to.

On June 2, agents searched a garage at 252 Whiton Street, Jersey City, and seized two wood and carpeted structures bearing the name "Clyde." On June 16, California agents searched a residence at 351 View Drive, Ukiah, California.

On June 23, FBI agents once again interviewed Loretta's brother, Nicholas. "I still haven't heard from her," he said. The agents played him a tape recording. It was from a call on November 20, 1998. Nick listened. It was the conversation between an unsuspecting Loretta—returning a page for John Rizzo—and a law enforcement officer. "I don't recognize either voice," he said.

Later, an agent made notes. Nicholas Marra was lying, he believed. Telephone records for Marra showed that he had called the Rizzo pager himself, as well as a cell phone Loretta had been using under the name of John Graskukas.

It was on June 24 that a grand jury in Erie County indicted James Charles Kopp on charges of murder in the second degree, reckless endangerment in the first degree, and criminal possession of a weapon in the third degree. But Jim Kopp was a long way from Erie County.

*   *   *

Brooklyn, N.Y.
Wednesday, October 6, 1999

The woman who called herself Joyce Maier walked into the brown brick building at 385 Chestnut Street, in the eastern corner of Brooklyn. Loretta Marra had lived with Dennis Malvasi in apartment 2D since March. There were some nice streets not too far away, quaint walk-up apartments, bustling shops and markets. But the immediate area around the building on Chestnut was not pleasant. Cabbies wouldn't come here at night. Loretta's apartment overlooked Liberty Street and F&H Auto Repair, which was protected by a chain-link fence crowned with razor wire. Across the street sat an empty lot overgrown with weeds and strewn with litter, a "Danger: Poison" sign marking the spot.

Loretta sometimes spoke with a neighbor named Carmen, and her friend Yolanda. Carmen was a tiny 78-year old from Puerto Rico, walked with a limp and had a black Chiuahaua named Chi Chi. She was a pastor, had her very own pulpit in her apartment where she addressed friends or those she helped off the street, preached the Rapture to them, told them the Good News: "God is coming, and the earth will be aflame! And you know who will burn? The wicked will burn. The wicked will burn!"

It is difficult making yourself disappear. It takes planning, energy, an inner radar detector—paranoia is your friend, unless it goes too far and you are sucked into your own vortex of obsession. Loretta was living such a life. Here she was, a devout Catholic pro-lifer, holed up in Brooklyn, underground, as her mother had been with the French resistance.

Scott Gardner Photo

The Brooklyn apartment building where Loretta Marra was in hiding.

Loretta opened the letter dated October 12, from one of her friends in Canada. A very nice one. It was addressed to "Jane," the name she had used when crossing the border to give birth to her son in Canada. "I pray for you," it said. "I pray that everything will change, and once more, freedom."

Outside it is dark, raining. A dirty American flag lies tangled and ripped on the fire escape of her neighbor's apartment. She can see, through her window, across Liberty Street, the car lot and razor wire bathed in security lights. Above her head in the apartment, water drips from a hole in the pockmarked ceiling. Pip. Pip. Pip. She moves past the lightbulb that dangls on a cord, and walks to the door, opens it just a crack. No such thing as a smoke-free apartment in this part of Brooklyn. But she has to think of her kids. Loretta lights a cigarette and inhales. Pip. Pip. Pip. She leans her shoulder and head against the wall, peering through the opening. She exhales, the smoke escaping into the corridor. She stares at nothing.

* * *

New York City
October 4, 1999

Monday morning. The special agent drove to work in downtown Manhattan. What car was it today? The Intrepid? The Taurus? FBI agents changed cars every day. In the interests of security? Nah. That's Hollywood stuff. Your car for the day was simply whatever was available in the company pool. Security? Hell, he couldn't even park in the underground garage at the office. Had to find a spot on the street like everyone else. He worked at 265 Federal Plaza, the Jacob K. Javits Building. In a part of Manhattan where so much of the architecture was striking, larger than life, the 41-storey dark blue- and gray-checkered concrete building, reflected the agent, looked so—federal government.

The G-man parked and emerged from his car, walked along the sidewalk to the side door for employees, the security guard nodded at him in recognition. Six foot four, angular and athletic, long casual stride. The herringbone, tan suit shimmered in the sun, dark shoes polished, tie with red-and-blue teardrop design. His hair combed back, perhaps a dash of mousse, the flecks of gray unnoticeable from a distance. Name: Michael A. Osborn. He was overseeing the biggest investigation of his career.

He lived in New York but there was no hint of a local accent, no drawl of any kind, no regional inflection. Where was he from, originally? "Can't tell you that." Which region of the country? Sorry. He spoke G-man, carried the act to amusing extremes. The bureau cultivated it. In a country of sharply divergent regional cultures and state laws, the FBI is national, loyal to nothing except the Constitution. Just the facts, ma'am. Osborn had been with the bureau for five years. This new case, while high-profile, wasn't a promotion, that's not how things worked. His field office was the logical one given the proximity of the suspects. And he, Osborn, was deemed to have the skills for the job.

It was a case rife with politics, religion, ends and means, "justifiable homicide," the kind of case where those being pursued, and their allies, saw the FBI as jackbooted assassins with uberfeminists Hillary Clinton and Janet Reno pushing the buttons. Abortion. Murder. Pro-life. Pro-choice. Osborn could not let himself dwell upon the politics, it was peripheral to the task. He had his orders.

Mike Osborn was pursuing a couple of people who were friends of James Charles Kopp, the wanted killer of an abortion doctor. That was his focus. He allowed himself to think about the night Dr. Slepian was killed, his kids beside him in the kitchen, the blood. That's the crime. You couldn't imagine Michael Osborn lying awake at night debating whether the shooter of an obstetrician was more worthy of FBI pursuit than the killer of a plastic surgeon. Enforce the law. It's all in the FBI oath.

His team was watching and recording somewhere close to the building at 385 Chestnut Street in Brooklyn on Tuesday, October 5. Agents working surveillance included Osborn, Robert Conrad, Joan Machiono. They saw a man who looked like Dennis Malvasi walk into the building. Two weeks later they watched a blue Mazda park in front of the building. They ran the plate: car registered to a Joyce Maier, driver's license obtained in that name, January 1999. The address given by the woman is not 385 Chestnut, but an American Mail Depot box. Agents obtained paperwork for the license and vehicle. They lifted fingerprints from the forms she'd filled out. The prints matched those of Loretta Marra.

* * *

Brooklyn, N.Y.
Friday, November 5, 1999

TV Reporter *(off camera)*: What do you think is going through his mind when he looks through that telescope at the doctor?
FBI behavioral expert: Target acquisition. Pull trigger, take in breath, pull trigger, kill.

Reporter: So he's not thinking anti-abortion thoughts?

FBI expert: No. He is focused solely on his mission, his covert military mission, as I'm sure he describes it to himself, and that is to acquire target and kill.

Host: I'm Mike Wallace. These stories tonight on *60 Minutes II*.

The videotape of the program continued. Loretta Marra and Dennis Malvasi watched, along with a man Dennis had known years before, and with whom he had recently become reacquainted. The *60 Minutes* episode had first aired two months earlier. The segment was called "The Fugitive." It was about a man wanted by the FBI named James Kopp, "believed to be a lone sniper assassin who picks off abortion doctors one by one."

(Images of flowers and mourners from Bart Slepian's funeral. FBI wanted poster for Kopp.)

Reporter: The FBI discovered that Jim Kopp was one of the busiest anti-abortion activists in the country, a legend within the movement.

(Cut to Jim's stepmother, Lynn Kopp)

Lynn Kopp: The children had some very strong disciplinary action against them.

Reporter: Like what?

Lynn Kopp: Beatings. And one of his daughters told me that Chuck had—had been very cruel to his wife.

Reporter: How do you think this impacted the kids, Jim in particular?

Lynn Kopp: They would be very protective of their mother, and there would be a lot of resentment towards their father.

(Cut to Dr. Garson Romalis in Vancouver recalling the morning of his near-mortal wounding in 1994.)

At that moment Loretta Marra spoke up.

"He could have killed him if he wanted to," she said.

Malvasi's old friend listened carefully, memorizing her words.

The agents would want him to remember them precisely.

"So what did Marra say, exactly?"

The man considered the question. He tried to remember.

"He could have killed him if he wanted to."

Did Loretta Marra mean James Kopp? That Kopp could have killed Romalis if he had wished to? Or was she using a generic "he," as in "the sniper?" First he was sure she had meant Kopp. Then he wasn't.

Malvasi's "old friend," was now a paid informant of the FBI. Code name CS1. The FBI had recruited him some months earlier. There was a second informant, CS2, working other people in the pro-life movement. As for CS1, his first task was helping to locate Marra and Malvasi. Now he was in regular contact with Dennis and Loretta and was being paid for solid information. He would engage the couple in conversation, work it around to Kopp. So far, Kopp's location had not been revealed. If Loretta knew where he was, she was still cautious talking about it.

Hopefully Loretta would loosen up, tell the informant where Kopp was, or better yet, try to contact him. But at this point it was not wise for the FBI to simply haul her in for questioning. If the FBI knew one thing about Loretta Marra, it was that she would not be intimidated and would never give up a fellow pro-life soldier. She felt that suffering was what being a true Catholic was all about, suffering for the truth, for a higher good. She would happily put out her hands for cuffing, her lips sealed to protect Jim from the government. He was innocent, after all.

* * *

Dublin, Ireland
Winter 1999

Dublin is a city that seems ready to burst at the seams, cars crowded on narrow streets, sidewalks and footbridges crossing the River Liffey

Scott Gardner Photo

Francis welcomed Jim Kopp—"Timothy"—into his hostel.

with crowds pinched like sand passing through an hourglass. "It feels," says a cabbie, "like half the fookin' country lives in the capital." It is a good place to blend in, to vanish, to be no one. Jim Kopp was in Dublin, in a tough part of town, among others who had no money and were also perhaps running from their past.

At a hostel he found a savior when he looked into the kind, pale, wrinkled face of an elderly Irishman named Francis. "Yes, yes, come in, come in," Francis would tell all visitors, his eyes as warm as a fireplace, his hands thick and soft. He was a retired furniture maker—retired, but still a joyful Catholic working towards a greater goal: delivering his soul to the Lord. He managed the Morningstar men's hostel, named after the star of Jesus, run by the Legion of Mary. The hostel didn't force religion on its guests but was Christian in approach, held services in the chapel. There was a picture and quotes from Saint Thérèse d'Lisieux on the wall—one of Jim Kopp's favorite saints, as it happened. Francis believed he had been sent to the hostel by God. He was 77 years old, his Irish lilt gentle when he spoke, barely above a whisper. But he was still spry enough to bound up the stairs two at a time. In the 400-year-old building, row upon row of cots lined the communal sleeping areas, the walls a faded yellow, not the grandest setting, but definitely an improvement from the street. At Morningstar, for two pounds a day, you could live your life in a respectable manner.

One day, a tall, thin man, glasses, half beard, showed up needing help. As always, Francis was there.

"What's your name, son?" he asked in his hushed voice.

"Timothy," came the reply.

Francis took the tired hand in his, and Timmy's life was saved. A nice man, Francis thought. Prayerful. But Timmy's life wasn't perfect, he made mistakes, as all who came to the hostel had done. Francis listened to Timothy's story. A real shame about his family, back in the United States, who apparently no longer accepted him, who had cast him out for being different. Francis felt for him. Timmy had his beliefs, others held them in disdain, so he escaped from the torment, hid from it. The others might come looking for him. It was important that he remain hidden at least for a while. Timmy said his family lived in New Orleans. He had lots of stories. One day, Timmy didn't show up for mass as he always did. He was gone, just like that, unannounced. Strange for him to leave so suddenly.

"Good luck to you, my son," Francis thought. "May the Lord look over you. And may your parents one day find you. Whatever happened, they must be so worried."

CHAPTER 15—TIM GUTTLER

Hamilton, Ontario
Monday, January 24, 2000

The Canadian arm of the international joint sniper task force held a press conference—with spokesman Keith McCaskill from Winnipeg, Hamilton police chief Ken Robertson, and Dennis McGillis from the Ontario Provincial Police. There was an announcement. The OPP had officially issued an arrest warrant for James Charles Kopp in the attempted murder of Ancaster's Dr. Hugh Short in 1995. No charges were announced in the attacks on Dr. Jack Fainman in 1997 or Dr. Garson Romalis in 1994. McCaskill added that the investigation would continue across the country, but refused to point the finger at Kopp in connection to the Winnipeg and Vancouver attacks. "We certainly know that Mr. Kopp may be a key to the investigations in Winnipeg and Vancouver," McCaskill said, describing Kopp as "a person the police want to interview."

What was going on? It had been seven months since the Erie County grand jury had indicted Kopp for Dr. Slepian's murder. Why had the OPP waited to file its charge? There was no new evidence, no break in the case. Investigators in Vancouver, Hamilton and Winnipeg had done all they could.

They had even pursued a possible link between Kopp and a fundamentalist Catholic sect called St. Pius X, which catered to

Barry Gray/The Hamilton Spectator

Hamilton police chief Ken Robertson addresses media.

Kopp's known preference for attending mass in the traditional Latin. There were St. Pius X churches in Vancouver, Winnipeg and St. Catharines—a city 40 minutes east of Ancaster. A story making the rounds in the Winnipeg congregation had Kopp attending Our Lady of the Rosary. It was even suggested that he had helped organize the mass, but no one could confirm it.

Hamilton police had scoured the woods behind Dr. Hugh Short's home several times looking for the weapon. They returned and searched again after the rifle was discovered behind Slepian's house, three years after the Ancaster shooting—but found nothing. Hamilton police had found the hair fibers in the ski hat at the scene, and developed DNA from it, but could not confirm whose DNA it was. The decision to finally issue an arrest warrant for Kopp seemed more of an attempt to rekindle media interest and encourage tips. Chief Robertson would only say to gathered media that Hamilton police had reviewed the evidence with the OPP, discussed the case with Hamilton's crown attorney, and decided to issue the arrest warrant.

The effectiveness of the task force had been called into question. In Winnipeg, McCaskill had publicly defended their work. He suggested FBI had caught a big break when Joan Dorn had called the police with Kopp's license-plate number in Amherst—it "was not exceptional police work," he was quoted saying in the *Winnipeg Free Press*. But the reality, despite the big announcement, pointed out columnist Susan Clairmont in the *Hamilton Spectator*, was that little was happening in the Canadian sniper hunt. At the same time the arrest warrant was issued, two of the three OPP officers who had been working with the task force were given new assignments. "We're not going to have these guys traveling the country searching for him," said one OPP official.

The Slepian murder had altered the nature of the Canadian investigation, the FBI had the resources—not to mention direction from the White House—to lead the effort to catch him. The Canadian police were primarily on the sidelines, the evidence they had gathered a reference for the American investigation. But for all that the FBI had learned about Kopp, for all the searches and forensic evidence and surveillance, 15 months after Bart Slepian was killed, they still had no clue where he was.

* * *

Dublin, Ireland
Spring 2000

The slender man with thick glasses and bleached hair moved among the crowd on Grafton Street. He loved Grafton, the redbrick street reserved for pedestrians. Shoppers, tourists, professionals, lawyers dressed in black robes taking a break from the nearby courthouse, schoolgirls at lunch, teenage boys on guitar singing John Lennon's "Come Together" to earn loose change.

Jim Kopp loved to blend in and walk the street, up and down, taking in every detail, thoughts swirling in his head. He worked on the local accent, but was still far from being good enough to fool a native Dubliner. He loved languages, the dialects running within each. He considered his spoken French, for example, to have a Caribbean lilt to it. No, he reflected, he would not speak Irish until he got it down perfect. Do not abuse the language, he mused, it would offend the people. Ireland was the right place for him to be, this country where God's law still transcended man's law—they hadn't legalized baby killing here.

He ducked into Bewleys, his favorite coffee shop off Grafton, climbed the wooden stairs to the second level and the James Joyce room, named for the city's favorite son. Jim Kopp had been on the run from the FBI for 17 months. Yet he frequented a place like Bewleys, which was a popular meeting place in the city. It was hardly the kind of dark corner where a fugitive would be expected to lurk. Despite his professed rejection of material things, Jim gravitated towards the trendy. Bewleys had energy, felt so alive. Had he not come this far? Was God not with him? The FBI tentacles were everywhere, he knew, but they had not found him. As he climbed the stairs, Jim could see the quotations stenciled onto the peach-colored walls, written in Gaelic, the language the Irish tried to preserve.

Is friotal aindéthe, Is bri na nadana. (I am the true word of the hidden gods, I am a word of poetry.)

Mise an ghaois/ Mise an deal bhadoir/ Mise gaoth ar muir. (I am the wisdom of the mind/ I am the conjuring sage/ I am the wind over the sea.)

Nurse a coffee, chat with a few of the regulars who knew him as Timothy, people like Peter, who was sacristan at a nearby church. And there was Terry, who had cerebral palsy and was in a wheelchair. Everyone on the street knew Terry.

Timothy rose, left his friends, walked to the end of Grafton. There is a war monument there—like a miniature Arc de Triomphe, it occurred to him—listing the death casualties for the South African War at the turn of the 20th century. He could read the scroll: Third Battalion: L. Murphy. Murphy. His grandmother's maiden name. He walked under the arch into St. Stephen's Green. A pond, fountains, lush green grass, palm trees—not an uncommon sight in

St. Stephen's Green, Dublin

Ireland—rows of tall elms. He thought of the place as a Garden of Eden. Do not linger long. Yellow reflective jackets. The Gardai—Irish police, on foot patrol.

Jim Kopp loved the city but hated his life, the anguish of running, the fear. Exhilaration one moment, despondency the next. Such extremes. Having left the Morningstar hostel, he now lived at the Ivelagh Hostel on Bride Road, in the Christ Church area of Dublin. It was an old part of town crowded with apartments, row houses, markets. He lived on the top floor of the hostel, room 191, in a cramped dorm-style room with an armoire, some shelves, a bed, and barely enough room to turn around. From his window he could see the courtyard of a vocational school, and beyond that the spires of St. Patrick's Cathedral. On the main floor there was a kitchenette where tenants made toast and snacks, a common room, dining area, everything painted pistachio green. Compared to Morningstar, this was high living. He lived under the name Tim Guttler, came and went as he pleased, said hello to the manager, staffers. He worked odd jobs, earned about 74 Irish pounds weekly. Kevin Byrne managed the place, a burly man with gray hair and

Scott Gardner Photo

Jim Kopp attended the church through the gate pictured at right, on a narrow Dublin street.

ruddy face who guarded the privacy of his tenants like a bulldog.

Jim Kopp was by now an expert at obtaining false identities. The names of the dead were perfect. He'd visit a cemetery, find the name of someone who would have been close to his own age. On July 4, 2000, he obtained a temporary driver's license in the name of Sean O'Briain, date of birth January 2, 1960. He put together a new résumé and submitted it to an employment agency.

* * *

Jim Kopp made a good Catholic effort to mortify temptation, but drinking did not rank as high on his list of sins to resist as others, especially in Dublin. His weakness was Bulmers cider. Pubs are Dublin's heart, places independent of time where the Irish take their worries out for the night and dance all over them. At pubs like O'Shea's, walls shake from people clapping and stomping to the sounds of Celtic Storm, the smoky room filled with faces that glow from the drink, heat, and uninhibited perfection of the evening. Young men and women, elderly, couples, singles, all joining as though part of a single body, feeding off the energy of one another. The mood peaks, incongruously, when the band launches into American standards like Kenny Rogers's "The Gambler," and John Denver's "Country Roads," hitting the chorus hard: "Take me home, country roads, to the place, I BE-LONG!"

True to form, Jim also spent time in the trendy, cobblestoned Temple Bar area, where tourists and students flock. There was a sports bar boasting 100 TV screens he visited to watch American football, see if his hometown San Francisco 49ers were playing. (Did he mention that he had a connection—apologies if he sounds like a name-dropper, he *hates* doing that— with Joe Montana, the Niners legend? Not a direct connection, mind you, but he knew someone who knew Montana quite well. And he had once met Mark Bavaro, too, the former New York Giants tight end—a big pro-lifer.) He hung with his Irish friends, had a few drinks, perhaps more than a few drinks, walked the streets with them late at night, feeling like a regular guy at times. But could he feel anything for long? The friends who knew him as Timothy had no idea who he really was. Did Jim even know the answer to that question? He had been on the run for 20 months.

Early one morning, the pubs closed, the streets barren. He moved alone, briskly but cautiously, down the street, pulled his jacket pockets inside out. It was a trick he had learned to deter pickpockets, show them he had nothing to interest them, which was in fact pretty much true. With all his experience, Jim liked to think there wasn't a city in the world he couldn't walk through in the middle of the night. But then, he had never been wanted for murder before.

His internal radar had never been more sensitive. Footsteps clicking on the wet pavement behind him. Heavy steps. Perhaps two men? Gardai? Interpol? FBI? He walked faster, turned down an alley. Don't think. Disappear. He felt his hands on cold metal as he pulled himself into the garbage Dumpster, sinking into the rot, the stench turning his stomach. Think about the shower, the inevitable glorious shower he could take in the morning. Suffer. Feel it. Be stronger from it.

Later, feeling secure again, he sat down to write, thoughts flooding his mind. His letters were a kaleidoscope of corny jokes, doodled happy faces, references to favorite movies and books, scattered Latin phrases, homilies attributed to his mother and father, Biblical passages. One letter, two, three, four, five. He wrote them all to the same person. He couldn't help himself. He sealed the envelope. On the back, he wrote a return address in German. On the front, he wrote the destination in his looping handwriting:

Ted Barnes
385 Chestnut Street
Apt. 2D/Brooklyn, N.Y.

* * *

Brooklyn, N.Y.
June 2000

Loretta Marra looked at her friend as he drove. He was Dennis's old friend, really, but over the last year or so she had grown to trust him, at least enough that he was driving Loretta and one of her sons to a walk-in clinic so the boy could get medical treatment. Loretta had kept a low profile but she wanted to quietly become active in the movement again. Federal law made old-style rescues too risky, but there were other ways to throw a wrench into the baby-killing business. One was to put industrial-strength glue into the locks at clinics.

"Would you be interested in scouting some clinics?" Loretta's friend—the informant—agreed.

"Hear from Jim lately?" he asked.

"Yeah. He's doing all right, but he said he needs money."

"We should get him some," the friend replied. "How would you do that?"

"It has to go through me. He'll certainly take it but he said he'll only take it if I approve."

Later they talked about morality and philosophy, Loretta's favorite topics. New York bishop Austin Vaughan had recently died. He was a hero in the pro-life movement, had been arrested many times. He had once warned pro-choice New York governor Mario

Cuomo that he was risking the fires of hell for his support of the killing of unborn children. When was violence justified in the war to save babies? The sniper who had killed Dr. Barnett Slepian, intentionally or not, had taken a definite position on the moral spectrum. "I think I'd be capable of killing, for God and a higher good," Loretta told her friend. Surely only a moral coward would rule out violence in all circumstances.

Special Agent Michael Osborn met with the informant. What did he have? Osborn listened as CS1 talked about what Loretta had said. Interesting, but not what Osborn was after. "Anything on Kopp's location?" he asked. "No. Nothing.

Loretta had been careful whenever Kopp's name came up. So far, all the FBI had court permission to do was listen to what CS1 relayed to them. They needed more surveillance, they needed a fly on the wall. In October, Osborn filed court applications to conduct audio surveillance on a car. CS1 had access to several vehicles. They'd put the bug in a car, have him take Loretta for a drive, get her talking. Osborn and Buffalo special agent Joel Mercer went before a judge to argue their case. They said the bugs were necessary for two reasons: one, to establish that Marra and Malvasi were themselves breaking the law by harboring a fugitive and obstructing justice; and two, the prime reason, to locate the fugitive himself, James C. Kopp. "There is probable cause," argued Mercer, that the couple will "further the conspiracy to harbor and conceal Kopp … and would talk in connection to facilitate, accomplish, and continue his status as a fugitive from justice and to continue to evade apprehension and arrest." On November 1, U.S. Court of Appeals Second Circuit judge Ellsworth A. van Graafeiland signed an order authorizing the FBI to bug a gold Chevy Malibu for 30 days "for the purpose of obtaining evidence concerning the location of a fugitive as defined in Section 2516(1) pursuant to Section 2561(1)(n)."

CS1 phoned Loretta. They chatted. She said she wanted to visit a friend in Oneonta, New York. Turned out she was in luck—her friend had use of a Malibu. He picked up Loretta and Dennis. He turned the conversation to a familiar topic. "So when do you want to scout clinics?" he asked Loretta. "Anytime you want," she replied. Osborn listened on the bug as talk turned to details about what type of clothing the friend should wear and which night of the week was best to glue locks at clinics. They moved to the bigger picture of the pro-life movement, where it was heading, use of force, and Slepian's death.

"I'm still not sure myself—you think the shooter was trying to kill him?" CS1 asked.

"You're always out there to maim," said Loretta.

"What's Jim's opinion on that?"

"I know he feels bad for Slepian's children. But he knows Slepian was not an innocent person, either. He was, morally, a guilty person."

The talk turned to Malvasi's surrender to police after blowing up an abortion clinic back in 1986, when Cardinal John O'Connor had urged him to turn himself in.

"I disagree with it," Loretta said.

"With what?"

"Surrendering."

"Why?"

"In my opinion Dennis had an obligation not to obey him. But he didn't know that."

"Would you have given yourself up?"

"No, I don't care if the Pope tells me to. He has no authority to tell me, to tell me to turn myself in for doing something morally praiseworthy. O'Connor's request was a sinful command."

Later they discussed whether the FBI was on to them. "If I leave the security of that address, you know," said Marra, "my whole life will fall apart again. I can't risk it." Loretta knew the government had come close. How did she know? asked CS1. Because they had questioned her brother Nick. But the FBI did not know where they lived. If they did, she knew, they would be breaking down her door by now.

* * *

Dublin, Ireland
November 2000

On November 26, Jim Kopp was issued a new passport, number
T895122, in the name of John O'Brien, date of birth January 2,
1960, parents Charles and Bridget O'Brien, from County Cork.
On December 14, he applied for a provisional driver's license under the name Daniel Joseph O'Sullivan, and took an eye test. He
was getting some work in construction, paid through the Irish
Nationwide Building Society, checks made out to Sean O'Briain.
In January, he got a part-time job at Dublin's Hume Street Cancer
Center using the name Tim Guttler. He did clerical work, a quiet,
unassuming man, avoided eye contact with anyone, walked with a
limp. The hospital was a few blocks from his beloved Grafton Street
and St. Stephen's Green.

Scott Gardner Photo

Jim Kopp attended St. John's Church near Dublin Bay.

On Sundays Jim Kopp attended St. John's church in a seaside
port town called Dun Loughanie, a short train ride south of the city
along Dublin Bay. St. John's had been an Anglican church before its

conversion to the St. Pius X denomination. The Society of St. Pius X is a breakaway sect of the Roman Catholic Church, rooted in disaffection over liberal church reforms. Canadian police hadn't been too far off the mark to follow leads linking Jim Kopp to the group. St. Pius X churches around the world still held their mass in Latin. Its fundamentalist Catholicism appealed not only to Kopp's faith, but also to his fascination with intrigue, power, connections. One of his favorite books was *A Windswept House*, by Malachi Martin, a novelist and Vatican insider. It is a dark tale about a global conspiracy of satanists and freemasons that threatens to take control of the Church—and is opposed only by the few Catholic traditionalists who cling to the old ways. It was fiction, but Martin claimed that much of it was true.

A typical winter daytime service. About 50 people. The smell of candle smoke, air so frigid inside the old building some parishioners wear coats. Before the service begins, total silence. A young woman kneeling in prayer, dressed in black, head covered according to the rules, a veil over her face. A rumpled man named Pat sitting in one of the back rows, holding his personal Bible, which is bloated, as if it had fallen into a bathtub long ago, pages worn and yellowed and patched with tape.

The priest enters, keeps his back to the congregation, says no words of greeting. To the uninitiated, the Latin mass is a hard, cold ceremony. The priest kneels at the altar and begins.

In nomine Patris, et Filii, et Spiritus Sancti. Amen. Introibo ad altarre Dei. *(In the name of the Father, and of the Son, and of the Holy Ghost. Amen. I will go up to the altar of God.)* Ad Deum, qui laetificat juventutem meam. *(To God, who gives joy to my youth.)* Judica me, Dues, et discerne causam meam de gente non sancta: ab homine iniquo et doloso erue me. *(Judge me, O God, and distinguish my cause from an ungodly nation: save me from an unjust and deceitful enemy.)*

Later, he gives a brief sermon. "It is time to wake up from our sleeping. We have the power to wake up from our lives, to overcome *materialism, to witness the supernatural life. God is a god of vengeance. He will strike the unjust. Some would say, there is no God, no hell. Oh, but wait until the day of judgment."*

At the end of the service, Jim Kopp—Timothy—liked to kneel and pray before one of the small altars along the side wall. Over time he talked about his life with a couple of parishioners. Said he planned to leave Ireland soon. Family emergency. Sad story. Timmy had to get to Germany to see his mother. She was dying.

CHAPTER 16—A MORAL IMPOSSIBILITY

Washington, D.C.
January 2001

On January 19, a new FBI surveillance warrant was signed by Southern New York District judge Whitman Knapp, for placement of a bug in a Ford Windstar van. (Knapp was well known in New York law enforcement circles—he chaired the 1971 Knapp Commission that held hearings into charges of corruption on the NYPD brought by Frank Serpico.) The warrant was good for the period between January 20–22, when Dennis Malvasi, Loretta Marra, Loretta's brother Nick, and informant CS1 were taking a road trip to Washington. Malvasi had invited his old friend to attend the White Rose Banquet.

The grandly named "banquet" was a small annual gathering held on the same weekend as the March For Life in the American capital. The march was a big mainstream event, the banquet a meeting of the pro-life fringe, where those who had taken the anti-abortion fight to violent extremes were honored. Malvasi was in the spotlight this year. Loretta, sensing that the authorities would be looking for her, kept a low profile. Before the banquet began at a suburban Washington Comfort Inn hotel, Loretta sat in the van in the parking lot, took out a pad and wrote notes for Dennis's speech. When Malvasi spoke, he lambasted pro-lifers who opposed violence in the abortion fight.

"I'm glad to be here today," he began. "This is the largest gathering of baby defenders I've ever had the pleasure of being with, and what a good feeling it is to see so many of you ... We've had around 30 years of abortion, and around 30 million mangled baby bodies. Year after year, pro-lifers get outraged, and the bodies pile up. Year after year, pro-lifers write angry letters to the editor, to their congressman, to their senator, and the bodies pile up even higher ... It is the baby defender who dares to suggest that the time for playing by the rules of the enemy is long past. It is the baby defender who dares to suggest the use of direct action to interfere between a vicious assailant and a helpless infant ... I will always be grateful to ... the ones who gave me moral and material support, before and after my arrest. I encourage you all to continue the noble work of supporting your local baby defender, from lock gluers to bombers, monkey wrench crews, arsonists and snipers. Your help makes all the difference in the world and to the babies themselves. Thank you and God bless."

Afterwards, in the Windstar, Loretta, Dennis and the informant talked about Jim Kopp. Loretta said that Jim had expressed interest in getting in touch with *Time To Kill* author Michael Bray. Perhaps Bray would be interested in assisting Jim upon his return to the United States, helping to find safe housing, money. Jim's name would never have to be used among anyone associated with Bray, he could just be referred to as a baby defender.

"I'm still interested in sending Jim some money," the informant added.

"That would be no problem," said Malvasi.

"But it has to go directly to Jim."

"Of course."

They drove the Windstar back to the hotel where they were staying, the Hampton Inn at 15202 Lansdale Boulevard. in Bowie, Maryland—Bray's hometown. On January 22, they headed home to Brooklyn. The next day, FBI agents walked through the doors of the Hampton Inn, searched hotel records and found a registration card under the name of Joyce Maier, a known alias of Marra's.

* * *

On Friday, February 2, New Jersey District judge Alfred Lechner Jr. approved a third bugging permit for the FBI, this time for a white Chrysler Grand Voyager, for the time frame February 3–4. Dennis and Loretta's friend was thinking of driving the Voyager to Atlantic City, where he had a contact at the Taj Mahal hotel and casino. He could put them up in two rooms, had some extra money to gamble, too. They could send all their winnings to Jim Kopp—wherever he was.

The next day, Saturday, on the drive from to New Jersey, CS1 asked Loretta about Jim. How was she communicating with him? It was email, she explained. A Yahoo! account she accessed at a local library.

"I'd love to meet Jim some day," the informant said.

"I could eventually arrange a dinner meeting with him."

"Really? How much?"

"You could get his autograph, talk to him. For $10,000."

At the casino Marra gambled along with CS1, while Malvasi stayed back in the room with their two sons. Loretta turned to her friend. She needed a break. "Have to go back to the room for a minute, check on the boys. Can you hold this a minute?" She handed him her purse and left the room for the elevators. There wasn't much time. How long would Loretta be? What if Dennis showed up? What if security saw him? He searched the contents of the wallet. Two PT-1 calling cards. A slip of paper. Two sets of numbers. A name. He got out a pen and started writing, finishing before Loretta returned.

Later, CS1 contacted Michael Osborn. The agent wrote down the numbers: 0113531872801; 0874106124. The first three digits—011—was the code for making an international call. And 353 was a country code—for Ireland. Osborn phoned the Buffalo FBI Field Office.

Osborn well knew that a lawyer could ultimately take issue with the search of Loretta Marra's wallet. The FBI had a warrant to bug the vehicle, not rifle through a woman's wallet: "*The search and seizure is presumptively unreasonable. Unquestionably, as of the time of the warrantless seizure and search of the wallet, CS1 was functioning completely as a government agent.*" Osborn would counter that his job was to gather evidence. Clearly he had not sought, nor obtained, a search warrant to go through Loretta's personal property. But the informant was acting on his own initiative. He was under no direction from the FBI on that specifically.

* * *

Dublin, Ireland
February 16, 2001

Jim Kopp ducked into the cyber café, smoke hanging in the air, computers lined up row upon row. He took his assigned seat at a terminal. On the run he had taken such care to keep moving, trust no one, bury his identity. So what was it inside that told him to reconnect with his past through a computer? Dangerous? No. He knew how to keep the FBI—"the Edgars," as he called the G-men—guessing. Do not send conventional email. The FBI could surely monitor it. Instead leave notes in cyber bottles. Write your email, store it in a draft folder on a Yahoo mail account. Do not hit Send, ever. Simply save it as a draft, let it sit there, like an envelope that never makes it to the mailbox. A second party can access the draft if she knows it's there and knows the account user name identification. A private pipeline—for Loretta's eyes only.

He logged on to Yahoo! email and typed the user name: aheaume@yahoo.com. It was named after a woman, real or imagined, named Alyssa Heaume.

Subject: quickie

He wrote in his cryptic, quirky way, the letter sprinkled with non-sequiturs, observations, inside jokes, French phrases, self-deprecation. He wrote about a possible trip he was planning.

What did Loretta think about it? He finished the email, saved it in the aheaume draft folder, logged off, paid at the counter and left. Dublin is five hours ahead of Brooklyn. Loretta would read the message when she got a chance to log on. The next day, February 17, he was back, at a different café. He typed a new message.

Subject: longer.

His present and future. Surely Loretta was the only one who would understand, who could offer something of value back to him. The mission? The babies? What should he do? He saved the email in the folder and left. Later that same day—joy. Loretta had read his messages and deposited her reply in the draft folder, couching her letter in code words and inside references:

On margins: the capital city of mom's birth to jackie area is fine with me, but I am nowhere near in the position you are to judge that. Anything at all you'd suggest would sound fine with me, because you are an if kind of gal, and you can talk big and act rich, as far as I'm concerned. Mech points out, though, that jackie, and the whole larger area of which jackie is but a part, is said to be under closer scrutiny these days because others have also thought of what you've thought of, with those others are said to be very, very naughty and so forth. I am simply ignorant on the facts of the matter. I understand where you want bmtm to occur. I believe I told you i was calling from one during our 2nd phone conversation, and you worried that i was out in the cold and wet, and I told you it was fairly sheltered, because I was in the very shadow of the establishment.

Loretta noted that "BMTM" would be best if it was just a phone call from Jim to her apartment. No talking, though, just ring the phone. The call would be the signal that he had not been detected, that he was safe, and they could go and get him. The email continued:

New RMC program is fine with me. I see several weighty advantages, both tactical and moral. Only drawback is the hideous emotional stress it will visit upon you. I think it will be incalculably more difficult in that sense than RSQA. Assuming, however, that you're at peace about it, the advantages are immense. In the RSQA type world there were two possible outcomes (not counting complete failure). One happened only once, we'll call that outcome number two, and the more common outcome is number one. Number one was always the desired one. I have with regret more bitter than you can imagine, come to hold that it is immoral to seek number one, that one has no right not to go for number two, if one is doing RSQA type stuff. There are now enough examples to form statistics, and the statistical rate of recidivism is just too high to justify pursuing number one, in my opinion. Now, this is a bummer. I mean to say, who wants to run around and set a goal like two over, and over? UEWW. RMC solves all that nicely. The recidivism rate is guaranteed zero which is of paramount importance, if the finality of number two is avoided, leaving options for happy endings all around.

When Jim Kopp sorted through his thoughts, he decided to reply, but on paper, by hand. He wrote a letter that he planned to send by regular mail:

"The descendents are the only ones in this blankety-blank town who will give me sacraments, knowing my background (good). But when the subject comes up they spend all their time trying to convince me I should never do it again (bad). And then in Passant they harp on the value of hidden penance to solve the world's ills, (good) to the exclusion of Ronald Reagan in principle (bad). This is all beaucoup frustrating to me, but it's also something of a moot point, since my efforts to get new papers have ground almost to a complete halt because I know not why. Is it due to a psychological lack of confidence on my part, a closet desire to retire, or because the papers are truly impossible to get? Some days I wake up and I want to go be a monk. Other reasons, but then I remember I can't go anywhere. Also, to get new real papers is a risk beyond the status quo where I exist (uneasily) on the black gray market (with no record of any sort).

Through all of this, the threat of what you said before we parted company last haunts me. The thing about retirement. I know I've asked before, but could I ask you your thoughts on this? It was the retirement thing you said. I clearly see I am force-retired from any run of the mill effort in the cause so dear to us, but do you also mean permanent retirement from R-squared? Because if so, I might as well go be a monk. The only thing that sticks in my craw about that is that it would require foreswearing R-2 in principle, and in perpetuity. That strikes me as a moral impossibility, wouldn't you agree? Let's assume it is, for a moment. Practically this leaves me in a sort of limbo where I am prevented anything like a monastery, but also practically prevented any return to the field. Now, limbo I can deal with one day at a time, etc., but from time to time I begin to hope or wonder, will I ever return to the field? I guess my situation resembles that of an aging movie star who has lost his looks, but has a hard time imagining picking up a new trade. I don't know the answer, but I'm sure your thoughts about retirement fit in somewhere. I hope to send hard copy as soon as possible, please don't despair, meanwhile, notwithstanding computer situation, you'd enjoy reading all the drafts there."

* * *

FBI Field Office
Buffalo, N.Y.
Tuesday, February 20, 2001

FBI agent Joel Mercer examined the phone numbers relayed to him by Michael Osborn. At least one of the numbers was in Ireland.

Mercer contacted the FBI's legal attaché closest to Ireland, based in London, England. The London office put a call through to Dublin and the Garda Sìoch·na, Extradition Section. The translation of the Gaelic title is "Guardians of the Peace." Extradition works in great secrecy, dealing as it does with foreign governments on sensitive matters. The Gardai agreed to work with the FBI to track down James C. Kopp, if indeed he was still in the country.

An Irish agent examined the phone numbers provided by the FBI. One of the numbers—0874106124—was for a cell phone registered to a Sean O'Briain. Detectives began asking questions around Dublin, showing photos of James Kopp. As the Gardai worked the streets, names started coming, rumors, then contacts, people who knew of a man named Sean O'Briain who fit Kopp's description. They learned that Sean O'Briain was an alias for Timothy Guttler. Word was that Guttler stayed at the Ivelagh Hostel. The Gardai paid a visit to Kevin Byrne, the manager. Timothy? He collected his mail. Went to work. Quiet man. Said hello now and again. That's it. He's gone now.

CHAPTER 17–PARTIAL SUCCESS

New York City
Thursday, March 1, 2001

The special agent left the FBI office in lower Manhattan, drove down Broadway, left on Chambers Street, past the New York City County Courthouse and the municipal building with the grand archway and golden statue of justice on top. Right on Center Street, quick left to cross the Brooklyn Bridge over the East River, the Twin Towers of the World Trade Center just off to the right and behind the car. Osborne headed up Brooklyn Bridge Boulevard, left on Atlantic Avenue, the low-rise buildings, subway cars emerging from belowground to raised tracks, rattling loudly. Finally, Chestnut Street. Surveillance.

Later, an agent watched as Loretta Marra and Dennis Malvasi left their apartment. All clear. The agent entered the building, opened the door to apartment 2D, went inside, quickly planted the bug, and left. Earlier that same day, Eastern District judge Nina Gershon had signed an order authorizing the FBI to install a listening device. The bugs in the automobiles had so far turned up useful information, but not Kopp's latest location or any hint of what his plans were. Osborn wanted ears in the apartment. The agents kept odd hours, sat on watch all through the night.

That evening, Loretta and Dennis talked about what they would say to other pro-lifers when trying to get assistance for Jim upon his return from Europe. "We should say, 'Jim is looking for work again, and he's willing to teach, train others.'"

Osborn listened. Kopp was planning to come back, and soon. And Marra and Malvasi planned to help him, and enlist others as well. The next day, Friday, New Jersey District judge Dennis M. Cavanaugh signed an order for another bug, this time for a red Ford Windstar and hotel rooms 1401 and 1402 at the Taj Mahal casino in Atlantic City. Saturday morning, Loretta logged on to a computer, opened her Yahoo! mail account, and typed in the user name.

Subject: all set

On Monday, she left a new message in the draft folder.

Subject: Thumb twiddling

She logged off the email and later surfed for information about weather conditions in Montreal. At 11 a.m. she opened the email again. "We have to get Jim's money," she told her husband.

"Why am I getting money for you?" Dennis said. "I'm the one who's going to meet him."

"True. You're gonna meet Jim. Jim told me to give $1,000 … for Amy. I'll take care of that, and leave Jim a note about it." Amy was Amy Boissonneault. Their pro-life friend had been diagnosed with breast cancer. Loretta phoned her brother, Nick, said she might come visit. When she got off the phone she told Dennis that he needed to keep checking the computer for new email while she was away. On Thursday, March 8, at 7:55 a.m., she left a new draft message in the folder.

Subject: Partial success

At 7:57 a.m. she left another.

Subject: Getting worried

What's going on, anyhow? Haven't heard from you in ages. Please let me know how you are.

Loretta left the apartment to visit a man named Richard Bruno. She had a letter to show him from Jim, and also a request. Bruno owned a chimney company and had employed Kopp for a time before he had gone missing. Bruno did not believe that Jim could ever hurt anyone—he was a prayerful, peaceful man. A holy man. Loretta explained that Jim had directed her to give money to Bruno, so that he in turn could give the cash to Amy. Jim wanted Amy to use it for alternative breast cancer treatments.

Later, Loretta talked to Dennis about plans to visit Nick on Saturday. Dennis would need to check the email account before leaving the apartment and joining her. "OK," Dennis said, "now, if he's coming to town then forget going there—if he's gonna be here tomorrow or Saturday, forget going there, right?"

"We'll have to talk," she said.

"Why don't we just take a cab and go hook up with him and bring him here."

"If he's coming to town." Michael Osborn listened to the recording. It was clearly a reference to James Kopp. He might be planning a return trip to the United States. But it also appeared likely that Marra and Malvasi would be out of the apartment on Saturday. That would be the time to move. Osborn had already applied for and received a "sneak and peek" search warrant. On Saturday, agents entered 2D, searched, photographed letters and documents. They found several false IDs for Loretta, including an Arizona driver's license.

In a new letter from Kopp, he had asked Loretta to obtain the birth certificate of a dead child that he could use for false ID. He also wrote that he had moved to another job to earn more money, and a manuscript he was chipping away at was coming along. And he raised the possibility of entering the United States perhaps through Buffalo or Niagara Falls, posing as a tourist. The agents carefully replaced the letter and other items and left. Where was Kopp, exactly? The letter did not say. And when exactly was he planning to return?

On Tuesday, March 6, Dennis picked up the phone in the apartment. Loretta was on the other end.

"Anything?" she said.

"No. There's been no messages. It's been ten days now."

"I'm worried."

"Don't worry, we've gone longer than ten days without contact in the past."

* * *

Dublin, Ireland
March 13

The cramped newsroom of the *Irish Mirror* tabloid pulsed with the energy of an afternoon deadline crunch. The paper had a small staff, maybe just four reporters. Phones ringing, ties loosening, epithets bouncing off the walls. News editor Mick McNiff's cell phone rang. The call display showed the number for his contact with the Gardai. He'd take that one.

"Yah. McNiff." Gardai headquarters was a few blocks up the street from the *Mirror* by sprawling Phoenix Park. McNiff listened to his contact and scribbled on his pad. The tip he was getting was big. Terrific story. A bonafide scoop. Seems the Gardai were working with the FBI to catch an American abortion doctor killer. The man, James Charles Kopp, had been living among Dubliners, even working at a hospital on Hume Street. Should the *Mirror* go with the story? The contact said nothing about holding it. Even if he had, it wouldn't have mattered. The *Mirror* didn't hold news. It broke news. That's what it would do this time.

McNiff passed the tip to a reporter. This was going front page. The next day, Wednesday, March 14, the *Mirror* published a story inside that said the FBI was flying in agents from America to work with the Gardai to catch the Yank James Kopp. On page one, it splashed as its main story a photo and headline pumping an exclusive interview with Muhammad Ali. American cultural icons like Ali always sold well at the newsstand. So did pieces like the second story, about the axing of an Irish TV program by the BBC. But over in the left corner was a photo of a man with a gaunt face and ragged beard. Kopp. The headline read:

EXCLUSIVE
Doctor
'killer'
hunted

Mick McNiff rarely regretted a bold news decision, but he felt the heat on this one. He got a call from an official with the Gardai who wasn't happy about it. "Couldn't you have waited just a day or two?" he said. Why had someone called McNiff with the tip in the first place? Was it possible that the police source was strongly opposed to abortion, and had leaked on purpose to give the American a fighting chance to escape Ireland?

The *Irish Mirror* coverage may have alerted Kopp.

Bernie Tolbert, the FBI's supervisor in the case, never heard anything to suggest that a member of the Gardai was trying to tip off Kopp. But he also knew anything was possible. As for McNiff, he mostly lamented one thing—that they hadn't splashed Kopp as the main story and art. Muhammad Ali was not the big story. It was Kopp! But then, when he first got the tip he had no idea how big it would all get—that within days, reporters from Fox News and CBS would visit their humble newsroom chasing the story.

The Gardai were close, but their target disappeared. The *Mirror*'s coverage may have been the cold hard knock that rousted Jim Kopp from whatever complacency had set in while living in Dublin. "Well," cracked one of the *Mirror*'s editors, "at least we know we have *one* reader."

* * *

It's a lovely journey by car south from Dublin along the coast. Emerald-green fields rolling towards rounded mountains and the Irish Sea, chimney smoke from tiny old homes lingering as a gray haze above the rooftops. Church spires mark each small town, Dalkey, Killiney, Bray, Greystones, Newcastle, Wicklow.

Jim Kopp had little time to reflect on the beauty of the countryside. He was leaving in a hurry. But where to now? The Gardai, FBI would expect him to fly out of Dublin. Or take a fast Seacat ferry from Dublin or Dun Laoghaire to Britain—once he crossed it would be a short trip to Holyhead in Wales, where he could hop on a train. But the train would mean many stops, opportunities for the police to find him. Better to leapfrog the U.K. altogether. Misdirection. Hitler had thought the allies would invade Europe at Calais. He had been fooled—the target was Normandy. Misdirection. Jim Kopp's target was not England. It was France.

There are two ports along the southern Irish coast where you can take a ferry directly to France, across the Celtic Sea and the English Channel. The port at a town called Rosslare is closest to Dublin. The main road leads down to a rocky beach and the passenger ferry terminal. One of the ferries that serves Rosslare is called the *Normandy*.

The vessel, which is large enough to carry shipping containers, tractor trailers and dozens of cars, has two dining rooms for passengers, a games area, a bar and small movie theater. Early evening, the horn sounds on board, engines rumble, water churns as the ferry lumbers out of port, ropes of white foam roll in to the shore.

Looking back at the Irish coast, sun setting, the sky a tapestry of pale blue and orange and navy, and darkness out at sea.

The captain's voice comes over a loudspeaker. "Good evening, ladies and gentlemen. We're anticipating light northerly winds. Shouldn't be too bad, perhaps just a moderate chop. A relatively calm voyage."

In the Celtic Sea, a "moderate chop" makes the vessel roll, dip, pitch. Keeping balance in the cabin showers is an athletic endeavor, even in relatively calm seas. In rough water, passengers can barely stand, stomachs turn and people retch. Items in the gift shop fall off the shelves.

The ferry has no phone service, televisions or Internet hook-ups—just small radios in each room with two channels bringing in classical music. On a clear night, six hours into the voyage the lights that dot the Welsh shoreline come into view. In your bunk you can feel the roll of the sea underneath, your body moving with each swell, tips of waves and spray hitting cabin windows with a hard smack. Roll, pitch, roll. Up on deck outside, a biting wind whips across the mist-soaked deck, slaps faces like a cold glove. It is peaceful, too, the engines humming evenly, water pounding the hull rhythmically, aqua and white foam churns and fizzes. Roll, pitch, roll. The ferry rounded Land's End, crossed the western edge of the English Channel, passed the Channel Islands. Daylight returned.

Around midday, 20 hours after the voyage began, the coast of France came into view. Jim Kopp was about to land not far from the D-day beaches. He believed that most people associated Second World War heroism with the D-day landings and it grated on him because his dad had served in the Pacific—the underappreciated theater. The ferry pulled past the long breakwater and into dock at Cherbourg. A bit farther east along the coast rose the steep cliffs at Pointe du Hoc, where American Rangers pulled off their audacious landings more than 50 years ago. Jim Kopp had arrived.

* * *

New York City
March 14, 2001

Special Agent Michael Osborn heard the news from the FBI field office in Buffalo, via the London branch. They had a bead on Kopp in Dublin, but lost him. The bureau was feeling the heat. They seemed so close. Loretta Marra remained the key. If for some reason Kopp ceased his contact with Marra he might drop off their radar completely. Osborn knew the email communications between the pair was key. They needed to act quickly. He needed to break into their shared account.

On March 14, Western New York District judge William M. Skretny approved a request from the FBI to "intercept electronic communications made to or through the Yahoo! account with the user ID of aheaume, registered under the name heaume, alyssa." The warrant also allowed the FBI to use "trap-and-trace" technology on the account—akin to tapping a phone line. All Internet servers have an Internet service provider or ISP address, a 32-bit designation written as numbers separated by periods. By tracing the origin of the ISP address used by Kopp—an Internet café, for example—the FBI could scan all material being sent from that address and isolate and read Kopp's messages. With the ISP address, they might be able to trace the file to a specific business using that server. But first they needed to search the Yahoo! account.

In Santa Clara, in the heart of Silicon Valley, FBI agents arrived at a collection of eight low-rise buildings in a nondescript commercial strip mall—the global headquarters of Yahoo!. They served the warrant and cracked the aheaume account. The emails saved in the draft folder had not been deleted. Back in New York, Osborn was soon analyzing the messages, in particular those written a month earlier, on February 17. He read and reread the code Kopp and Marra used. "DV"; "Ronald Reagans"; "on margins"; "Jackie area": what did it all mean? Jim Kopp would always remain certain there were code words the Edgars never figured out. But Osborn's people cracked most of them. "DV" appeared frequently in his correspondence. He loved to throw around Latin. DV is the acronym for *Deo volente*: God willing.

Kopp and Marra discussed his future, whether he should he return "to the field." They talked about "outcome" number one and two. Number one referred to wounding abortion doctors. Number two meant killing them. Number one, wrote Marra, is the desired option, but the "rate of recidivism" is high—abortion doctors may return to work after being wounded. "Ronald Reagans" or "R-squared" was a reference to the assassination attempt on President Reagan's life. "Jackie area"? Jackie might be a reference to Loretta's son, who was born near Montreal, "Jackie area" was probably that part of Canada. Loretta had also written: "Mech points out that jackie is said to be under closer scrutiny these days, because others have thought of what you've thought of, with those others are said to be very, very naughty." Mech was Dennis Malvasi. And jackie—Canada, or Canadian Immigration, the Canadian border—was under scrutiny of late. Kopp's reference to "on margins" meant international borders. "Capital city of mom's birth" was a reference to Loretta Marra's mother, who was born in Paris.

Osborn wrote out his analysis of the emails and passed it to the Buffalo office. Murder suspect and fugitive James Charles Kopp is likely in the vicinity of Paris, plans to fly to Montreal in order to return to the field—to shoot more doctors.

CHAPTER 18—WORRIED BIG-TIME

Dinan, France
Thursday, March 15, 2001

It is a steep climb from the marina up the cobblestone Rue du Jerzual in Dinan. The cool damp air smells of moss and wet stone. Closer to the top, the scent of fresh baguette and pastry arrives. "Dinan," if spoken with an anglo "n" on the end will draw a blank stare from a Frenchman. Jim Kopp focused on getting the pronunciation perfect, prided himself on speaking proper French. You show respect for the locals by earnestly trying to speak the language so as not to mangle it. No need to pull any Ugly American routine, he felt.

The town, encircled by 13th-century ramparts that once guarded it from invaders, sits atop a hill overlooking the Rance River valley in France's Brittany region. On the outside of the ramparts, down in the lower town, is the marina. Sailboats set out and wind their way north along the Rance River to the Golfe de Saint-Malo and, ultimately, the Atlantic. Dinan has 11,000 people but feels much smaller, a village trapped in a medieval time warp with its half-timbered, moss-dappled homes, some of which tilt from the weight of their 600 years, as though ready to fall at any moment. He walked inside the 12th-century Basilique Saint-Sauveur in the town center near the clock tower on Rue de l'Horloge. It was dark inside, smelling of old stone. A massive crucifix rose above the altar. Purple, yellow,

Scott Gardner Photo

The Mouline Meen hostel, where Kopp stayed in Dinan.

and green light burst through stained glass.

Dinan is in one sense a tourist destination, not so much for North Americans as for Europeans. It still feels isolated, a four-hour drive from Paris. Jim walked among the locals, tourists, past the post office, banks—and two police stations, local and national. There were brasseries, crepe shops, lingerie stores, cyber-cafes. Jim Kopp got a room in a hostel in the lower city, not far from the marina. It was a drive alongside the river, through a thickly forested area, across a narrow stream, to the lone stone building called the Moulin Meen— an auberge de jeunesse, or youth hostel. He had one of the several bunk beds in room 14, second level. He met a young Japanese man and they engaged in long conversations. The hostel manager was Benoit Benetou, a man with a thoughtful face who spoke English well. The thin American appeared unremarkable to Benoit. He merely seemed adrift, like so many of the young people who stayed there.

Jim decided to take an impromptu trip to Paris, a two-hour ride by train. There he visited a place that always beguiled him. Behind Notre Dame Cathedral is a parkette, and belowground is a monument lacking the ornate design of most everything in Paris. It is a Holocaust memorial called Memorial de la Déportation, remembering the French Jews who were captured and gassed by the Nazis. He descended the steps, the walls white and rough textured, the corridors tight, tomblike, all sharp angles. Words were etched on the wall as though put there by fingernails. And, visible but untouchable through a grate, were buttons, thousands of them, lined up to mark each death. So many innocent lives sacrificed on the altar of ideology. Just like the murdered babies, Jim Kopp thought. On the wall were quotations: "The day that people will have understood who you were, they will bite the earth with sadness and remorse, they will water it with their tears, and they will build temples to you." Later, he walked along the Champs d'Élysées at his languid pace, his lungs filling with crisp spring air, moving past shops and cafés, Parisians sipping red wine on patios and breaking baguette. The folksy tune entered his mind, and then the words:

> Lately I wonder what I do it for
> If l had my way
> I'd just walk through those doors
> And wander down the Champs d'Élysées
> Going café to cabaret,
> Thinking how I'd feel when I find
> That very good friend of mine.

Joni Mitchell—"Free Man in Paris!" The lyrics and music flowed through his soul, from the angel poet he had held close to his heart since his teens in Marin County. He sang it to himself and it brought a smile. She was speaking to him. Trapped as he was on the run, he had for the moment escaped, gliding along on Joni's rhythms. Later in the evening, he walked Rue St.-Honoré, which ran near the Louvre, the smell of crepes in the air, traffic jammed on the narrow street. Like Grafton Street in Dublin, Rue St. Honoré had the kind of upscale shops that someone of Jim Kopp's means could never patronize.

He had a package he needed to mail. In the envelope was a letter he had written, with more quirky references, cryptic messages, a collection of thoughts and tangents that reflected the cross-currents in his labyrinthine mind. He included some articles he had printed off the Internet. One that amused him bore the headline "Meteorite Iron Found in 'Tomb of Queens'" about a tomb discovered by a team of archeologists in a place in Syria called Umm el-Marra. Marra. Perfect! He sealed the envelope, addressed it to Ted Barnes, Brooklyn, N.Y., and dropped it in a mailbox.

* * *

Brooklyn, N.Y.
March 16, 2001

On Friday, March 16, an envelope addressed to Joyce and Ted Barnes arrived at a post office in Brooklyn. It had a Paris, France, postmark. The FBI special agent picked up the envelope with a gloved hand and opened it. Michael Osborn took photos of the envelope, then pored over the contents and photographed each page. James Kopp had been a busy guy. There were dozens of pages in the package, Internet printouts, newspaper articles, handwritten letters. Osborn made notations referencing each item in the package:

- Handwriting: "C.S. Lewis wannabee; neverbee"
- Article: "Our Lady of Fatima Said in 1917"
- Birth certificate John O'Brien
- Birth certificate Daniel Joseph O'Sullivan
- Death certificate Daniel Joseph O'Sullivan
- Two passport application forms
- "Letter from Father Emily"
- "Meteorite Iron Found in 'Tomb of Queens'"
- Article: "The Society of St. Pius X in Rome"

Osborn placed the papers back in the envelope and resealed it for delivery to Ted and Joyce Barnes. Three days later, on March 19, a Federal Express package No. 40055766270 arrived

at a Brooklyn sorting station. The intended recipient was Ted
Barnes. Osborn reviewed the contents, took photos and wrote
out notations quoting the start of each item. Most were letters
handwritten by Kopp:

- "I guess my situation …"
- "Anyhoo, my boss …"
- "add in xo above"
- Miller and Boissonneault addresses
- "Just got the pix"
- "Yes, I need help"

Osborn resealed the envelope. Later, after she had received
the package, Marra wrote a new email in the Yahoo! draft folder
for Kopp's eyes.

Subject: I got your snail

Osborn wanted to widen the net further. He applied to put a
tap on phone conversations. On March 21, Eastern New York District judge Reena Raggi signed an order allowing the FBI to listen
to phone conversations between Loretta Claire Marra and James
Charles Kopp on three phone numbers: 718-647-9440, 917-833-
1317 and 917-826-8520.

* * *

Dinan, France
March 21, 2001
9:45 a.m

Jim logged on to the Yahoo! account. It was coming up on 4 a.m.
in Brooklyn. He typed an email:

Subject: now now now now now now

Dear person, this keyboqrd [sic] *is all frenchied up.* [The key-
boards in France have small but vexing variations from North

American models. The "q" is where the "a" should be, for example.] *The sooner I get about 1000, the sooner you see this smiling cherubic face ... DV.*

He saved the message in the folder. and wrote two more emails. He told Marra to send $20 to Jean Aubrigon c/o La Poste, Dinan, France.

Meanwhile, that morning in New York City, Michael Osborn read the messages. "DV." *Deo volente.* It was Kopp all right. And he had made a big mistake. He had just announced his location. Got him, Osborn thought.

In Brooklyn, Loretta logged on to the account. She turned to Dennis. "He says the computer is 'all frenchied up,'" she said. She wrote a new email at 1 p.m.

Subject: on my way

Will send the $20 ... my cellphone number is in the stuff you haven't read. My hard line is listed in the phone book under the name you snail me at. The hard line is safest.

The money was wired from a Brooklyn Western Union office to Jean Aubrigon in Dinan. Loretta wrote another email.

Subject: 20 Sent

Money has been sent. I have as much $ as you need.

The next morning, Loretta was back on the computer checking for new messages from Jim.

"Anything?" asked Dennis.

"No," she said.

"Probably doesn't have money to get online."

"I'm afraid he doesn't have enough money to get himself back."

On Friday, at 4 p.m., Jim Kopp entered the cybercafé in Dinan. He typed two messages.

Subject: thank You God Almighty qnd [sic] *his little helpers*

He wrote that he needed more money. The escape route was still open. How would he communicate with Loretta upon arrival? He wrote another email.

Subject: Jackie

*jackie route unless you wave off..... very happy you're there ... will
need rest/medicine when i get there.*

Loretta and Dennis discussed options. Should they send someone to France to help Jim? Perhaps Sabine Goodwin, a friend who
lived in the U.K., could do it. What about all the email messages in
the folder—should they start deleting them? What about Jim calling
them collect, was that safe? Loretta logged on to the computer and
wrote a reply:

*Jackie is fine with me, I know of no problems.... Can't we please
make the bmtm just you calling me from a pay phone when
you're in town on my lovely, friendly, safe and clean hard
line and telling me where you are and I (or mech) come get
you any hour day or night? we are convinced 100% that the
mere fact of you being undiagnosed enough to stand around
on the street and make phone calls is complete proof that
you are not diagnosed at all. Can't wait to see you. You can
get as much rest as you need here, and we can likely get any
prescription meds you need.*

She saved the message and logged off. Osborn read the exchange.
"Bmtm" had been their code for Kopp's escape route. "Jackie"—they
were still planning to come back to the United.States via Montreal.
"Undiagnosed"—they thought Kopp was moving about undetected.
Not quite.

* * *

In Dinan it was 11:19 a.m. on Saturday, March 24, and 5:19 a.m.
in Brooklyn. Jim had been unable to collect the money from the
Dinan post office. He typed three messages.

Subject: ouestern onion, c'est horrible
*Can't get the $20 without the control number. Send the number
on the email account right way and then send $50 after that and $600*

after that, each time place a message with the control number for that
transaction … I will study your bmtm plan and comply exactly. When
I show up, I should be an 'uncle' from Paris.

Loretta read the messages and talked to Dennis about finding a
24-hour Western Union ("ouestern onion") office. Loretta phoned a
friend. Did he know of one? She phoned Western Union. Meanwhile,
Jim couldn't help himself any longer. The email seemed to be working
so well, he was undetected. Perhaps he simply yearned to hear her
voice. He had to phone. Just before 3 p.m., he dialed. Loretta picked
up. It was nearly 9 a.m. Brooklyn time. It was Jim.

"Having some trouble with the French mail clerks," he said.
"You know the French, you have these virgin bitches protecting the
Honor of France who think I'm committing fraud."

They chatted some more. Everyone back home sends their
love, Loretta said.

"Well let them love me with cash," Jim quipped. They ended
the call. Loretta turned to Dennis.

"He sounds OK, but like he's under really extreme pressure," she
said. "He's just talking the way he does when he's under pressure."

"What's he want you to send him?" asked Dennis.

"James?"

"Yeah, how much money do you have to send him?"

"Three hundred."

Dennis asked her if she wanted to do the Western Union transfer herself. Loretta went with a friend to Western Union and wired
Jean Aubrigon $300. And then she wired $300 more. The friend was
CS1—the informant, who was still on the job, still hoping to reap
reward money if he could help capture Kopp. He managed to grab
the receipt from the wire transfer, fold it up and tuck it into his sock,
before getting back in the car with Loretta. Later, he found a phone
book and called Michael Osborn: Kopp was still in Dinan.

Back at the apartment, Loretta and Dennis continued planning.
Should they contact their friends for help with Jim due back soon?
What would be better for travel from Montreal to New York, bus or

train? They needed to dispose of some of the files and letters. How secure had their emails been?

"You shouldn't stay online so long when you're writing him messages," said Dennis. "Who else is using the account? And who established it? We have to get rid of the papers. I'll wrap them in newspapers and throw them in the recycling boxes in the subway."

And what about their eldest son Louis? Would he recognize Jim when he arrived?

"We'll call him Tony," said Dennis. "And if he says he looks like Jim Kopp, I'll just say, 'yeah, he does look like him.'"

On Sunday, Judge Nina Gershon approved an FBI application to continue monitoring two cell phones that Dennis and Loretta were using: numbers 917-833-1317 and 917-826-8520. That night Loretta left a new email message in the account. Osborn recorded the time of the message as 9:58 p.m.

Subject: dauphin—not crucial to read right now
You will be introduced as Mr. Tony Barret, a friend of ours.

On Monday, Loretta wrote two more messages. She also received four phone calls. Osborn and his team listened. The caller did not identify himself, but by now they knew Kopp's voice, could quickly recognize the tired cadence and diction, his accent at times verging on a southern drawl but never quite getting there. Kopp told Loretta he couldn't get the $300 she had tried to send. There was still a problem with the test question used by Western Union agents to confirm the identity of the recipient, and also with the money transfer control number.

Let's try again, said Kopp. Send $70 to John O'Brien in Dinan. Loretta agreed to do so within the hour. She immediately went to Western Union and wired the money. This time, the money got through. Later that day Loretta and Dennis scanned online for news of the manhunt for James C. Kopp. They also examined a map and located Dinan.

"I talked to him," said Loretta. "He had problems with the wire. He's using the name John O'Brien. I can't believe all he's going through."

Later, Loretta and Dennis talked about the future. What if they were caught? What if the FBI showed up one day to knock down the door? What if they were filmed entering the Western Union office? Their fingerprints were all over the place there. They had used it too much. Couldn't they have just mailed American cash overseas and let Jim exchange it for francs? What about tracing Jim's calls to their apartment? They agreed to get rid of the pink Western Union receipts.

"If you get picked up," said Dennis, "I'll get released and grab the boys."

"You might get released, but they would definitely detain me."

Tuesday morning Jim sat at a computer in Dinan and typed an email. Then four more within the span of a few minutes.

At 7:23 p.m. in Brooklyn, Loretta wrote Jim.

Subject: 1950 FF in CASH ON THE WAY

Dennis went to Western Union to wire $50 to John O'Brien in Dinan. He waited, then phoned Loretta. "Check the control numbers to see if Jim has picked them up," she said. Loretta phoned a contact named Sabine Goodwin. Would Sabine be able to get money to Jim in France? Next she phoned a contact at a monastery near Dinan. The contact said he could get a FedEx package to Jim. She went to the FedEx depot and sent a package containing 300 francs to the monastery. On Wednesday Loretta gave Dennis instructions on what to do if Jim called while she was out. Then she left the apartment, turned on her cell phone and called Sabine. When she returned, she logged on again to see if there was any message from Jim. There was nothing.

* * *

On Thursday, March 29, the phone rang in Loretta's apartment. It was 9 a.m.

"Hello?"

"Listen closely."

"Yes."

Michael Osborn's ears burned as the bug picked up the conversation. Kopp.

"I need to get out of this town because I am H-O-T," Kopp said.

"Really?"

"Oh, not super H-O-T. Now, you've got no red lights at your end, right? Nothing in the news?"

"Nothing in the news, no," she said.

"I mean, just answer the obvious stuff. I listened to some French news last night and there was no—no big deal. Do me a favor. In the next day or two I'll get in contact with you, but do some thinking about—about Oz. Do you know what Oz is yet?"

"I think so."

"Then I will send some letters. From Oz."

"Right."

"Oz. Dookesland. And to ROI, too."

Osborn listened. Oz? ROI?

"Then I'll return to the capital city of Dookesland and go to Jackie."

"OK," said Loretta.

Oz. Dookesland. Phonetic. Probably a play on Deutschland. Germany. Capital Berlin. He wants to fly from Berlin to Montreal. Misdirection. Kopp will mail letters to friends in the United States and the ROI—Republic of Ireland—from Germany. Need to put out an alert, thought Osborn. Kopp plans to move, and soon.

CHAPTER 19—SAYONARA

Jim hung up the phone after finishing his conversation with Loretta. It was about 3 p.m. Later, he walked through the center of Dinan. Thursday was market day, a festive atmosphere, the town square packed with kiosks, the smells of old cheese and fresh baguettes. Vendors sold meat, vegetables, fruit, clothing, and wine in old bottles with homemade labels. There was a carousel for the kids.

He walked into the post office. Behind the counter stood the clerk, whose white hair belied his youthful, animated face. The bearded man asked about a package left for a Francis Teller. The clerk checked. Jim prayed it would be there. The package was in. There were 300 francs inside.

"Merci. *Bonsoir,* good evening." Jim Kopp left through the sliding doors of La Poste, down six steps to the street. It was now nearly 4 p.m. He saw a police officer, a common sight in that part of town, with the police station nearby.

"*Bonsoir,*" Jim said.

"*Bonsoir,*" replied the officer, who turned away. Jim walked on. How many times had he had brushes like that with police officers? There had been so many random encounters over the last several years, any one of which, he mused, might have put him on a slow boat to Siberia. He vanished into the crowd in the market. Past La Belle Epoque Pizzeria and the courtyard beside the market where the carousel turned around and around, carnival music swirling up into

Dinan police officers Christian Joncour and
Henri Tardy took down Kopp.

the air. Past the *hotel de ville*, along the Esplanade de la Ré-sistance, and le Jardin du Val Cochere ("Garden of the Little Devils") on his right, and between rows of 150-year-old Platane trees, which were bare and gray, with bulbous joints at the top. The historic ramparts of Dinan were to his left. He moved past the Tour de Beau-fort, and the statue of Duclos, Mire de Dinan 1704-1772.

Oz. A coarse language, German, which is no doubt why the French hold it in contempt. French being the language of beauty— according to the French!—but German, the language from which English actually derives.

He walked the length of the promenade, about 100 meters. Then up the hill, along Rue du Fosse, up the stairs. His legs had to be tired, but when had Jim Kopp not been tired in the time he had been sleeping?

English, derivative of the German, dominates the world: the language of commerce, bad enough for the French, but more than that, worst of all, the language of diplomacy! Diplomacy, a French creation, although the great statesmen, at least in Kissinger's book, were men like the Brit Castlereagh, or Austrian Metternich, and Kissinger—good Nixon man, was German, although he officially renounced his citizenship. Kissinger. If H. Kissinger hadn't done his thing in '73, I'd have been on a one-way flight to Saigon. Me and Walt. Our draft numbers were high probability. Then Kissinger's peace accord. Gord Liddy, the hotheaded egotist, screwed everybody with Watergate. Dad would have never touched Watergate, would not have soldiered along in the ranks if he had accepted the offer to go to D.C. Dr. Steinfeld, Nixon's Surgeon General told me so, years ago. True story. Go ahead. Ask him. Ask him how his daughter is. She was gorgeous.

Along Rue d'Horloge. Past the Hôtel de la Tour d'Horloge, a creaky, heavy-beamed old building. There was a tiny Madonna perched above the doorway of the store next to the hotel like a guardian angel. A few more steps and he would be out of the narrow side street and into the crowded square.

Germany. Austria. Grandpa's birthplace. Dad. The Marine, who was there, the crucible of death, Japan, and what would Dad have said now about my—success? Success by what measure, I suppose, but of course that's the point, Jim, you idiot. Hmm: "Jim Kopp's struggle is the struggle of modern post-Christian civilization." Yes. And the central point of it all is, will we strive to protect the weak? Will we? Where are we going? Quo Vadis?

He felt a hard hand grab his shoulder. It exerted a forceful grip, an unfriendly one. How long had it been since he felt anyone grab him with force? It had once been such a staple of his life as an activist, used to be part of the game. There were two of them. Plainclothes. Large men. He struggled against the man squeezing his shoulder. It was no use. They twisted his arm behind his back, drove his body to the ground.

"La police! La police!" Jim Kopp yelled.

Perhaps he was trying to convince police that he was not James C. Kopp, the American fugitive. Or was it a last desperate attempt to sell someone, anyone, a bystander, on the idea that he was a victim, being attacked by thugs? An elderly woman approached the two men who were pinning down the thin, gaunt man, and hit them over the head with her umbrella. The man she thought to assist may have looked weak, but his appearance belied his strength. They had to fight to keep him in place, force his hands behind his back for cuffing, facedown, cheek grinding into the cobblestone. A car pulled up and he was pushed into the backseat. A brief drive to the police

Dinan post office where Kopp retrieved his money.

station around the corner. Silence in the car, Jim Kopp saying not a word. Escorted inside the station and down the hall, right turn, into a small, square overnight holding cell that was located right next to the drunk tank.

What had gone wrong? His situation, prior to his arrest, had hardly been perfect, but he was ready to move, had enough money to get on a train, ultimately get to Germany, mail his letters, meet up with contacts, get to Canada, New York, and back to Loretta—and to the field. He did not know that the day before his arrest, local police had received a fax from the authorities in Paris, via the FBI. A man named James C. Kopp, who was on the FBI's Ten Most Wanted List, was in Dinan, and planning to run. He could be armed and is dangerous. He had been using the post office to retrieve money being wired from the United States. Circulate his photo to post office employees, see if anyone recognizes him.

The next day, the haggard-looking bearded man had stood in La Poste, feverishly rubbing rosary beads. The clerk named Christian Guillot studied him. When James C. Kopp left the post office, Guillot phoned the National Police. If the man returns, the

Scott Gardner Photo

Prison in Rennes, France, where Kopp was taken.

clerk was told, phone us immediately. Later that day, he returned and retrieved an envelope. He left the office. Guillot phoned the police: he had come back. Guillot followed him out, saw a uniformed police officer standing on the corner. He motioned to the officer to follow Kopp. The officer started to move, but suddenly realized two plainclothes detectives had arrived. Their names were Christian Joncour and Henri Tardy, both 25-year veteran cops.

They followed the fugitive as he walked around town, up the hill, down the narrow side streets, waiting for the right moment to arrest him. Kopp did not turn around, but it appeared that he was quickening his pace. He was almost in the main square, where he could disappear into the crowd, when they made their move. At the station, Captain Pascal le Taillendier searched Kopp. His passport said he was John O'Brien, from Ireland. Then Le Taillendier found two more Irish passports—one for Sean O'Briain, and one for Daniel Joseph O'Sullivan. He also found instructions written in French on how to operate a semiautomatic pistol, a scrap of paper with a written reference to a Western Union transfer for 300 dollars in the name of Francis Teller, and the 300 dollars cash.

Kopp was placed in a small cell. National French police drove from Rennes, the regional capital, 30 minutes away, to take Kopp back with them to the prison facility there. They loaded James Kopp into a vehicle in Dinan and drove along the river to the Moulin Meen hostel. He was taken upstairs to his room to collect his things. The Japanese roommate was there, astounded at what was going on. His friend Jim Kopp looked at him and grinned.

"Well. I guess it's *sayonara*," Kopp said.

* * *

Buffalo, N.Y.

That afternoon, when agents in the Buffalo FBI field office heard the news there were high-fives all around. Bernie Tolbert answered the phone in New York City. The agent on the other end had some good news for him. Kopp was in custody. Got him. Funny how things work out. Tolbert was no longer with the bureau. He had retired a month earlier, taken a new job as head of security with the National Basketball Association. He had thought about staying in the FBI just a bit longer, to see the Kopp investigation through to the end. They had been so close to nabbing him in Ireland. But he knew it was time to move on. The new job took him to Barcelona, Tokyo, Paris. But the Kopp case would never be far from his thoughts.

When Tolbert left the bureau in February, he spoke with Lynne Slepian. The investigation had brought them very close. He tried to convince her that the case would remain a top priority with the bureau, even though he was leaving. And now, right after Bernie Tolbert heard the big news, he phoned Lynne. No answer. He called her cell phone. Lynne was at the doctor's office with her mother.

"Hello?"

"Lynne—it's Bernie. You sitting down?"

"That all depends—what do you have to say?"

"I told you we'd get him. And we did." A long pause. He could sense Lynne's emotion. He heard her begin to cry. Then the widow and the retired FBI agent were both in tears. Tolbert burst with pride over the work his old team had done. Some of the guys back in Buffalo had a poster made for him, the James Kopp wanted poster with "captured" splashed across it. Eventually he had it framed and matted and hung like a prized trophy on the wall of his NBA office on Fifth Avenue in Manhattan.

* * *

Brooklyn, N.Y.
March 29, 2001

That afternoon rain clouds gathered, a damp chill in the air. Loretta Marra had been at the cramped, dingy laundromat a block away from her apartment at 385 Chestnut Street in Brooklyn. Her cell phone rang. It was Dennis. The news had spread. In France, where it was now evening, James Charles Kopp was in custody.

"I'll be right home," Loretta said. She hung up, then phoned him back again. "Clean up the computer," she said.

Dennis killed the files. Loretta neared the outside of the building, towards the front door, when she saw FBI agents moving towards her. She was not about to submit quietly, she didn't have it in her. She took a FedEx receipt out of her pocket and ripped it up, then pressed speed dial on her cell phone.

"Put the cell phone away," said an agent, grabbing her arm.

She hung on to the phone and screamed—not a scream of terror, but a prolonged war cry, one of warning for Dennis, perhaps.

"Put the cell down now!" yelled the agent over her shriek. "Right now! Drop it! Drop it!"

The agent was on her now, turning Loretta around, forcing her hands up on the wall. Two uniform New York Police Department officers who happened to be nearby came running. Loretta saw the cops pull their guns. FBI agents flashed their badges for the police to see. A heavily armed FBI SWAT team moved upstairs to the apartment. The team had been well briefed on Dennis Malvasi's violent history. Do not treat him lightly. He had blown up clinics. Take all precautions. Agents pushed Malvasi to the floor in the apartment, cuffed him, then escorted him outside. The couple's two boys, ages five and two, were in the next room, looked after by agents.

Malvasi knew the drill. "I've never met Kopp in my entire life," he told agents. "I don't know this man."

Neighbors emerged from the building, hearing the screams. They were shocked to see the photos of Marra and Malvasi in the newspapers the next day. Arrest warrants were processed charging that the couple had harbored and concealed "a fugitive, James Charles Kopp, and did aid and abet in his movement in interstate and foreign commerce to avoid prosecution."

Agents searched the apartment, collecting evidence. They found documents stuffed in the back of the toilet. They found letters from Kopp, Irish phone numbers, library cards for Joyce Maier, an address for Amy Boissonneault, an Internet printout from a group called the Pensacola Pro-life Hunt Club, a false Arizona driver's license in Joyce Maier's name, a social security card and birth certificate for one Rose Marie Carroll. They also found two Canadian birth certificates for Loretta Marra's two sons, bills for electricity, gas, telephone for Ted Barnes, a driver's learner permit for Joyce Maier. There were receipts for $4,381 in gold and silver bars—and four bars, plus cash, stuffed inside the base of a lamp, along with Marra's legitimate passport in her own name. There were pages from the Army of God Code of Conduct handbook, and seven pages from the website of the Canadian Abortion Rights Action League—including pages listing abortion clinics in Quebec, Ontario and British Columbia.

After the arrest, agents Michael McAndrew and Christy Kottis drove Marra to the 75th Precinct at 1000 Sutter Avenue in Brooklyn. After processing, Marra was driven to the U.S. Eastern District New York courthouse in an FBI van. She still looked for a way out.

"As I see it, you two have three options," she told the agents from the backseat. "One, is to quit doing what you do altogether."

The agents said nothing.

"The second option is to do your job but to stop persecuting Christians. The third option would be the heroic and Christian thing to do, which would be to pull the car over right now, let me out and give me 20 dollars."

The agents still said nothing.

"Look, I'm not insane. I don't actually believe that you would let me out, but that would be the heroic thing to do."

CHAPTER 20—ST. PAUL 4:18

Lewisburg, Tennessee
Tuesday, April 3, 2001

Five days after the arrests of Kopp, Marra and Malvasi, the phone rang at a farmhouse in Lewisburg, Tennessee. Susan Brindle picked up. It was John Broderick, the lawyer who had once defended her sister, pro-life radical Joan Andrews. Broderick talked to Brindle about the arrest of Jim Kopp in France. He was going to see Jim on Thursday. "Any messages for him?" he asked.

"You're seeing Jim?" Susan said, the name sounding more like "Jeem" in her southern accent. "Can I go with you?"

"Susan—"

"I'll raise the money. Please. Can I go?"

Susan Brindle had been a pro-life activist for years, although not as high-profile as Joan. She hadn't seen Jim Kopp in years. Susan had first met him at a pro-life convention in Atlanta in 1987, gave him a ride one day. A real decent man, she thought, really holy. A pacifist, too. She didn't want to believe he was guilty of murder, but needed to ask him in person and see his reaction to be convinced. Broderick agreed to Susan's request. He would get her in.

"There's someone else I'd like Jim to meet," she added.

That "someone" was Bart Slepian's niece, Amanda Robb.

Bart's death had hit her hard. She went on tranquilizers. Amanda

Scott Gardner Photo

Kopp's lawyer in Rennes, Hervé Rouzaud–Le Boeuf

started thinking about her uncle's killer, maybe too much. She went to a shootings range, felt an assault rifle rock her bones as she tried to blow holes in human-shaped targets at 100 yards. Amanda's writing career had included a daytime Emmy nomination as part of a team writing television shows like *All My Children*. Now she was researching an article on Kopp, on the shooting, its impact on her own family. She wanted to meet her uncle's killer.

Her phone interview with Susan took place on the day of Jim's arrest. The call had been prearranged, the timing was a coincidence—although Susan felt there was deeper meaning. She didn't believe Jim had shot Dr. Slepian and she believed the call was a sign that Jesus was welcoming Amanda into Jim's life. So she would try to get Amanda an audience with him.

The next day, April 4, Broderick, Susan, and Amanda each flew to Paris and met at Charles de Gaulle Airport. Together they took a train west to Rennes. Amanda agreed that for the first visit it would be just Susan and Broderick. At that time, Susan would prepare Jim for meeting a special visitor.

* * *

Rennes, France

Hervé Rouzaud–Le Boeuf rose early, dressed, looked out the window towards the old stone building a few blocks away. A room with a view, mused the lawyer with a grin, his pale blue eyes twinkling. The building down the street was the Rennes Court of Appeals. No matter how many times he saw it, the power of the building as a symbol never failed to strike a chord. It was where actions of the state were called into question, under the dispassionate protection of the French Constitution, by criminal lawyers such as himself, the place where justice must be done and must be seen to be done.

Rouzaud–Le Boeuf cut a jaunty figure as he left his apartment building. He looked rather like the late Canadian prime minister Pierre Trudeau: modest height, silver-gray hair of liberal length poking out from underneath a black fedora, leather briefcase in hand, maroon shirt, tweed jacket, black scarf for the nip in the air. He was 54 years old, from a city in Brittany called Vannes, where they spoke not French but Breton. His office in Rennes was on Rue Bonne Nouvelle, first floor, near Place Sainte Anne. In his office he kept prints of ships and nautical maps, a tribute to his father, who had been a captain on oceangoing cargo vessels.

He had not been surprised to receive the call requesting that he represent an American fugitive charged with murdering a doctor. A legal service had recommended Rouzaud–Le Boeuf. He was an obvious choice. He spoke fluent, elegantly formal English and was well versed in international law relating to extradition. He took the case. The lawyer knew that Mr. Kopp was accused of committing a murder in New York State, had fled the United States and ended up in France using false passports. The Americans wanted to extradite him for trial.

His thoughts turned immediately to the most pressing issue. Did Kopp face the death penalty if he was shipped back to the United

States for trial? Rouzaud–Le Boeuf was well aware of the American fondness for the death penalty. Their new president, George W. Bush, inaugurated in January, had signed death warrants many times as governor of Texas. His new attorney general, the conservative John Ashcroft, a former Missouri senator, supported capital punishment as well. But he also knew that New York State had more liberal politics than other parts of the country. France, and the entire European Union, had outlawed capital punishment. The European Court of Human Rights had declared capital punishment "a form of torture and degrading treatment."

Rouzaud–Le Boeuf considered death sentences just one of the peculiarities—and shortcomings—of the American justice system when compared to that of the French. It was not that Hervé Rouzaud–Le Boeuf was anti-American. Not at all. Let us just say the American legal system did not ring as true to him as the British, and therefore the Canadian, and particularly the French, which he favored above all else.

He brushed up on New York criminal law. Under former governor Mario Cuomo, a Democrat, there had been no death penalty. But Republican George Pataki had beaten Cuomo on a law-and-order platform that included the restoration of capital punishment. When Bart Slepian had been murdered, Pataki called it an act of terrorism and a cold-blooded assassination. The sniper, he added, should be caught and put to death. As Hervé Rouzaud–Le Boeuf prepared to meet James Charles Kopp for the first time in jail, he was well aware that his task was to save the American's very life.

* * *

The Rennes prison is a sprawling, worn, old complex with towering walls. James Charles Kopp was led into a visitor's meeting room, and waited. He looked drained, weak. A cold he had been fighting didn't help. Susan Brindle and John Broderick were brought in. Jim's eyes met Susan's, his tired face looked relieved. An old friend.

"Thank goodness you're here," he said. "When John said you were coming I knew everything would be all right."

She was instantly struck by how terrible Jim looked. She took him off to one side. There was something she had to ask him.

"Jim, you know, good people, God bless them, paid for my ticket to come over here. I need to be able to tell them—you need to look me straight in the eye, be really honest with me, because—tell me, did you do this, or not?"

He looked her in the eye, unyielding, no pretension, no false sincerity, no nervous smile, no fidgeting. "Susan. I did not do this. I did not do it."

She felt relief. She'd never believed he could have done it. And now, looking into his blue-gray eyes, hearing his voice, she was certain of it.

"You have to tell everyone, hold a press conference and tell everyone I didn't do this," he continued. "No one knows. Tell them, please."

Later, Susan said she needed to ask something else. "Jim, there's someone I want you to meet, she's here in Rennes. Her name is Amanda, and she's Barnett Slepian's niece."

His niece? Here?

"She's a smart girl, I've spoken with her. She's a pro-abort but she's as honest as can be. She's tormented. Will you see her?"

"Susan, please, please," he pleaded. "I don't want to. Just tell her for me, can you?"

"Can you do this, please, for my sake, can you? Just tell her what you told me. She has a right to meet the person accused of killing her uncle, and to learn the truth, for the sake of her own soul."

* * *

Hervé Rouzaud–Le Boeuf arrived at the prison, was escorted to the meeting room to see his client, and quickly discovered he was not alone among those wishing to offer Mr. Kopp advice. He saw the woman with dark hair. She had an American southern accent. He took her hand in a chivalrous gesture. His English seemed from another time, words rolling off his tongue with precision and distinguished élan.

"It is most pleasant to meet you."

No matter what he said, Hervé Rouzaud–Le Boeuf sounded like a diplomat holding court at a cocktail party. She was introduced to him as a "legal clerk" but seemed more a friend of Mr. Kopp's. There was a lawyer there, an American named John Broderick. A colorful man, this Mr. Broderick, caricature of the avuncular Irish-American, tall, gruff, booming voice, viselike handshake. A strong personality. But then, James Kopp had a strong personality, too, Rouzaud–Le Boeuf could tell that from the start. Very opinionated. Kopp did not seem to mesh well with Mr. Broderick, they did not seem to share the same views, not today, anyway. There were loud disagreements. Eventually the French lawyer sat with Jim, away from the others. Now was his chance to take the measure of his client. Rouzaud–Le Boeuf looked into the mans eyes. Mr. Kopp was clearly agitated, frightened, surely in need of rest. Understandable. But the lawyer needed to know the truth.

"Mr. Le Boeuf. I am innocent."

The lawyer studied him. Kopp spoke in detail of the road to his arrest, rambling at times, going off on tangents, but repeatedly stressing his innocence. Rouzaud–Le Boeuf had stared into many faces over the years, both the guilty and innocent. Looking at his new client, he was convinced. It wasn't so much what he said, or that he had an airtight alibi—he did not. Rather it was the genuine way he talked. By the time he left the prison, the lawyer had no doubt. He had not been sitting next to a murderer, he thought.

* * *

Susan spoke further with Jim. There was so much she wanted to know. Why had Jim planned to return to the United States right before his arrest? Why not just stay safe in Europe? "It's insane, Jim, you're free, why come back to America?"

"Because I heard that Amy had cancer."

What? Amy? What, Susan wondered, does Amy Boissonneault have to do with this? She hadn't seen Amy in at least a year. Amy was 34 years old, 12 years Jim's junior, and was the best friend of Susan's daughter. Susan had no idea Jim felt so close to Amy. He told her he had tried to send Amy money so she could undergo alternative cancer treatment. "I heard she had cancer," he said, "but at her age, it was low risk, I thought she'd be OK, but when I heard it went to her brain I had to get back to America. I had to tell her that I love her—and ask her to marry me."

Susan's eyes teared up, and so did Jim's.

"For the first time in my life," he continued, "I feel that Jesus wants me to have a wife and kids."

Jim had felt affection towards Amy for a long time. Perhaps he never revered her in the same way as he did Loretta, but Jim was attracted to Amy and admired her. Jim likened Amy to Mother Teresa. Both women were gentle, saintly, on the surface, but underneath were also tough as nails. Jim loved that about her. Amy called herself a tough farm girl. Jim knew the feminists would hear that and miss the point. She was delivering calves with her bare hands when she was ten, he liked to say. You could find her in the dead of winter up on a friend's roof fixing a hole. That's the kind of woman she was. He took a piece of paper from his pocket and handed it to Susan. It was from a magazine, a picture of an engagement ring.

"You're thinking, 'Jim is crazy, he's finally lost it,' and I understand that," he said. "But I need you to do this for me. I need you to find this ring, have it blessed, and then call Amy's father, ask him for permission."

"Permission? Jim, her father is going to give his blessing for his daughter, who has cancer, to marry a man who is accused of murder, who's been gone two and a half years? It's insane!"

"I know, I—"

"Look, I'll ask her, but not her father."

"No-no-no, just ask him, just say, 'Mr. Boissonneault, if Amy didn't have cancer, and if Jim wasn't in jail accused of murder, would you allow him to date Amy?' And if he says no, then don't ask her. I'll just pray. I'm meant to wait. But if the answer is yes, can you find her, bring her over here to me?"

Susan left the jail that night, thoughts swirling, caught between what her heart and her mind were telling her. Her heart won out. Back at the hotel, she spoke to Amanda Robb. Jim had not killed her uncle, Susan was sure of it. And Jim was about to become engaged.

"Jesus is going to work a miracle," Susan said. "I just know they're gonna get married and have babies."

Amanda couldn't believe what she was hearing.

The next day, Bart Slepian's niece was introduced to Jim Kopp. She expected to meet him in a room divided by Plexiglas. But in the Rennes jail they sat in a private room, only a wooden table separating them. Jim carried a Bible with him. Amanda, a writer, soaked up the atmosphere, took the measure of this man Kopp, made mental notes. He was tall, lean. Baby-blue eyes. Handsome? Yes, she decided, maybe even shockingly handsome. He offered his hand.

"Hi, I'm Jim," he said.

She shook his hand and quietly muttered, "Amanda."

Amanda later wrote an article about the meeting, and her quest to find Kopp, and sold it to *New York Magazine*. It ran under the headline "The Doctor, The Niece And The Killer." She wrote:

> "There was a long silence, and to fill it I told Jim two people
> had sent their love to him via me. The instant I mentioned
> the second person's name, Jim curled into a fetal position
> and sobbed … Eventually he choked out that he thought
> this person hated him. He pulled himself together, saying,
> "If you wait long enough, everything in life comes back to
> you." Then he started rambling … His narrative was a tangle
> of strands about victim souls, abortion, his "calling" to stop

it, his destiny, my uncle's murder, and fleeting mentions of his "fiancée."

"I didn't shoot your uncle," he said. "But I'm going to plead guilty and do the time—25 years straight up—because someone of my religion did." This hung heavily in the air. I worried I was going to throw up. As I felt my face twitching, Jim smiled beatifically and changed the subject to movies. He suggested I watch *Pay It Forward*, which he said was the story of his life ... He then urged me to see *There's Something About Mary* and quietly added that I looked like Cameron Diaz ... It suddenly dawned on me that my uncle's killer was flirting with me."

Amanda Robb told Jim she wanted to understand him, asked if she could write to him. He agreed. A guard entered the room to escort him back to his cell. He handed Amanda a Bible. Inside, he had written "To Mandy." Only her family had ever called her by that nickname, she reflected.

* * *

Before leaving Rennes, Susan Brindle spoke to Jim about Amy one more time. Amazing thing. Susan had called home and spoken to her sister about Jim's proposal to marry Amy. And her sister Joan said that out of the blue Amy had called, said she was coming to town, would stop in to say hi. Susan relayed the story to Jim and he smiled. God was directing everything! Susan finally said goodbye to Jim. She took the train back to Paris. That night she searched for the ring Jim had requested, went store to store for several hours, until, late in the evening, she found a small jeweler who had it. She bought the ring and took it to Notre Dame Cathedral to get it blessed. No priest was available, so she returned the next morning to early mass and got the ring blessed. Then she caught her flight to New York. Susan called Amy's father early the next day. He knew she had been in France visiting Jim Kopp. "How are you, Susan? And how was Jim?"

Susan got around to asking. "Mr. Boissonneault, can I ask you a really strange question? If Amy didn't have cancer, and Jim wasn't in jail, would you ever allow him to ask her out? I just need to know."

"Kind of an odd question, don't you think?" he said.

"I know, I know. But I need to know."

"It's not really up to me. It's up to Amy."

"Thank you. And God bless."

Susan went and saw Amy, who was visiting Joan's home. They walked in the backyard past a statue of the Blessed Mother. "How is Jim?" asked Amy. "Does he talk about his friends?"

"He does. He talks about you."

"Me?"

"He talks about you, he really cares about you."

"What are you talking about?"

"He loves you, Amy."

Amy stared at her, bewildered. "What? Jim? I always—I always thought of him like a priest, in a way. Never thought of him in that way."

Susan smiled. That was how she had always felt about him, too. "Jim did say that you went on a date once," she said.

"A date?"

"Yes, to an antique store or something."

"That wasn't a date!"

"Well, Jim doesn't go out alone with girls, and you two were alone. To him it was a date."

Amy was shocked. She didn't know what to say. Susan drew the engagement ring out of her pocket.

"Jim asked me, Amy, to ask you to marry him."

Amy started to cry. Susan did too. "You can tell him to ask me in person when I see him in France."

It was all too much. But miracles happen, right? Maybe Amy would get better, and Jim would get out of jail, and—and they could get married, maybe even live in France. But Amy was dying, they had no future, did they?

Susan, Amy, and Susan's daughter flew to France and visited Jim in the Rennes prison. They met as a group, then Amy and Jim met privately. The women left the jail and walked outside its walls to a specific spot Jim had told them about. Just stand there and listen, he had said. It was dark. They could barely hear, but were sure they could make something out.

God bless him. He was singing hymns.

Susan felt Jim had a beautiful voice. Not everyone was a fan—his singing drove his cellmates crazy. He had shared a cell with a Brit who was being extradited. They got along at first, but after a while he asked to be moved because Kopp sang his hymns, loudly, at three or four o'clock in morning. Amy made one last visit to see Jim. He did not propose to her. She asked him not to. She did not have much time to live, she was certain of that. Before they said goodbye, Jim elicited a promise from Amy. They would not tell anyone about their relationship, or what was said in private. They would take the secret with them to the grave.

* * *

Rennes, France
Tuesday, May 8, 2001

On May 8, the U.S. Justice Department formally submitted a request to the French government for the extradition of James Charles Kopp. A deadline was set for the end of the month for the French courts to decide the matter. Under the extradition treaty between the two countries, no one arrested in France for a crime committed in the United States could face a penalty harsher than a convict would face in France. As the deadline neared, American officials speaking for Attorney General John Ashcroft insisted that the death penalty remain an option should Kopp be found guilty of murder. This, even though the European Court of Human Rights had previously ruled that no individual could be extradited from any European country without a guarantee that capital punishment be taken off the table. The French Court of Appeal in Rennes would make the final decision on the matter.

Hervé Rouzaud–Le Boeuf considered the situation an intriguing one. His client had broken no French law. Perhaps he might be charged with illegal entry to the country, using a false passport and so on. Perhaps. Might get a couple of months in jail. After that? If the extradition failed, Mr. Kopp could stay in France or go elsewhere. No Western European country would send him back to the United States to face the death penalty. He could remain in legal limbo indefinitely.

Hervé Rouzaud–Le Boeuf faced something of a dilemma. On the one hand he could hope that Ashcroft would agree to drop the death penalty. But that would mean extradition and a murder trial for his client, a possible life sentence. On the other hand, maybe it would be better if there was no deal at all. Then French justice would determine Kopp's fate. Rouzaud–Le Boeuf had many long talks with his client. The American was an engaging man, highly intelligent, but could be volatile at times, unpredictable. He talked of his family, his father. He told a fantastic story of how he ended up in France: he had learned that the Archbishop in Ireland was a homosexual, had started telling others about the fact, and some clergy urged Kopp to get out of the country. Yes, in their early conversations, Mr. Kopp seemed quite agitated, at times unbalanced.

The day neared when the Court of Appeal in Rennes would make its extradition decision. Rouzaud–Le Boeuf received a phone call. He should appear in court immediately. There he was handed the faxed letter. It was from the U.S. embassy in Paris. The Americans would not seek the death penalty for James Charles Kopp. Rouzaud–Le Boeuf smiled. His client was going to live. Of course, the Americans had little choice. They could not risk losing Kopp altogether. And, if Kopp was innocent, as his lawyer strongly believed, then he would be ultimately acquitted. How might Kopp fare in New York? He had retained a high-profile Buffalo defense lawyer named Paul Cambria. He would of course still need to navigate the American legal system and its sideshows—the media frenzy, the money, courtroom histrionics, plea bargains. In America, Rouzaud–Le Boeuf reflected, innocent men sometimes end up in prison, admit to crimes they did not commit.

There was something else that worried him. There was a signature missing on the letter from the U.S. embassy—Ashcroft's. It should be there, he thought. This was an important case, shouldn't the attorney general himself make the decision? Now, on the other hand, it was unthinkable that top American officials would renege on such a promise. It would be a gross violation of international law. But there was still that risk, however small. On June 7, Rouzaud–Le Boeuf got what he was looking for—a public statement from Ashcroft on the extradition agreement:

> James Charles Kopp committed a heinous crime that deserves severe punishment. We need to send a strong message that, no matter what our differences are, violence is not the solution. The FACE laws were created to ensure that violence against individuals providing legally available health services is not tolerated and will carry a stiff penalty, and I intend to enforce those laws. Shortly after the arrest, the French government, pursuant to its law and practice, asked the United States to assure it that the death penalty will not be imposed or carried out. Nevertheless, I have been working to ensure the United States' ability to pursue strong punishment for this terrible crime. I wanted to make sure that our nation would not be constrained by limits placed on Kopp's extradition by France, preventing us from seeking punishment outlined by our laws and our Constitution, such as the death penalty. Unfortunately, in order to ensure that Kopp is not released from custody

and is brought to justice in America, we have had to agree not to seek the death penalty. I share the sentiments of Dr. Slepian's widow, Lynne Slepian, that if the choice is between extraditing Kopp to face these serious charges in a United States court or risking his release by France, the priority must be Kopp's return.

On June 28, the Court of Appeals in Rennes ruled that Kopp should be extradited to the United States for trial. But to Jim the game was just beginning. He was a lawyer's son, after all. He decided to challenge the court's decision. If he could delay his return, all the better. And if the ruling was by some chance overturned, he could remain in Europe indefinitely. As for the death penalty, he didn't trust any of them back home, not even the pro-life conservative Ashcroft, whose hands were surely tied on the matter. The abortion industry was bigger than any one man. They all wanted him to suffer. The Edgars were no doubt putting the full-court press on anyone he had ever known or loved back home, he thought. No, once the Americans got him back home, all bets were off. He was certain "The Government" would never cease trying to make an example of him. And that meant that a lethal injection might still await James C. Kopp.

* * *

Rennes, France
Spring 2001

As Jim Kopp waited for the appeal court to rule, he wrote letters to family and friends. Now was his chance to explain the last two and a half years. Jim was certain the FBI had given his brother, Walter, who still lived in California, a rough ride. In his mind's eye he could see the men in dark suits and sunglasses hounding his twin brother. *"Yeah, uh, gee, Walt, we think you oughta co-operate—seems we found this stuff called DNA at the murder scene.*

James Kopp's DNA. Couldn't be anyone else's DNA. Well, unless of
course the killer had a twin. You reading us here, partner? Jail is not
a pleasant place to be, Walt ..."

He wrote Walter, protesting his innocence, defending his convictions:

> I have been framed. I guess I just wanted to make certain
> you knew there was no deal on the table and likely not to
> be with the way I have been drawn and quartered before I
> even got to court. They knew they didn't have to deal, not
> after the job they have done on me ... I don't blame you
> one bit if you are upset and frustrated. Me too, you know. I
> didn't do this. But one thing I am guilty as hell about is my
> religion and beliefs, especially pro-life. In that regard I'm
> no different from all the people being put in new graves in
> Israel and Beijing ... I know this is hard. You are suffering,
> through no fault of your own, for your brother's religion.
> Many people in Russia and China are dead over this. You
> are so kind to keep asking to help when all I gave you, via
> the movement, not via killing anybody, is grief. I guess
> what I'm trying to say is that it is my religion and belief
> that bother the powers that be. If I were not pro-life, they
> would have not gotten this far. Actually, they would never
> have thought of it. I would be no greater a suspect than
> you are ... My current lawyer, who I hope to keep, hates
> pre-trial publicity. But there is another set of lawyers out
> there who I have no control over who want to show the
> world about how I have been framed.

In another letter to Walt, he further developed his self-portrait
as innocent fall guy:

> If I could name who shot Slepian, I would. But I do not
> know for certain. I suspect I'm in trouble because I can

make a good guess. But it's nothing they don't already know. Even if the FBI knew I did not do it, it's too late for them to change horses and stick the blame on someone else. Do not to be ashamed is my word. I would think that's good enough. But most people only believe what they read in the newspaper.

He wrote a long letter to Susan Brindle, intended as a message for all his friends to see—and he knew the Edgars would be reading it at their leisure, too:

The Peace of the Lord be always with you, but especially today!

I don't like writing generic letters, i.e. letters intended for more than one person, but I am out of paper and stamps, and so many people have written. Also, it is tedious to repeat things, to the point where I don't repeat them, and even good friends, as a result, are clueless.

As I told the extradition judge here, I am innocent of this terrible thing, and I desire to enter an American court as soon as possible to clear my name. Any delays toward that goal are procedural in terms of the slow grinding of the wheels of justice. Some advantage accrues to my defense lawyers in that they can prepare a defense.

Preparing a defense in this sense does not mean merely establish my alibi and things like that, things I could have attempted two and a half years ago. "Preparing a defense" means becoming familiar with the bizarre twists against me. For example, you would think that hair or carpet fiber appearing in a forest is laughable enough, and not hardly worth refuting, especially as both appear in connection with the stealing of my car from an airport parking lot. But suppose other defects appear in the hair itself; and you can get the hair omitted by pointing this out? Do you see what

I mean? These are the sorts of decisions Mr. Cambria (my lawyer) must face. All of this stuff has to be evaluated on its merits, even if its appearance is ludicrous.

Why did I run away if I'm innocent? This is what everyone wants to know. The answer is a person, not a thing or an idea. The person is Maurice Lewis, R.I.P., who was poisoned in Canada in 1996, roughly.

Maurice's body was found in a truck parked on the side of the road. His body had lain there two days. The official cause of death is "no apparent cause" or trauma—nothing except that he was dead. The RCMP report indicated the presence of someone who cleaned up the death scene before the RCMP got there (Royal Canadian Mounted Police— like CHPs, or State Troopers in the United States). Why do we know this? The RCMP makes no reference to any wrappers, papers, soda cans or bottles or bags that one would associate with eating a snack. The only people I know with no food wrappers in their cars are people who only eat in restaurants on long drives. Maurice Lewis was not such a person. All pro-lifers eat cheap so they can save money to pay for the expenses of pregnant women, which Maurice Lewis did do.

I spent six weeks alone with Maurice in a strip cell in Rome, when we were beaten. I know about him. So, the death of Maurice weighed on my mind in Fall 1998, when the first news of the FBI seeking me as a witness came on the news (i.e. if that's how they treated Maurice, what about me?). Then there was the matter of the 1985 San Francisco trial against me for charges of assault with a deadly weapon. I was acquitted, but what a pain! I was not interested in repeating that experience.

Then there were outstanding warrants in a jurisdiction where I had just finished suing (unsuccessfully) the warden, who, (before I sued him) had murdered two inmates, crushing them to death in a trash compactor during an escape attempt. (Don't worry, he won't sue me for libel, this is an open fact demonstrated in court—the prosecution merely needed an eyewitness.)

So let's review the bidding, as Nancy Kopp would say:

a) Maurice Lewis;

b) San Francisco, AWDW (i.e. I have already been charged with things I didn't do);

c) Pittsburgh warrants (exposure: 4 years.)

Even so, when I heard I was wanted for questioning, I tried to turn myself in through a Vermont lawyer, Dan Lynch ... and lo and behold when I called an intermediary, Dan had become a judge. This gave me pause. (Can you turn yourself in to a judge?) Sounded awfully ex parte to me.

So, the run theory prevailed. If I had it all to do over again, I probably would not have run away. But that's hindsight.

If the above does not make sense, please ask any veteran rescuer, any veteran object of U.S. lawsuits, or for that matter (esp. about Maurice ...) anyone familiar with Mena witness murders (*New American Spectator*), (No I am not a conspiracy theorist ... yet).

My spirits are good. I look forward to a vigorous defense. My eyes are on God, I am looking to Him to free me. I am tired of running. The evangelical chaplain here gave me a tape of hymns by 2nd Chapter of Acts. Here is my favorite:

I'll be free at last, to lay it all down/Free at last to wear my crown

And the sun will never rise again/For he will be my light

My heart will never never never/Break His heart again.

I pray for you all. Please write, don't be afraid. Send it unsigned through a lawyer if you wish. I'll figure out who you are. God bless you.

Please remember my chains,
Jim

Remember my chains. It was a quote from St. Paul's letter to the Colossians, 4:18.

CHAPTER 21–"A PRO-LIFE SCALP"

Buffalo, N.Y.
Summer 2001

Buffalo lawyer Paul Cambria Jr. had a national reputation. He had defended the right to free speech for clients such as porn king Larry Flynt and shock rocker Marilyn Manson. At 54, he had practiced law for nearly 30 years. He contributed regularly to a website devoted to legal questions regarding pornography and free speech. He rode a Harley, was once featured on the cover of *Rolling Stone*. The press loved him. He once admitted that he wanted to be on O. J. Simpson's legal Dream Team "in the worst way," and quipped he was relieved he wasn't hired to defend Timothy McVeigh because his skills might have got the Oklahoma City bomber acquitted.

Once Cambria took the case of James C. Kopp, the buzz began. He was very good, but some of Jim's friends felt he needed a committed pro-life attorney, someone to make the philosophical points. Others, like Susan Brindle, thought Cambria, who was not known as a pro-lifer, was perfect. Morality, abortion, religion—that was not Cambria's game, and that was not at issue in Jim Kopp's case, or at least shouldn't be. Cambria would have credibility with a jury. He could stand up there and say: "I am pro-choice, I lament the death of Dr. Slepian. But Mr. Kopp did not pull the trigger." In addition, Cambria would be expensive, very expensive. But donations

Jim Kopp's lawyer, Paul Cambria Jr.

from pro-life supporters were coming in. Susan told Jim, whatever it costs, they would raise the money, because that's how much they believed in his innocence.

Meanwhile, controversy over Jim's case raged online. His supporters charged that the FBI had fabricated evidence to deliver a pro-life scapegoat for pro-choice forces in Washington.

"Regardless of whether Jim Kopp actually committed this crime or not," wrote one commentator, "the Clinton-Reno Department of Justice was going to have a pro-life scalp and his was as good as any. In a nation governed by amoral people who see the judicial system as an instrument of politics rather than justice, that's just the way the game is played."

It didn't add up, did it? Jim had friends all over the country, and no one had ever seen any sign he was capable of shooting anyone. He never talked about it. If anything he seemed destined to be a priest. That FBI mug shot, it didn't even look like Jim. Physical evidence? The police can't find the rifle used to shoot Slepian, yet finger Kopp for the murder anyway. Then, more than five months later—presto—they find not only the rifle but hair fibers supposedly linked to Kopp all over the place. It was all there: planted evidence; unlikely killer; biased law enforcement. It all had echoes of the O. J. Simpson case. A lawyer of Cambria's caliber would make hay with the inconsistencies.

* * *

The charge against Loretta Marra and Dennis Malvasi was upgraded from conspiracy to harbor a known fugitive to a more serious charge of obstruction of justice. In the summer of 2001 they applied to be released on bail. Their trial had been moved from Brooklyn, in the Eastern District of the State of New York, to Buffalo, in the Western District. Malvasi had a Buffalo court-appointed lawyer named Thomas Eoannou representing him. Marra retained a Long Island lawyer named Bruce Barket, who had defended pro-life clients in the past.

Barket was a stocky 42-year-old devout Catholic with dark hair and an olive complexion that reflected his Lebanese-Italian heritage. He had once stopped practicing law to study for the priesthood, but returned to his job and made a considerable reputation defending the underdog. He won the New York State Association of Criminal Defense Lawyers Gideon Award, for representing people who could not afford to pay. Barket disdained the description "pro-life lawyer," but he made no secret of his beliefs, or of the fact that he wanted to add the notion of protection of the fetus to the quilt of American civil rights.

Barket had fought some controversial cases. He continued to represent Amy Fisher, who had made headlines in 1992 as a 17-year-old high school student who had an affair with a married man and wound up shooting his wife in the head, nearly killing her. Dubbed the Long Island Lolita by the tabloids, Fisher pleaded guilty and was sentenced to 5 to 15 years in prison. In 1998, she claimed she had had a steamy affair with her first lawyer—prior to Barket taking over her defense—and that he had forced her into copping the plea to avoid the tryst being revealed. "What took place," Barket said after becoming her lawyer, "is sad and despicable." In 1999, Fisher launched a $220-million lawsuit against five corrections officers who she alleged had raped her. She later dropped the suit. The judge said that her lawsuit "read more like a cheap dime-store novel or a script for a tabloid television show than a pleading in a federal lawsuit." Barket had earlier requested a new criminal trial for Fisher, claiming that the district attorney handling the case had made plea-bargain promises that were not kept. It would not be the last time that Bruce Barket argued that he had been misled by a prosecutor in a plea bargain.

Loretta Marra wrote a letter to the presiding judge, Richard Arcara, arguing for her release on bail. She said she was no flight risk. All of her friends were known to the FBI in any case, she had nowhere to go even if she wanted to, and two little boys she needed to care for, one of which she was still nursing at the time of her arrest.

"I don't mind being incarcerated," she wrote. "It has a lot in common with the monastic lifestyle, a lifestyle which holds tremendous appeal for me ... If you set bail, I will never give you cause to regret it, I will not flee. I swear this to you on my salvation. As a completely convinced Catholic there is no more binding oath I could possibly conceive. I have hesitated for days to write this, so much does the oath terrify me to take it. I will die rather than break it. Thank you and God Bless You."

The judge denied her bail.

* * *

In Buffalo Paul Cambria spoke to the media about his client's continued fight against extradition from France to the United States for trial. "Ultimately," Cambria said, "I want him back here, and he wants to come back here to fight these charges. But his French attorney has been telling him to keep fighting extradition." Early in October, the French court rejected Kopp's appeal. There was still one other appeal he could make, this time to the Superior Administrative Court in France. He filed that appeal, too. And then, several months later, he decided to abandon the fight.

In May 2002, Hervé Rouzaud–Le Boeuf spoke at a news conference in Rennes, saying that his client intended to prove his innocence upon his return to the United States, and viewed the trial as a chance to clear his name. Why did Jim Kopp give up the extradition fight? There may have been reasons only he understood, but he was perhaps motivated by what was happening to Loretta. Could he use his extradition as a bargaining chip to free her? It ate him up thinking of Loretta in jail, denied bail, two young boys at home who needed their mother. At one point in the extradition delay, he floated an idea to U.S. Justice Department officials. Kopp said he would agree to return to the United States while secretly giving his consent to leave the death penalty on the table—putting his own life at risk—if the Americans would in turn let Loretta walk free. Surely the feds would jump at the opportunity. Loretta was small potatoes, he thought, it's Kopp they wanted on a gurney.

Was the suggestion genuine or was he playing another game?

Loretta, through Bruce Barket, urged Jim not to take such a drastic step. Was he that confident he would be acquitted of Bart Slepian's murder? Or was he putting on an act to impress Loretta? Friends of Jim's thought there was something else that may have prompted him to give up his extradition fight. An obituary had appeared in the *St. Albans Messenger* newspaper in February:

ST. ALBANS/FAIRFAX—Amy Lynn Boissonneault, 35, of St. Albans, formerly of Fairfax, died peacefully of breast cancer on Monday evening, Feb. 18, 2002, at her home in St. Albans in the presence of her family and friends. Amy was an avid traveler and made many trips and pilgrimages across North America and Europe to include Italy, France and Ireland. She also enjoyed art, poetry, writing letters, summer sunsets at the lake, snowstorms, gardening, Jane Austen movies and New York City. Amy will be remembered for the things she treasured most. Her strong faith in Jesus Christ, her love of the Church and its saints and her family and friends. She enriched the lives of so many with her inner beauty and contagious smile. Her love of life and dedication to others were an inspiration to all who knew and loved her.

Memorial contributions, in lieu of flowers, may be made in Amy's memory to Good Counsel, Hoboken, N.J., or to the Franciscan Friars of the Renewal.

* * *

Buffalo, N.Y.
Wednesday, June 5, 2002

The U.S. Department of Justice jet arrived from Paris and touched down at the Niagara Falls air force base. On board were several U.S. marshals, the Amherst chief of police, and James Charles Kopp. He returned facing two trials. The State of New York had charged him with murder in the second degree, reckless endangerment in the first degree, and criminal possession of a weapon in the third degree. The federal government charged him with using deadly force to interfere with the right to reproductive health services.

Amherst police chief John Moslow, far left, and FBI officials address the media before James Kopp appears in court.

First he was taken to the federal courthouse in downtown Buffalo, escorted into the room by federal marshals and police. He was arraigned before magistrate Judge Hugh Scott on the federal charge. If found guilty, he faced a sentence of life in prison without parole. Paul Cambria filed a not-guilty plea on Kopp's behalf. Jim Kopp wore wire-rimmed glasses, a rumpled dress shirt, green work pants and navy canvas slip-on shoes. He had a rolled-up *Magnificat* magazine, the Catholic periodical, in his back pocket.

"Are you James Charles Kopp?" asked Scott.

"Yes, sir."

"Do you understand your right at this time to remain silent?"

"Yes, sir."

Kopp didn't say anything else, but he had instantly made an impression with the media. How could this man be the infamous sniper? His was not the fierce face that had glared from the FBI most wanted poster. Reporters described his thick glasses and boyish face. A slight, meek, wisp of a man with a loopy grin. The public had a new picture of James C. Kopp. Perhaps he wanted it that way. Few could see the wiry forearms, large hands, the blue-gray eyes that seemed to grow darker when he was angry, or the six-foot frame that never looked quite that tall because of his hunched gait. And no one could see the intensity that burned within him.

Judge Scott remanded Kopp into custody. As the marshals escorted him out of the court, he noticed a friend in the gallery, a pro-lifer. "Joe! Hi, Joe!" Kopp said, grinning, before being led into an elevator and down to where more armed marshals waited in vans and jeeps and sedans.

Paul Cambria addressed reporters. "He's very upbeat—very much looking forward to the process." Cambria added that the trial would not be about abortion.

A reporter asked why Kopp had fled in the first place if he was innocent.

"It wasn't because he's guilty. You'll find that out as we begin to try the case. There is a very plausible and innocent explanation for his actions."

The next day he was arraigned in state court and pleaded not guilty to the charge of second-degree murder, which carried a maximum sentence of 25 years to life. Cambria promised the media the trial would be a dogfight. One legal analyst said the resourceful Cambria would "have a field day" picking out weaknesses in the prosecution's case, including why it took police five months to find the murder weapon, and challenge them to prove that Kopp had bought it. In effect, the defense lawyer would put the FBI and police themselves on trial. The analyst added that everyone was anxious to see Paul Cambria take on the top prosecutor in the Buffalo DA's office.

* * *

"Life in prison would be difficult, certainly—it always is," Joseph Marusak said, his blue eyes staring unblinkingly into those of the jurors. "But he'll still be able to get up every day. He'll be able to breathe every day. What about his victim?" It was a Thursday in October 1998. The 20-year-old man charged with murder watched the prosecutor work the jury, trying to convince them that the accused deserved to be strapped to a gurney and have potassium chloride pumped through his veins, stopping his heart—that he, Jonathan Parker, deserved to die. Parker was Joe Marusak's first death penalty case. He had, weeks before, managed to get Parker convicted for murder. Now he was going for the ultimate sentence.

At that time, three years after Republican governor George Pataki had brought back capital punishment to New York State, only one other person sat on death row. Parker had shot decorated Buffalo police officer Charles (Skip) McDougald, father of four. A controversial case. The selection of an all-white jury for Parker—who was black—had drawn criticism. But then the victim had been black, too. Parker had been arrested a few times prior to the shooting on drug and weapon offenses. Before the jury Parker apologized to McDougald's family. He was sorry, truly sorry, for the tragedy he had caused. But Marusak argued that Parker had forfeited his right to live when he aimed a loaded semiautomatic pistol at the police officer's heart.

"If Officer McDougald had been able to steady his aim and kill the defendant, would that action have been justified?" Marusak asked. "If that action was justified, how can the death sentence not be?"

The presiding judge in the case was Michael L. D'Amico. He watched Marusak pour it on, taking the jurors back to the fatal night, putting them in the slain cop's shoes, recounting the final hours of his life.

Prosecutor Joe Marusak

"He had no clue as he got out of his car that he had an invisible target on his chest. Then the explosion shreds your heart. You reach for the gun out of instinct, your lungs filling with blood and the life going out of you—can you grasp the brutality of this?"

As Marusak spoke, the cop's widow fled the courtroom in tears. Marusak was Catholic, raised by devout parents, attended mass regularly. Through most of its history, the Roman Catholic Church had supported the death penalty. But by the end of the 20th century, Pope John Paul II opposed capital punishment as "cruel and unnecessary." U.S. Supreme Court justice Antonin Scalia, a Catholic, supported the death penalty. If Marusak felt any personal conflict on the issue, he could not let it affect his work in court. He kept his views to himself. But he also felt that arguing in favor of the death penalty in a court of law did not make him a bad Catholic. He hadn't requested the Parker case. It was assigned to him.

Marusak was 44 years old but looked much younger, had thick dark hair with flecks of gray, the pale blue eyes alert, skin unwrinkled, athletic build. He spoke with the distinctive Western New York accent, so when he said his name it sounded like Maroozyak.

He was in court on Saturday, October 24, 1998, as the jury returned to render its decision on the sentence for Parker. They deliberated 17 hours over three days. There was one woman on the jury who had refused to be swayed. Parker would live, serve life in prison with no parole. Joe Marusak lost. Marusak kicked himself over it. He should never have accepted that woman on the jury. During jury selection, she had opined that she supported the death penalty only in very rare circumstances. Marusak had thought he could prove to her that the murder of Skip McDougald was one of those times. He had been wrong.

As if by way of a rematch, faces from that courtroom would meet again. It was the evening before the verdict, on October 23, when another verdict had been rendered in the woods outside Bart Slepian's home—when the sniper had condemned Slepian with a high-powered rifle. The judge in the Jonathan Parker case, Michael D'Amico, would oversee the case that spawned from that night. And Parker's lawyer, John Elmore, would join the legal defense team for James Charles Kopp. His opposite number would again be Joe Marusak.

When Lynne Slepian heard that Marusak was appointed to prosecute Kopp, she spoke to Glenn Murray, Bart's former lawyer and friend. "The prosecutor's name is Joe Marusak," she told him. "Is he good?"

Murray smiled to himself. How many times had Joe kicked his ass in court? Every time? Yes, every time. "Lynne, this guy works 20 hours a day. He is every defense lawyer's nightmare. He's the best there is."

CHAPTER 22—THE USUAL SUSPECTS

Buffalo, N.Y.
Thursday, August 29, 2002

In order to establish the identity of Bart Slepian's killer for the jury, Joe Marusak returned to witnesses who saw the suspicious jogger near Bart's home in the days leading up to the murder four years earlier. He needed them to ID Kopp in a police lineup. Five men filed into the room on the third floor of the police station. They were fillers, all of similar age, weight, height and skin tone to Kopp. A theatrical-makeup artist added a beard and mustache to each, to resemble his appearance in October 1998. A hairstylist added Kopp's coloring, although two of the fillers were close enough that they didn't need it. Kopp was brought in to a different room and, under the eye of Paul Cambria, also made to look as he had back then—now clean-shaven, he was given a fake beard.

In the viewing room, the witnesses were instructed to say nothing to each other. They sat in the first two rows in assigned seats and were handed identification sheets to write on. There would be two lineups. Each man would wear glasses for the first one, and take them off for the second. Cambria was told that he could place the defendant in any of the numbered spots he wished, but he declined the offer. The lineup entered the viewing room. None of the men were permitted to make any gestures or speak. Each man stepped forward separately, made four quarter turns, then returned to his spot. For the second lineup, each man walked a different route towards a designated spot five feet from the one-way glass through which the witnesses were watching.

Detective Daniel Rich from the Erie County DA's office spoke to the witnesses. "If you recognize anybody on the stage that was involved in the incident for which you are viewing the lineup, please record the number that he has on his chest. If you don't recognize anybody on the stage, leave it blank."

One of the witnesses was Dolah Barrett. She held a master's degree in sociology and special education. She had seen the plodding jogger back then. Never seen him before in the five years she walked that route. She looked at the men in the lineup and wrote down a number. Jim Kopp's number. A high school social studies teacher named Daniel Lenard was another. He identified Kopp as well. So did Mary Jo Brummer. Landscaper Kenneth Dewey stared at the faces. One of them looked familiar, but he was not sure. Hadn't the jogger seemed taller? He left his sheet blank.

Marusak obtained a court order for Kopp to provide blood and hair samples, as well as handwriting samples to see if it matched the writing found on the SKS rifle purchase application document retrieved from the pawnshop in Old Hickory, Tennessee. FBI forensic chemist Julie Kidd constructed DNA profiles from hair and skin traces found on the green baseball cap and binoculars left at the shooting scene, and on the toothbrush recovered from Jim Gannon's attic. She compared the DNA from the evidence to that in Kopp's sample. The profiles matched. The odds were at least 1 in 280 billion that the DNA recovered at the crime scene belonged to someone other than the accused.

Among other evidence Marusak gathered for presenting in court were eight exhibits in a file labeled "FBI photos from Canadian investigation." He also had two dozen rolls of film documenting anti-abortion protests in the Philippines, where Kopp had been, and multiple rolls of film from the FBI's search of a home on Buck

Hollow Road in Vermont, where he had lived for a time and where the FBI had seized a Smith & Wesson handgun, two empty bullet clips and two boxes of cartridges.

Marusak and Cambria shared information, as they were required to do. And evidence started leaking to the media. Cambria spoke to reporters and confirmed the rumor that the prosecution had testimony from an unidentified woman—who was in fact Jennifer Rock. "We have been told by the prosecution that one of my client's friends supposedly drove him to Mexico after the homicide," Cambria said. "That's all they've told us. We don't even have the name of the witness who supposedly said this."

Marusak felt confident. He imagined Kopp standing there in the police lineup, seeing the beards on the other guys, knowing the witnesses had to be picking him out. The DNA evidence, the handwriting, the knowledge that Jennifer Rock would testify against him: Kopp could see it coming, this avalanche of evidence. He's got to be feeling the pressure now, thought Marusak, sensing this wave building against him.

As the summer wore on, Marusak worked the case every night, every weekend. It had to be that way, it was the way he approached cases, they became part of him. He needed to be at the top of his game. He forced himself to eat often to keep his energy level high. There was so much evidence against Kopp, but there were also the conspiracy theories. The defense would surely milk them, sow doubt in the minds of jurors. He had to bring them up, counterpunch. Marusak had no wife, or kids. He had never married. You throw yourself into cases like he did, you don't meet many women. He did not necessarily embrace his fate on that score, but he accepted it. His usually rigorous exercise regimen went out the window. He added 16 pounds to his five-foot-eight frame, pushing him over the 140-pound mark, still trim by most standards, but not what he demanded of himself.

He met with Lynne Slepian several times. He was impressed by her will, her strength, as they went over evidence, photos, details. She always had a pot of coffee, food ready for him.

This widow and mother had a black hole in her life, and yet, on the outside, she wore a stolid mask as she tried to keep a sense of normality in her sons' lives. What Lynne Slepian's boys must have gone through—and continued to go through—having seen their father bleed to death on the kitchen floor. Joe Marusak's father had died young, of a heart attack, in 1989. Joe had not been a kid like the Slepian boys. But he too had watched his father die in front of him, on the kitchen floor.

* * *

Buffalo, N.Y.
July 2002

A trial date for Loretta Marra and Dennis Malvasi was set for August, as the couple continued to be held in a Buffalo prison. If they were convicted of obstructing justice they would each face up to ten years in prison and fines of $250,000. They had already spent 15 months in jail. Marra's lawyer, Bruce Barket, continued working to reach a plea bargain with the prosecution. He argued that she should be released because, he argued, she had helped persuade Kopp to give up his fight against extradition from France and return to the United States to stand trial. Federal prosecutor Kathleen Mehltretter argued that Marra should receive no such credit. But then the prosecutor had her own reasons for reaching a plea deal with Marra-Malvasi. She felt a full-blown trial for the couple would mean calling witnesses who might also be called during the Kopp federal trial—which might hurt the case against Kopp.

On August 13, federal judge Richard Arcara postponed Marra and Malvasi's trial to September, giving lawyers from both sides time to work out a deal. The lawyers arrived at one: Marra and Malvasi would plead guilty to obstruction and receive a reduced sentence of 27 to 33 months. In addition, the couple would not be required to testify against Kopp. On August 21, Arcara flatly rejected the agreement. He thought the punishment suggested in the deal was far too light. Several months earlier, he had presided over Marra and Malvasi's preliminary hearing. He had heard evidence of emails between Kopp and Marra, in which Kopp talked about whether he should "return to the field." Arcara felt the emails reflected "conversations about returning to the field of shooting abortion providers." He believed that Marra and Malvasi had committed serious crimes, including perhaps acting as accessories after the fact in the murder of Dr. Slepian. He declared that the couple's case would go to trial, and set a date of September 24.

In September, Marra filed a motion to dismiss the charges against her. It was rejected by the prosecution. On September 23, the day before the Marra-Malvasi trial was to begin, Kathleen Mehltretter decided she would in fact support Marra's request to dismiss the charges—including obstruction of justice, conspiring to obstruct justice, and aiding and abetting the flight of a fugitive— and instead bring a single lesser charge of conspiracy to harbor a fugitive. She asked for a new trial in the Eastern District of New York, in Brooklyn, at the conclusion of Kopp's trial. Marra and Malvasi agreed to the proposal.

Arcara was not amused. The veteran judge was angry at what he called the prosecution's "manipulative tactics" and "blatant judge shopping." But he added that the law presumes the prosecutor is the best judge of whether a pending case should be terminated. He had little choice but to do as Mehltretter asked and dismiss the obstruction charges against Loretta Marra and Dennis Malvasi. They would return to Brooklyn to stand trial.

* * *

Buffalo, N.Y.
Summer 2002

When it came time to select a judge to hear Jim Kopp's murder case, there were several in the Buffalo area expressing interest. But whoever presided over the trial was walking into a political minefield. The Western District administrative judge, Vincent E. Doyle Jr., had a decision to make. He turned to the judge who had made the least noise about the case.

He phoned Judge Michael L. D'Amico. "There are quite a few who have asked about it," Doyle said. "Which is one of the reasons I don't want to give it to them. Will you do it?"

D'Amico paused.

"Or let me put it this way," Doyle said. "Do you have any issues with doing it?"

D'Amico knew what that meant. Doyle wanted to know if D'Amico had any issue with taking on a case where abortion was front and center. Doyle had already heard from Kopp's lawyer, Paul Cambria. Cambria said he had no intention of making abortion the central issue, but was definitely worried that he might wind up before a judge who was inclined to crucify Kopp for political reasons. Doyle had asked both Cambria and prosecutor Joe Marusak to submit names of judges they thought would be best suited for the trial. D'Amico thought the exercise was asinine. But his name was on both lists.

D'Amico was 56 years old, from the Buffalo area, married with two kids. He had a casual courtroom manner but he did not suffer fools gladly. He had a modest office with dark wooden interior, deep maroon leather chairs, American flag behind his desk. Through the connecting door was Courtroom Number One, where the assassin of President William McKinley had been convicted in 1901. Historians said that trial "involved themes that would resonate far into the brand-new century: a dangerously unstable individual on the fringe of society … the obligation of the bar to defend the indefensible, and a media circus surrounding the public trial."

D'Amico had never taken a public stance on abortion. Judges seeking election in New York State cannot discuss, or campaign on, their position on abortion or other issues such as the death penalty. In New York State, cases involving the death penalty are assigned to specially trained judges whose names go into a rotation. But there is no such system in place when the trial involves other controversial issues such as abortion. D'Amico's silence made him Doyle's choice for the job.

"In the event I assign it to you," Doyle asked him, "will you take it?"

"Not if you can find someone else who wants it," D'Amico said. "If you can, go with them, it doesn't matter to me. But if you need me, I'll do it."

* * *

Buffalo, N.Y.
October 2002

In October, Jim Kopp shocked everyone involved in his case when he declared he wanted to replace Paul Cambria with Bruce Barket, Loretta Marra's pro-life lawyer. Judge D'Amico considered the request. Kopp was taking a huge risk. In court, the judge warned him of the potential problems, including a possible conflict of interest for Barket to represent both parties. Kopp replied that he was aware of the issues and was not concerned. Joe Marusak stood and added that Marra could benefit from Kopp making incriminating statements about himself, which could in theory be encouraged by Barket. It angered Kopp to hear Marusak go on like this.

"I'm not comfortable with Mr. Marusak discussing strategy," he said to the judge. On October 22, D'Amico allowed Kopp to switch lawyers. Speculation in the media was that Cambria wanted out anyway, that he did not want the trial to turn into a forum on abortion, as Kopp appeared to desire. And money was drying up for Kopp's defense. Cambria told court that his firm received money from someone who said there were many people donating to the cause of his defense.

"The funds that were paid to our firm have long been exhausted," Cambria said. "And in any event, the funds were not donated to Mr. Kopp personally. As a result there are no funds currently held by us for his benefit. Indeed, I arranged for Mr. Kopp's state defense expenses to be paid by the county of Erie due to his indigent state."

In Barket Kopp now had a lawyer ready to argue the case the way he wanted. "Whether people want to hear it or not, this case is all about abortion," Barket told reporters. "I'm absolutely pro-life and abortion is an abomination and a scourge on society. It's a sign of a twisted society that our government wants to put a man like Jim in prison while allowing more than a million babies each year to be killed by abortions."

Marusak countered that he would focus on the facts proving the murder of Dr. Barnett Slepian by James Kopp was planned and deliberate. The sniper's motivation was a moot point. Marusak had kept himself ready for whatever curves were thrown at him. But even he couldn't anticipate the twists to come.

* * *

Erie County Holding Center
Tuesday, November 12, 2002

Jim Kopp loved intrigue, misdirection, unpredictability; it informed his world view and the way he conducted himself, even among close friends. A movie buff, he loved classic whodunits like *The Maltese Falcon*. He loved *The Usual Suspects*, in which Kevin Spacey is the seemingly pathetic small-time crook who turns out to be a criminal mastermind hoodwinking police. In the final scene Spacey's character, a supposedly pathetic man known as "the cripple," is released from custody; seconds later, the star detective realizes he has let the real villain go, and Spacey has already turned the corner and disappeared. Fooled them all.

In prison Jim came to a decision. He was about to surprise them all again. Through Bruce Barket he arranged a meeting with two veteran reporters from the *Buffalo News* named Dan Herbeck and Lou Michel. He had never before spoken to journalists. He wanted to tell them something. Kopp, Barket and the reporters sat down in a room in the Erie County Holding Center. Jim Kopp calmly announced that, before he would take any questions, he wanted to make an official statement.

"To pick up a gun and aim it at another human being, and to fire, it's not a human thing to do," he said. "It's not nice. It's gory, it's bloody. It overcomes every human instinct. The only thing that would be worse, to me, would be to do nothing, and to allow abortions to continue."

Then he did the unthinkable. He confessed to shooting Dr. Barnett Slepian.

"I did it and I'm admitting it," he said. He described a version of events that became his new defense, and sparked a whole new controversy. He claimed he had been shooting to wound. "I never, ever intended for Dr. Slepian to die. The truth is not that I regret shooting him. I regret that he died. I aimed at his shoulder. The bullet took a crazy ricochet, and that's what killed him. One of my goals was to keep Dr. Slepian alive, and I failed at that goal."

He laid it out. Planned the shooting for more than a year, scouted locations, planned escape routes. Scouted six Buffalo-area abortion providers. Slepian's house was ideal because it backed onto a wooded area. He had been in position, ready to shoot, on two earlier occasions but was not able to lock down on the target.

He described that night. He was in the woods watching the house, waiting for Slepian to appear. He showed in the kitchen, put something in the microwave oven, left the room. He took aim at the spot where he anticipated the doctor's left shoulder would be when he came back. Although he was an "expert shot" the shooting had gone wrong. He fired only once because he saw Slepian fall. It saddened Kopp to learn he had died.

The reporters asked more questions. Barket encouraged Kopp to answer most of them, but on occasion cautioned him not to say anything. He wouldn't talk about whether anyone had assisted him in any way. Would not explain why he buried the rifle and other evidence in the woods. And why had he done it at all? Kopp answered that one.

"Why do you think I used force against Dr. Slepian when he was within ten hours of taking the lives of 25 babies? The question answers itself." The misconception people have about him, he said, was that he is a "peaceful man who would not harm anybody."

They asked him how he felt about the comparison between his actions and those of the sniper who was terrorizing the Washington, D.C., area. The question angered him.

"Any reasonable person could see a distinction between me and the D.C. sniper. Why was Dr. Slepian shot? The obvious answer is to save children. If you did the same thing to protect a baby that was one day old, it would never be considered a crime."

And what would Kopp do if he were acquitted and returned to the street?

"I would do something."

Herbeck's and Michel's story was splashed across the front page of the *Buffalo News*. The morning it ran, Joe Marusak was alone at home, listening to the early news on the radio. The lead story was that James Charles Kopp had confessed. Marusak couldn't believe what he was hearing. He had an inkling that Kopp wanted to make some kind of statement before the trial began. But he didn't know what Kopp might say, or who he would say it to. He was shocked that he'd give an interview to reporters at this stage, period—and confess to boot. It was bizarre. Never seen anything like it. The case had completely changed, but Joe Marusak stayed focused, his mind leaping ahead to the new approach he'd have to take. He had already prepared an argument in case the defense took the position that James Kopp had shot, but not meant to kill, Slepian.

The blue-gray eyes saw the screaming headline in the *Buffalo*

News: "KOPP CONFESSES." Well. To a Catholic, confession means an act of a penitent disclosing his sinfulness before a priest in the hope of absolution. He didn't appreciate the misuse of the word. Confession? Not quite!

His friends and supporters were shocked by the turn of events. Why did Jim Kopp admit to shooting Slepian, and now? He had repeatedly denied that he was guilty. Hadn't he? Perhaps not. When he was in jail in France he told friends he was "innocent" and that he "didn't do it." Did he mean innocent of shooting Slepian, or innocent of killing him? He frequently played with semantics, played with words and their meaning. What was it that he had said to a throng of journalists when he was led from a French court to a waiting police van? "The question you should be asking is, 'Who killed Dr. Slepian?' That's the only question you should be asking." Who killed Dr. Slepian? Had he been telegraphing all along that, despite his denials, he had in fact shot the doctor, but had not meant to kill? Or that God had taken Bart Slepian's life?

The big question was, "Why?" Why throw himself on his sword like that? Jim Kopp was many things, but unintelligent was not one of them. He knew he stood a shot at acquittal. So why confess? Kopp told the *Buffalo News* reporters it was because he was haunted by the living victims, Dr. Slepian's wife, her sons, and also that he felt guilt over misleading his supporters all this time. He wanted to finally tell the truth—about what he did, and why he did it. That's what he told the reporters, anyway. Ah, the media. *Romanita*.

CHAPTER 23—BIBLICAL FIGURES

Brooklyn, N.Y.
November 2002

A week after Jim Kopp's carefully choreographed confession to the *Buffalo News*, Loretta Marra was escorted out of the Erie County Holding Center in Buffalo, and Dennis Malvasi taken from a federal facility. They were both transported to a prison in Brooklyn for trial. A new bail hearing was scheduled for the following week. Marra had high hopes that she might finally be released. She listened as Bruce Barket made his appeal to Judge Carol Amon for her release. She had been in jail for 19 months. Loretta teared up when Barket mentioned her two young sons.

The case had been assigned to an Eastern District prosecutor, but Western District prosecutor Kathleen Mehltretter appeared in court as well, at the request of the judge, to answer questions, given her background in the case.

"In your opinion," Amon asked, "do Mr. Malvasi and Ms. Marra pose a flight risk?"

"I believe they do, Your Honor," replied Mehltretter.

Anger surged through Loretta Marra when she heard Mehltretter speak. Loretta had been denied bail previously, wasn't this latest denial expected? It was as though this time, she truly expected something different. Something had gone wrong. The judge agreed with Mehltretter. No bail. Marra snapped.

"You lying bitch," she said.

* * *

Buffalo, N.Y.
Monday, March 3, 2003

People from all walks of life filed into the courtroom for jury selection in the trial of James Charles Kopp. The accused stood and smiled at the people who would decide his fate. In the wake of Kopp's confession, District Attorney Frank Clark, Joe Marusak's boss, said the strategy had not changed. It just meant there were fewer facts in dispute. They no longer had to prove Kopp pulled the trigger. They just needed to prove that he intended to kill in order to get a murder conviction.

Kopp was an admitted sniper, and that fact drew an even more radical stripe of supporter to attend the trial—those who felt that shooting Bart Slepian was justified. On the sidewalk outside the courthouse, four pro-life demonstrators handed out flyers. The flyers called for the jury to acquit "baby defender James Kopp." One man spoke to reporters and said it was a case of justifiable homicide.

Nearly 200 potential jurors went through orientation and filled out questionnaires on the first day of jury selection. A 16-page questionnaire asked whether close friends or relatives had ever belonged to any group that advocated a certain viewpoint on abortion, and whether they had read the *Buffalo News* story in which Kopp admitted shooting Slepian. Judge Michael D'Amico cautioned them to be honest about their opinions. "The issue of abortion may be raised during the course of this trial ... Whatever your view may be, it does not disqualify you from serving on this jury," he told them.

Jim Kopp watched the jury selection proceed, the faces of strangers pass before him. What was it his dad used to say? "Juries don't care what you know, but what you can prove."

The next day, March 4, Kopp again turned the trial upside down. He decided to reject trial by jury, he wanted his fate decided by judge alone. And there would be no testimony, no cross-examinations. Instead it would be a "stipulated fact" trial. Counsel on both sides would still have an opportunity to present their arguments in court, but the essential facts of the case would not be at issue at trial. Instead the judge would be given a list of critical facts agreed upon on in advance by the defense and prosecution. Wasn't Kopp's best strategy calling all of the government's evidence into question, debating the details in court, chipping away at the prosecution? Kopp had caught everyone by surprise once more. My God, thought D'Amico. Does Kopp have any idea what he's doing? Joe Marusak was shocked as well. He had never seen such a maneuver at this stage of a murder trial. What was Kopp thinking? Jim Kopp, the lawyer's son. Courtroom strategist. He had, years before, expressed his view on stipulated-fact trials. In the "Rescuer's Handbook" he had written about them as an "underrated" strategy. "But don't use a stipulated trial," he had cautioned, "unless you are pretty sure they have you dead to rights."

Judges have a responsibility to ensure that any accused person receives an effective defense, particularly in a case as serious as murder. D'Amico knew that Kopp's best defense rested with a jury trial. So the judge told him, repeatedly, that he should go with a jury.

"Do not presume anything about me, Mr. Kopp," he warned. "If you want my personal opinion, go with a jury. But it's your call. You have an absolute right to waive a jury. I can't stop you." There were numerous reasons to stick with a jury trial, D'Amico said. There were no guarantees either way, but with a jury, if he could just convince one of the 12 jurors that he was shooting to wound, Kopp could get a hung jury. D'Amico even assigned an independent counsel to talk to Kopp about the decision. The appointed lawyer met with Kopp

Scott Gardner Photo

Kopp is led into Courtroom Number One.

for six hours. He returned to D'Amico and said the accused was fully aware of his rights, but this is the way he wants to proceed, he was not budging. Bruce Barket, for his part, told Court TV that he was "comfortable" with Jim's new strategy. "Reasonable people can differ," he said. "Jim gets to make the call. I'm along for the ride."

Why did Kopp waive a jury? Privately, D'Amico had his own theories. A stipulated-fact bench trial meant the case would be brief. The judge had already ruled that TV cameras would not be permitted in the courtroom. That meant Kopp would not have a soapbox to talk about abortion. So why bother with a drawn-out jury trial? Or maybe that wasn't it, maybe Kopp decided that a long trial would mean the prosecution could trot out witness after witness, friends of his—maybe Loretta. He didn't want them exposed that way. Or, thought the judge, it might be as simple as money saved by a short trial. Barket would incur expenses traveling back and forth to his home on Long Island. Whatever donations Kopp had received had dried up, especially since his confession. D'Amico had no choice but to grant Kopp's wish. In all, 400 jurors had filled out the 16-page questionnaire, but none would hear the case.

* * *

Erie County Hall
Buffalo, N.Y.
Monday, March 17, 2003

James Charles Kopp entered Courtroom Number One handcuffed, wearing tan pants and navy blazer with a bulletproof vest underneath. He wore square wire-rimmed glasses, his rust-brown hair brushed to one side. Visually he remained a paradox, a man accused of cold-blooded murder who looked meek and even frail. One woman in the gallery thought he looked handsome, maybe even strikingly so, with his full lips. Another thought he looked like a geek at best, downright ugly at worst, with a "gaping fish mouth." Seeing him in person for the first time left people with a vague sense of unease. There was just something about him.

He wasn't the kind of figure most people associated with the FBI's Ten Most Wanted List. He was no Timothy McVeigh, with the square Marine jaw, brush cut, menacing stare. Handcuffs? They looked ridiculous on Kopp. This, wrote one reporter, is Atomic Dog? This is the sniper who evaded the FBI, Interpol, and the RCMP for 28 months?

When they weren't on Kopp, all eyes in court were on Bart Slepian's widow, Lynne, who sat quietly, surrounded by family and friends, wearing a black suit, her blond hair pulled into a ponytail. Support from friends was so strong there seemed to be a force shield around her, one that kept even the most aggressive reporters from trying to talk to her. When Kopp entered the courtroom he avoided her stare. But he paused to nod and smile at pro-life radical Michael Bray in the crowd. Kopp seemed to have little chance of acquittal, given the admitted, damning facts, and no jury to massage. All the defense had to work with was Kopp's intent.

Judge D'Amico took his seat.

"Your Honor," began Joe Marusak, "the first matter this morning is People of the State of New York against James Charles Kopp, under indictment 98-2555-S01."

D'Amico asked Kopp questions to ensure, for the record, that he still wanted to proceed the way he had requested—a stipulated-fact trial, and by judge alone—and that Kopp consented to the facts that Marusak was about to present. "And before I approve this stipulation and your desire to proceed in this fashion, Mr. Kopp," said D'Amico, "let me just ask you a couple of basic questions. You are healthy today, physically and mentally, no problems, no drugs, alcohol or anything like that?"

"No, Your Honor."

"You have a degree, a college degree?"

"Yes, sir."

"In what?"

"Biology."

"That's a bachelor's degree?"

"Master's."

"So you don't have any difficulty understanding what we're talking about?"

"Right."

"And no one has made any representations to you on what the verdict will be?"

"I got to guess, Judge."

"You can guess."

"Sure. And other people have guessed in my presence."

"But whatever guess you have in mind no one has represented to you that that's what is in my mind?"

"That's correct."

Kopp answered in the affirmative to the questions. But there was a caveat. Kopp and Barket had made an addition to the agreed statement of facts the night before, which was agreed to by Marusak. Kopp was already casting an eye to his future trial on the federal charges.

The addition read: "Mr. Kopp specifically reserves the right to challenge in any way he chooses, including attacking the veracity of the witnesses, the same facts if any other prosecutor's office seeks to introduce this stipulation or its contents in any other criminal or civil proceeding."

Specifically, Kopp and Barket were casting doubts on Kopp's admission to the *Buffalo News* reporters: "The People do not stipulate to the truthfulness of the defendant's statements referred to in Exhibit No. 39. It is only stipulated that the defendant made the statements contained in the [*Buffalo News*] article."

"But," D'Amico said to Barket, "you are not disputing the recited testimony contained in this stipulation of facts, that it is truthful and accurate?"

"For this proceeding," said Barket.

"Of course."

"I mean—"

"You are not acknowledging that it is. You are simply not disputing?"

"Right, Your Honor," Barket said. "I just want to make one thing clear. It is not his intention in any way to make any kind of admission at this point in time that would be admissible at any future proceedings, specifically with respect to the matter in Federal Court. He reserves the right to, later on, challenge the accuracy, veracity, truthfulness of witnesses today we are agreeing for this proceeding the court would consider."

What were Barket and Kopp getting at? That the facts they were willing to agree to at this trial—facts that could send Jim Kopp up the river for the rest of his life—were not necessarily the truth? If they were not the truth, why was Kopp agreeing to them?

"Very well," said D'Amico. "I think it's as clear as can be made on the record here where we are and where we are going. So are we ready to go?"

"People are ready to proceed," said Marusak. "The People and defendant stipulate that the defendant shot Dr. Slepian with a rifle on October 23, 1998, at or near 187 Roxbury Park in the Town of Amherst, County of Erie, State of New York, and that Dr. Slepian died from the resulting gunshot injuries." Marusak launched into

a point-by-point recitation of the facts of the case. He named witnesses by name who "would" testify—meaning, if a conventional
trial had been held, they would testify under oath to the facts he
was describing.

Marusak wanted to illustrate that Kopp had not only pulled
the trigger, but that he wanted to kill Bart Slepian, get away with
it, and was indifferent to the harm his action brought to Slepian's
family. He used overhead projections to show where Bart, Lynne,
and their sons had been at the moment the bullet came through
the window. "Judge, as Mrs. Slepian stood at the nearby kitchen
island talking to her boys, she heard a 'popping noise.' She and her
two sons were within approximately ten feet of Dr. Slepian when
the bullet struck him."

Marusak described the police response to the shooting. Some of
the details contradicted Kopp's version of what happened. Marusak
said a witness would have been called who had been 14 years old at
the time of the murder. Her name was Jessica Mason. She had been
jogging with her mother just after 10 p.m. They heard police sirens,
got in their car and went to see what was happening. They parked
in a driveway on Aspenwood Drive and could see Bart Slepian's
house. Jessica noticed a man crouched behind bushes two houses
down from Slepian's. He wore a dark, hooded sweatshirt. She saw
him run from behind the bushes to a small, dark car idling in the
driveway of the house and get into the passenger side. The car then
sped away. It was the first suggestion that Kopp did not act alone,
that he had someone driving a getaway car.

"We'll never know who the driver was," said Marusak.

The court would have heard from Patricia Osborne, who
sold Kopp the rifle in Tennessee. The court would have heard
that Kopp practiced at a rifle range. Other witnesses would have
included FBI agents, Lynne Slepian, Jennifer Rock, Kopp's sister, Anne Rodgers. Amherst police would have reconstructed
the shooting scene, explained how he carefully marked trees
so he could locate the hiding place for his rifle in the dark.

The prosecutor took the court along on the short ride taken by the military-style, full-metal-jacketed, 7.42 x 39 millimeter bullet fired by the Russian-made SKS rifle.

"At the close range of this shooting, the bullet went straight through the body without any significant deflection. This is a military bullet designed to punch holes in material as well as in people."

Marusak outlined the autopsy findings. "The bullet actually severed and obliterated approximately two inches of Dr. Slepian's spinal cord, backbone. The cause of death was a gunshot wound to the back."

He touched upon one potentially weak piece of evidence. An FBI firearms expert had test fired a bullet from Kopp's gun, recorded the rifling marks in the barrel, and compared them to the bullet that killed Slepian. They did not match exactly. This, said Marusak, quoting the FBI expert, was because "it is not uncommon for the rifle's barrel to change with each shot so as to preclude the finding of a reliable connection." That point was controversial among ballistics experts. After hundreds of shots, a barrel's rifling marks might start to change. But from one shot to the next? Questionable. Barket and Kopp could, in theory, jump on that discrepancy, couldn't they?

"I will, Judge, at this time offer that if you consider it necessary as the trier of fact, to view the rifle and a bullet," said Marusak.

"I have seen them before, Mr. Marusak. That's not necessary," D'Amico answered.

Marusak consumed nearly the entire day with a meticulous, detailed presentation. He could not editorialize, color the statement with his own opinion. He would have a chance for that in his closing remarks. The methodical account of the facts was designed to prove to D'Amico that James Kopp had accomplished everything he had planned to do.

D'Amico was impressed. The judge looked at Bruce Barket. "It's your understanding that's the complete stipulation?"

"Yes, Judge," said Barket.

"Yours as well, Mr. Kopp?"

Bruce Barket, Kopp's lawyer—and Loretta Marra's as well

"Yes, Your Honor."

The judge looked at Barket.

"Anything from the defense?"

"No evidence, Judge, besides the stipulation."

That was it. No evidence. Barket could defend Kopp in his closing argument, but would offer no evidence, no testimony, to take the sting out of anything Marusak said. "OK," said D'Amico. "All right, Mr. Barket." He had to convince the judge that Kopp's goal was wounding Dr. Slepian. But if that was Barket's intended focus, his argument strayed. He explained why Kopp took up arms—he was defending the shooting itself. "Jim was not motivated by hate, politics, malice or vengeance. He was motivated out of the love he held and still holds for the children scheduled to be aborted the next day ... The court should render a verdict of not guilty because Jim Kopp was justified in his view in using force, even deadly force, to save the lives of the unborn children that were about to be aborted."

"Deadly force?" "Justified?" It did not sound like an argument that Kopp intended to wound. Barket continued, arguing that Kopp's good intentions were reflected in his decision to confess. He could well have continued denying he had shot Slepian, gone before a jury and quite possibly been acquitted. "I'm thinking of Jim in Biblical figures," Barket said, "who in times of crisis ran and denied, even the Lord, Peter. Jim did that when he was confronted with what he had done ... [but later] he admitted the truth."

He tried to make the case that there was nothing in Kopp's history to suggest he would ever want to kill anybody: "This is not a situation where there are four or five other shootings of abortion providers that resulted in their deaths and Jim can be tied to those shootings."

Four or five other shootings? Kopp was prime suspect in four other doctor shootings, three in Canada, had been charged by Hamilton police in the sniper attack on Dr. Hugh Short. Everyone in the courtroom knew about the other attacks. But these shootings were not part of the evidence, were not facts agreed to by both prosecution and defense in the stipulation. If the trial was by jury, the jurors would have been prevented from knowing about that background. They would know only what they heard in court. But a judge trial is different. And in this case, D'Amico was familiar with all of the context—knew what was presented to a grand jury to obtain the indictment against Kopp. He knew all about the trail of the sniper.

What was Barket doing? He sounded like he was making the connection to suggest the earlier wounding of physicians had been intentional, and the killing of Slepian a fluke: *Jim Kopp had meant to wound Slepian, just like all the others, but this time, failed.* But if that was his strategy, Barket did not expand on it, did not openly play that card. Perhaps he felt he didn't need to—D'Amico knew the details, perhaps he would take what happened in the Canadian attacks into account on his own. But if that was the hope of the defense, it was misplaced. D'Amico blocked the other shootings from his mind, or tried to, because that evidence was not in the stipulation, it was off the table.

Barket continued. The margin between life and death is so slight, he argued. Consider the SKS rifle. How accurate was it? Jim was a good shot, but sliding it in and out of the holster in the ground, perhaps it affected the firearm. Even a hairbreadth misalignment could shift the bullet off target by inches, cost Dr. Slepian his life.

It was Barket's most effective point yet. There had been questions about the rifle's accuracy after FBI agents test fired it and disassembled it. And then there was the path of the bullet. The autopsy report suggested the bullet had taken an odd turn inside Slepian's body. The round had entered the victim at "an extraordinarily odd angle," Barket argued. The bullet entered the back of his left shoulder; had it gone straight through and exited cleanly out the other side, perhaps the doctor would have lived. But instead it had ricocheted, striking a lung, his spinal cord and several ribs. This had been the conclusion of the autopsy. But Marusak had an expert in gunshot wounds undertake a study of the case. The expert said that high-powered metal-jacketed bullets do not bounce around when they strike a target, they bore through. So which report to believe? Barket argued that the autopsy report was the most reliable, not the study done "by somebody paid years later to rebut" it.

"The ricochet," he said, "in all likelihood is another factor that contributed to the unintended death of Dr. Slepian."

Barket made a point of disputing Marusak's claim that Kopp had been seen by an eyewitness getting into a getaway car—driven by someone else—near the Slepian home. That evidence had nothing to do with Kopp's guilt or innocence. Was Barket trying to undermine the notion that a friend of Jim's had helped him?

He started to conclude. D'Amico should find the courage to find Kopp not guilty, he said. This case was an historic opportunity. "Now, frankly, Judge, I don't envy you at this point in time. By waiving a jury Jim and I have lifted a heavy burden and placed it on your shoulders. The question will become whether or not the law will be fairly applied to James Charles Kopp, even if the majority of the people don't like the result dictated by law ... Did he intend to kill Dr. Slepian? Absolutely not."

Barket invoked the names of John Fisher, Thomas More, and Richard of Wales, "all three public figures, a bishop, a judge and a politician. They were confronted with the most divisive issue of their time, the supremacy clause of Henry VIII, who insisted on everyone signing. Richard took the oath and received Wales as his reward. More and Fisher refused and were beheaded ... As we stand here now we must admire those two men who withstood even the pain of death and the demands of the majority in order to do what their conscience dictated. Richard received Wales as his reward for his whole life. Fisher and More received their reward all through eternity."

D'Amico was not impressed. Barket was not arguing points of law, he reflected. Was he suggesting that Kopp should be acquitted in order for the judge to save his own soul? That the judge's conscience should scream for acquitting Kopp?

"If you convict Jim Kopp there is no doubt that you will be hailed as a hero publicly for a time. I would respectfully suggest to you, judge, if you acquit him, as the law dictates, you will be a hero in the eyes of the truth for eternity."

"Thank you, Mr. Barket," said D'Amico. "Mr. Marusak?"

CHAPTER 24–GRACE AND AMMUNITION

Joe Marusak was not accustomed to handling stipulated-fact trials, with no witnesses to cross-examine. This was his chance to perform. "There is a factual theme in this case and it is this," he began. "This defendant, James Charles Kopp, twisted the meaning of the sign of the cross so he could justify to himself his own deadly use of the sign of the crosshairs."

A peaceful man? Devout Catholic? Just a cover to stalk and kill. "If anything, the Catholic Church stands for peace. The two greatest commandments according to Jesus Christ: love God with all your heart, soul and mind, and love your neighbor as yourself. He loved Dr. Slepian. Another phrase from Christ: 'Judge ye not, lest ye be judged.' Kopp took the role of police, prosecutor, grand jury, judge, trial jury and executioner all in one. Took it on himself." As for intent, "the natural consequences of his act were, a very bloody, gory death, a bullet that bore a hole literally right through him, I mean sliced him in half practically where all of the major blood vessels, capillaries to the lungs, the aorta, the heart, I mean everything vital about us in our blood circulation system is built in our upper body. And that's where the defendant aimed. And that's where he fired. And that's how Dr. Slepian died … You don't need to be a forensic pathologist to understand that. You know where the heart is. Blood vessels. Lungs. This defendant surely did, a master's biology graduate."

The meek, mild-mannered facade was Kopp's way of evading detection. He manipulated and deceived and lied to the relatively young, like Jennifer Rock, and the old, like James Gannon. "Do you think they knew they were helping someone who murdered?"

Marusak quoted from the confession Kopp had made to the *Buffalo News* reporters. "The defendant said, 'I made every effort possible to make sure Dr. Slepian would not die. It's the easiest thing in the world to kill somebody with a rifle. It's very difficult to injure them if that's your goal. Any idiot can see that it wasn't meant to be fatal.' Any idiot? Have you ever heard such brazen, unadulterated arrogance? Is it just because he's got a 3.87 out of 4.0 and we are just not at the level of his intellectual prowess? Is that why the rest of us are idiots? Is there some sophistication going on in Jersey City that we just don't know about, us backward hicks from Buffalo?"

Marusak was on a roll. Kopp was a zealot. Religious terrorist. Self-serving. Arrogant. "Say grace and pass the ammunition." Kopp was frustrated that the law of the land permitted abortions. Dedicated his whole life to stopping it. Lived a celibate life. "And the frustration is chewing him up inside, he can't get rid of abortion. In our democratic republic, he can't get rid of it."

Marusak shifted the scene back into the woods behind Bart Slepian's house, pointing to a photo, Exhibit 12, of the darkened backyard the night of the shooting, and the shattered window with the blind half-closed. It's almost eerie looking out of that darkness. The man is at home, his back and his side are turned to the outside, and he thinks he's in the comfort and security of his own home, with his wife and children. And the high-powered bullet rips out of that darkness, puts the darkness into the lives of the Slepian family forever."

The window shade may have been pulled halfway, said Marusak, but finding Kopp not guilty would be like pulling the shade down the rest of the way, and failing to "see the defendant's implausible, self-serving admissions for what they are. I know you won't do that, Judge. I know you will look at all the evidence with the calmness, with the fairness, but with the critical analysis, that every trier of fact needs to do. And I submit to you, if you do that, you will find him guilty as charged, intentional murder in the second degree. Thank you."

"All right," said D'Amico. "I anticipate a decision by tomorrow afternoon, if you don't have a problem with that, say, between 2 p.m. and 3 p.m. Make plans accordingly. "Any questions, gentlemen?"

"No, Your Honor," said Marusak.

"No, Judge, thank you," said Barket.

"See you tomorrow."

That night, D'Amico mulled over the facts. It was not going to take him much time to make his decision. But there had been a defense presented and he had to take it seriously—that Kopp, like others in the pro-life movement, was not the murdering kind. Kopp's confession that he shot Slepian was big, of course, but not definitive in the case. There have been people who have confessed to crimes they didn't commit. D'Amico didn't weigh the confession in a vacuum. Indeed, he felt the prosecution didn't need it to convict Kopp. It's just one piece of evidence, and the pool of evidence was deep. Barket hadn't mounted a defense like Paul Cambria would have, had not tried to make hay with the delay in police finding the rifle. But D'Amico wouldn't have found that very persuasive anyway, he thought. What, the police planted the gun? What's more plausible, he reflected, that they simply couldn't find it during the winter initially, or that the police planted it? What makes sense? Are you kidding me? Does anyone really believe that the police decided seven months after the murder to bury a weapon that turns out to be the one that fired the shot?

The next afternoon, D'Amico took his seat just before 2:30 p.m. He looked at Kopp, who as usual wore a blue blazer and tan pants. The judge wasted little time. "I have concluded, Mr. Kopp, that you are guilty as charged."

Kopp turned to Bruce Barket and smiled. Was it a nervous smile? Sheepish smile? Sarcastic smile? Journalists in court tried to decide.

It was, like everything about him, hard to tell. Court was adjourned, Kopp led from the room by police. In the gallery, a group of friends gathered around Lynne Slepian. She said little. There were no tears, or cheers. Sentencing was set for May 9. At that time, Kopp would have his chance to make a detailed statement, explain himself.

After the verdict, journalists, searching for answers, called his stepmother, Lynn Kopp, in Texas, for a reaction. She, too, wondered why it had it taken Jim so long to confess to the crime. "He said he didn't mean to kill but that he meant to protect unborn children," Lynn said. "Isn't that a contradiction? If you did it, if you had such intense feelings, why hide from them after you've done the deed?" Kopp already held his stepmother in low regard. Did he read her comments? He read everything. The liberal media, the pro-death media, had gone to his stepmother for comment on his case. He burned. And smiled. He expected nothing less.

Among his friends in the pro-life movement, both in the mainstream and on the fringe, there were many opinions about him once he admitted shooting Slepian. There were those who supported what he had done, who said it didn't matter if he intended to kill the doctor or just wound him, who argued that the violence was entirely justified. Others did not openly approve of shooting abortion doctors, and could not believe that Jim would ever shoot anybody. They believed the FBI was framing him. But once he confessed, they had to concede that Jim had lied and, apparently, was capable of violence. Friends were saddened by what Kopp had done, and criticized his actions. Then there was Joan Andrews, one of his earliest inspirations in the movement, and others who remained torn over whether or not he was guilty. They had thought of him as such a low-key man, so gentle. Could he be covering for someone else? That kind of sacrifice would be so like him. But then, he had confessed. He was a truthful man. She had to believe what he said.

Susan Brindle never could figure it out. Either Jim confessed because he did it, or he was so messed up that he felt confessing was what God wanted him to do. Either way, she prayed for him every day. And, God bless him, if he did it, or conspired to help someone else pull the trigger, he should pay the price.

James Gannon was as shocked as everyone else by the whole thing. But if Jim said he did it, it must be so. Gannon followed the official church line. He opposed abortion, and capital punishment, and murder. If abortion is the same thing as killing, then how is killing one more person, a doctor, going to help society? Gannon was among those friends who visited Kopp regularly at the Buffalo Federal Detention Facility, where he was being held. They wrote letters, and when they spoke on the phone, Jim's voice sounded so clear, like he was right around the corner. "So you mind if I stop by for a couple of days?" Jim joked. Gannon laughed.

But there were times when it wasn't easy having a friend like Kopp. He used to tell people, "One day you'll get a letter from me and it will seem completely out of character, and you'll be like, 'Jim, what the hell is this?'" Gannon wouldn't hear from him for weeks without explanation. Sometimes Gannon's letters to Kopp at the prison were returned unopened. He could not understand why.

Jim's sister, Anne, spoke to the media. She could never believe her youngest brother would shoot anyone. Jim was a wonderful person. But obviously he had taken his cause to a level she could never imagine, or condone. In fact, she even wondered if Jim had left evidence at the murder scene on purpose. Perhaps he wanted God to decide his fate. It would be God's will if he was caught—or got away.

"Jim might have thought, 'God, I don't know if what I'm doing is entirely the right thing to do, so I'm going to leave it up to you,'" Anne said. "'And if you want them to catch me, I'm going to put my hat out here so that they'll have no problem catching me. I'm willing to face the consequences.' He left it open so that God could bring all the force down on him if necessary."

When the calls from reporters did not cease, Anne decided to issue a special kind of statement. She hung a sign in front of her home. It read, "All we've known about Jim is that he works after the model of Martin Luther King."

* * *

Sentencing Hearing
Erie County Hall
Buffalo, N.Y.
May 9, 2003

Jim Kopp's only hope was that he and Bruce Barket could convince Judge D'Amico to choose a lighter sentence, perhaps 15 years instead of the maximum 25 to life. D'Amico received letters from Kopp's brother and sister asking for leniency. They told the judge they all enjoyed a normal family life growing up, and Jim was once a regular guy. Somewhere along the line he had gone off track, but he had come from a good family, he is a human being. Please have mercy. It wasn't the first time they had written him. Earlier, they had urged D'Amico to ensure their brother got a fair hearing at trial.

In court, D'Amico first had to deal with a motion raised by Barket. He had proposed, just two days earlier, to delay sentencing until after Kopp's trial on the federal charge of using deadly force to interfere with the right to reproductive services. That way, Kopp would not run the risk of incriminating himself by anything he might say at the sentencing. D'Amico rejected the request. "With all due respect to the federal authorities," he said, "I can't operate on their timetable and I have no idea what their timetable is. We are going to proceed. Go ahead, Mr. Marusak."

Joe Marusak presented an even darker, more detailed profile of Kopp than he had in his closing remarks in March. He took the court back to Kopp's early days in California, his middle-class life, the Eagle Scout, honors student at UC Santa Cruz, how he followed his girlfriend to Texas, got his master's degree in biology. "But he never used that scientific talent," Marusak observed. "We don't know of any steady employment that he undertook in the field of science." He cataloged the arrests, more than a hundred of them, Kopp's dual identity as peaceful man of faith and sniper, his manipulation of friends. "He developed, basically, fraudulently and deceitfully a Jekyll-and-Hyde personality, consciously. He convinced everybody—every FBI interview[ee], every acquaintance of his, to a person, is effusive that this man wouldn't even hurt a fly. He lived a lie for 20 years."

Kopp belonged in the company of the radical Army of God—"the army of lunatics"—and Marusak likened him to Oklahoma City bomber Timothy McVeigh. "He is nothing more than a dangerous sociopath, plain and simple." He countered Barket's argument at trial that Kopp had confessed to shooting Bart Slepian simply out of a desire to tell the truth. No: Kopp merely saw the mounting evidence against him and tried to cut his losses. "That's why he confessed, not out of any sense of duty or honesty or a Christian ethic." Kopp believed himself to be "somehow morally, intellectually, religiously superior to all of us. In his own eyes, Judge, this defendant has cast himself—and I emphasize, in his own eyes—as God's avenging protector of the unborn. From the Spanish Inquisition to the Twin Towers disaster, religious zealots have rained terror on their victims. He's no different. He will never be open to rehabilitation. He's manipulated and lied his entire life."

Marusak quoted from conversations between Kopp and Loretta Marra that the FBI had recorded—"and we know how close Ms. Marra and the defendant are," he added. Marra had told Kopp about the love of his supporters back in the United States. "Let them love me with cash," Kopp had said. "Let them love me with cash," Marusak repeated. "That's part of the Catholic religion, isn't it? Part of Christianity? Love your neighbor. Give me money. Let them love me with cash."

Jim Kopp sat in his chair, his blood boiling. Marusak, a Catholic, was attacking him personally, but worse than that was attacking his faith, his Catholicism. That, to Kopp, was beyond the pale. Marusak next appealed for a stiff sentence on behalf of Bart Slepian's widow, who was seated in the gallery. He spoke of Lynne's courage, the impact the murder had on her sons. And he spoke of Bart, read testimonials about his work ethic as a physician and as a father.

He quoted from a letter by Dr. Carole Lieberman, who had gone to school with Bart in Belgium. "His faith and his religion did not counsel him against abortion. And although, personally, I don't think he would have wished that in his own family, he recognized and respected the law that allowed a woman to make that choice … And I understand very well the moral opposition to abortion. But this is not about abortion. This is about murder. A man who would murder such a man as Bart deserves the harshest sentence allowable by law."

Marusak returned once more to Lynne. Mother's Day, he said, was in two days. "By God, this woman, Mrs. Slepian, if there ever was a good mother, she's it." He read a letter to the judge from Lynne:

I'm speaking on behalf of our four children: Andrew, age 20; Brian, age 18; Michael, age 15; Philip, age 12. Overnight they went from average everyday boys to the objects of every media source in the country. Philip was only seven when his dad died. I think he's probably been affected the most, because there is just so much that he can't remember about his dad. My sons are angry, and so am I. But there is no way to bring my husband and their father back to us. He was such a proud man, and a very private person. All this attention would have made him so uncomfortable. The only thing that would make things a bit better would be to ensure that Mr. Kopp never sees the light of day again. He is an evil man and does not deserve to have his life back again.

Marusak couldn't resist taking one more swipe at Kopp's interpretation of Catholicism: "This defendant alleges he is motivated by his Christian beliefs. I'm reminded—I don't know if you have seen

Godfather II, where Al Pacino plays the role of the Godfather. And he's at his son's baptism and he goes through the Catholic prayer where he's announcing how he rejects Satan and evil. And while he's doing all of that, his henchmen are killing the five other Mafia family guys. So out of his mouth is this profession of Catholic belief, when his actions are that of nothing more than an assassin. If that's being a hero, well then, so be it."

Now it was Bruce Barket's turn. He did not invoke the intent-to-wound argument. He had bigger fish to fry: morality, religion, the rule of law, and how history shall judge everyone in the long run. But first he defended Kopp's character, tried to take some of the sting out of Marusak's scathing attack. "You listened to Mr. Marusak paint Jim as a cowardly assassin. I have gotten to know Mr. Kopp over the last year or so and that's simply not true. He is not a sociopath. He is calm. He is rational. He is sane. I know that Jim Kopp is intelligent. He is caring, generous. He is slow to anger, quick to forgive, very modest, deeply spiritual. He's a prayerful man with a humble heart. He is also an honest man, scrupulously honest. Jim Kopp is a good man … If Jim wanted to continue to fool people, he had an opportunity to do that. He had the means to do that. And there is a substantial chance that we wouldn't be here today at his sentence. He might very well have been acquitted."

Barket turned to abortion. "Jim has a set of beliefs that are not inconsistent with a large majority of people in this country. He believes that abortion is intrinsically evil. The answer why Jim Kopp is here, I think, comes from a society that encourages mothers to bring their unborn children to doctors not for care, but to be slaughtered in horrific and unimaginable ways."

Barket next turned to the argument that shooting Slepian was justified. The simple syllogism cannot be refuted, he said: all innocent life is worthy of protection. Unborn children are innocent life. Therefore unborn children are worthy of protection. And the Catholic Church supports force, too, even deadly force, to protect others, contrary to what Marusak had said. Barket attacked the sanctity of the rule of law. "Our Supreme Court, as honorable as it is, also once indicated that slavery was a choice. They said African-Americans are nonpersons. They have said that unborn children were not children and it's OK to kill them."

The law had been wrong on slavery, segregation and it was wrong once more, on abortion. "The fact the Supreme Court has declared abortion to be legal does not answer its morality. Abortion is immoral. It's an intrinsic evil. Jim Kopp is a hero. And today I think he will become a martyr." Barket said he was reminded of the famous abolitionist John Brown. Brown had long advocated violence to resolve the great social issue of his day and had once led a band of men in a deadly attack on neighbors who advocated slavery. He had later tried to lead a slave rebellion, and had been hanged for that. "One hundred and forty years later, we see John Brown as a hero. There is a shrine built to him for freeing slaves. The judge in his trial is a historical footnote."

D'Amico was once again underwhelmed by the presentation. He was not hearing Barket make an argument. He was making a speech, a statement. He's telling me how I can be a hero, the judge thought. Barket's approach was not sitting well with him, not at all. What are you talking about, Mr. Barket—I'm supposed to have courage to impose a minimum sentence, thereby sending a message about *my* moral convictions? Don't presume what my moral convictions are. Or am I supposed to base my ruling on your convictions?

Barket concluded by saying that Kopp deserved the minimum sentence, "to reflect the complexity of the issues involved" and to vindicate the other victims in this case, "the unborn who are killed by abortions every day." Finally, he took a swipe at the FBI. At the same time as "hundreds of agents, thousands of work hours and millions of dollars were spent in hunting down, capturing and prosecuting James Kopp, and making America safe for abortionists," real terrorists, in al-Qaeda, were plotting the 9/11 attacks. "To law enforcement, I would say, stop using your resources to protect abortionists. It is akin to protecting the slave owners. History will not judge you kindly. The fact abortion is legal is not the final word on whether or not what Jim did is moral or immoral. Thank you."

"Thank you, Mr. Barket," said D'Amico. "Mr. Kopp, anything you would like to say in your own behalf?"

CHAPTER 25—SUPERNATURALLY WICKED

Marshals took the cuffs from his wrists. He stood up from behind the table he shared with Barket, shuffled to the lectern at the front of the courtroom, five armed sheriffs now gathered in a ring of security around a man who looked as if he was not strong enough to rip a sheet of paper. This was his chance, four and a half years after his run from the law had begun, his chance to account for himself, to unravel the mystery of how young Jim Kopp from Marin County became the sniper James Charles Kopp. He looked thinner and paler than in March. He wore the usual blue blazer that hung loosely from his frame. He organized his stack of papers.

"Yes. Good morning, Judge. On October 23, Judge, in 1998, late at night I shot Dr. Slepian. Let me explain a little bit about why and how." At first his voice registered barely above a whisper. Judge D'Amico asked him to move closer to the microphone at the lectern. "All right. This is not easy for me to talk about, Judge. I want to make it clear that this information I'm about to give is not why I shot Dr. Slepian. However, it does explain how I went from someone who had, let's say, an intellectual understanding of an abortion to someone who had a much stronger feeling about what abortion really represents in the United States.

"In large measure it began really in 1980, at Stanford Hospital, California. I saw a baby killed from abortion that had attained eight months' gestation. If I had not seen this, I doubt I would ever have ended up here. Murder is not something to be voted on, any more than rape or robbery. Anyone who wants to understand what abortion is really about must see the body of a child first before they speak. Dr. Slepian was perfectly qualified to speak about abortion. He saw many bodies.

"In 1987 I witnessed the first forced abortion I ever saw. I was told that because of an injunction I could not try to stop it. I wish I had anyway. A woman with polio in both legs was dragged, sobbing and pulling back, to the door of the mill—we use the word mill, Your Honor, because a clinic is where you walk in the door, sit and you walk out healthy. That cannot be used to describe an abortion mill, where the woman is basically messed up for life and the baby is dead. A woman with polio in both legs was dragged, sobbing and pulling back, to the door of the mill, where two nurses reached out, grabbed and pulled her in. She was walking with calipers and braces on her. Any sidewalk counselor in America can tell you of similar incidents. I can talk all day about this."

He saw it all, with his own eyes. And other forced abortions, too. The women emerging from the mill, weeping, sobbing, scarred in body and mind, destined for endless drug and psychotherapy treatments, perhaps committing suicide. They are brainwashed, browbeaten and bullied into abortions, usually by men. There was more. Kopp talked about his speech to the young prostitutes at Juvenile Hall in San Francisco. How he had been "the first westerner" to hear eyewitness accounts of forced abortions in China. He touched on what he saw as key historical moments in the abortion war. Forced sterilization. Hitler. "This is covered really well in a book called *QB VII* by Leon Uris. I can't tell you how much I recommend this book. It connects sterilization, abortion, and ultimately the Final Solution."

Just minutes into his statement he was already all over the map. Those in the courtroom hearing him speak for the first time were amazed. Journalists who were barred from using tape recorders, as is the usual rule, scrambled to write it all down but could not keep up. But this was Jim Kopp speaking the way he always spoke when engaged in heavy conversation. He was back at the hostel in Dinan spelling out his world view for a friend, his mind processing his scattered thoughts, connecting the dots.

"Here's a quote: 'In view of the large families of the native population'—now this phrase, native population, means Polish, Gypsies or Romanians and Jewish people, bear in mind—'it could only suit us if girls and women in that native population had as many abortions as possible. We could not possibly have any interest in increasing the non-German population.' That's a quote from Adolf Hitler."

A central belief of pro-life activists is that, if only people are exposed to the reality of abortion, the effect on patients, the trauma of the unborn baby, and can learn the historical context, they—not the hardcore pro-abort ideologues, of course, but those in the middle or with little commitment—will see the light. Their eyes will be opened to the truth. And so Jim Kopp was once again the teacher. But what good could this possibly do with D'Amico and the sentencing? Kopp quoted Margaret Sanger, the founder of Planned Parenthood, a favorite target for pro-lifers.

"Here's another quote, from 1939: 'The most successful educational approach to the Negro is through religious appeal. We do not want word to go out that we want to exterminate the Negro population.' We find that quote in a book called *Margaret Sanger, Father of Modern Society*. Obviously, Judge, she agreed perfectly with Hitler about the notion of the master race. What she contributed, that Hitler didn't, was technique."

He tried to draw a connection between Hitler, Sanger and Bart Slepian. He looked down at notes he had made from an article written by Amanda Robb, Slepian's niece, who had visited him in the jail in France. "Now, the next quote, Your Honor, I will make very clear, I didn't find out until 2002. It comes from the niece of Dr. Slepian."

But then Kopp was off on another tangent. "There was a film called *A Matter of Choice*, in the 1980s. Very influential. There was another film made at the same time showing a forced abortion where a woman at the last minute wants to jump off the table. Very common thing, and the nurse does a verbal slapping. You don't actually give someone anesthetic like Novocaine or whatever, but you use your voice to get them to sit down and shut up and stop. Women and men who have come out of the profession of killing children, they can corroborate all of this.

"Anyway. In this movie *A Matter of Choice*, they interviewed this Dr. Allred in Los Angeles. He made an extremely similar comment to the one I'm about to tell you. In any event, Dr. Slepian's conversation actually took place in 1997. Dr. Slepian, when asked why he did abortions, answered that it was 'part and parcel of keeping the minority quotient manageable.'"

Kopp looked at D'Amico.

"Judge, wouldn't it be nice to say that was a casual remark? That it slipped out and we wouldn't hold Dr. Slepian to that? I say no, Judge, it's perfectly 100 percent consistent with the racism and genocide that began with Margaret Sanger, took a little detour through Germany and wound up back again in Western New York in 1997. Keeping the minority quotient manageable. Dr. Slepian also said, 'Abortion is killing potential life. It is not pretty. It is not easy.' This is a direct quote from him. The inner seed of that quote sounds like the Pope."

Kopp claimed to be quoting Bart Slepian from an article written by his niece, Amanda Robb, for *George* magazine. Amanda had written about how James Kopp changed her family's life when he shot and killed her uncle. She wrote about the night she received the phone call telling her that Uncle Bart had been shot to death, and later about meeting Kopp in jail. The piece for *George*, and the other articles she had written, offered private glimpses of the Slepian family. They were well written but also uncompromising in their bluntness and included some characteristically pithy quotes from her late uncle. Not everyone had appreciated her airing of the family laundry. And now, in court, Bart Slepian's assailant was quoting the dead man's niece to try to justify the shooting.

Rick Schwarz, Bart's longtime friend from med school in Mexico, later heard about the quote mentioned by Kopp—"keeping the minority quotient manageable." It didn't surprise Rick that Bart might have said such a thing. But he would have been joking; it would have been meant as a private, dark-humored quip, certainly not meant for publication or to represent his position on abortion. That was his sense of humor, and others shared it. In Mexico, there were a couple of guys who had joked that what overpopulated Mexico really needed was a good abortionist. Bart wasn't one of them, but it was something he might have joked about.

But in court, in front of the judge, reporters and the doctor's widow, Kopp had just taken Bart's quip and used it to try to paint his victim as a racist. The problem was that Kopp had not turned to Amanda's original article for his quote. He had lifted it from accounts of the article he had read on the Internet. Those online accounts got one important word wrong. Bart had not said "minority quotient." In describing his rationale for performing abortions, he told Amanda that it was "Part and parcel of keeping the *misery* quotient manageable."

Kopp did not let up. "Of course Dr. Slepian had to kill lots of black babies down at the abortion mill, red babies, Mexican babies. Black women today get twice as many abortions as non-black women per capita. There are twice as many abortion mills located in the inner city as elsewhere, and this is all part of Margaret Sanger's agenda." Kopp had still not moved to the issue of his defense, and the only argument that could possibly persuade D'Amico to show leniency in sentencing: that Kopp had intended to wound Slepian, not kill him. Instead, Kopp appeared to be arguing that Slepian deserved to die. The critical issue, to Kopp's way of thinking, remained whether he was justified. The key was: the fetus is human, and therefore shooting someone to protect it from termination is justified.

He quoted the Pope. Abortion is killing a living creature. A law that permits abortion is an immoral one and must not be obeyed. These babies are being torn apart. "What about the use of force to try and stop abortion? What does the Church say about that? St. Ambrose said, 'He who does not repel an injury to his fellow, if he is able to do so, is as much at fault as he who is able to, who commits the injury." That citation is in *New Catholic Encyclopedia*, page 593."

Remorse? Would Kopp show any to help his case? Doctor killer Michael Griffin had recanted his actions, apologized, expressed regret. It saved him from the death penalty. "It's customary at sentencing to talk about remorse," Kopp said. "I have already spoken in the newspaper about my feelings about the suffering that Dr. Slepian endured and his family endured. I stand behind these words today and forever. These feelings, Judge, have to be held in balance, though, for the children that were killed by Dr. Slepian. I estimated 25,000. That's my estimate based on how many hours he worked down at the mill and so forth. It's actually a conservative estimate based on a 13-year career of child killing. But more importantly, I have to hold these feelings in balance with the concern I have for the children that were about to be killed by Dr. Slepian on October 24, 1998. Just to give you an impression, Judge: 25,000 is a number. Stalin said one death is a tragedy and a million is a statistic. You can fill this courtroom top to bottom, put the caskets, one casket for each child involved, fill this courtroom and one half of another."

Did he really believe his numbers? By his "estimate" Slepian would have had to perform more than five abortions every day, 365 days a year, over his entire career.

"Even if I failed at my goal to preserve Dr. Slepian's life, nonetheless, I would be the only one I know of in this case who even had a plan whereby at the end of the day, both Dr. Slepian and his victim will still be alive. Who will advocate for the children? Why should the safety of Dr. Slepian be put above the safety of weak, vulnerable children, when Dr. Slepian had every opportunity to stop killing, and the children had no opportunity to run away from him?"

Slepian, Kopp said, had been stubborn. "The first abortionist doctor was shot in 1992. Possibly many hundreds of doctors quietly left the field after that. Any doctor who remained in the field was and is exposing himself to actual danger. If it were not so, why would the FBI have warned Dr. Slepian the very day he died?"

He talked about the fatal night. Family members in the kitchen? Kopp said he never saw them and wouldn't have pulled the trigger if he had known they were there. Shoot to kill? If he had meant to kill, "why not shoot him in the head? If my intention was to kill the guy flat out, why not shoot him in the head? I had a better shot, considering how restricted the angle was, to shoot him in the head than shoot him anywhere else."

Finally, he explained how he did it. He buried a tube in the woods behind Slepian's home, then inserted the rifle, which was wrapped in vinyl. He covered the opening of the tube with dirt, leaves, branches. He returned several times—early morning, late at night—to retrieve the weapon from the holster and wait for the right moment to shoot. "After I shot poor Dr. Slepian I put the gun in the hole to keep it from being found. This took no time because the opening of the hole was inclined in such a way you didn't have to dig and, you know, dig this hole."

He was reiterating what the police and prosecution had said. But he now denied painting markings on trees, even though he had agreed in the stipulated facts at trial that he had used them to help locate the rifle's hiding spot. "I simply have no clue how they got there and who put them there. I never saw them. I'm utterly clueless about all this. I located the gun-hole easily myself because it was under a very characteristic bush. I never had any problems finding the weapon that way."

Like Barket, he also now disputed the notion of a getaway car, even though that, too, was in the stipulated facts. No, Kopp said, he went back through the woods, on foot, between a cul-de-sac and a tennis court, retrieved a hidden bicycle. "A few doors down I passed a dozen or so young people engaging in some sort of spontaneous party or meeting in the middle of the street."

He presented his new account in detail that suggested either that it was true, or simply that he knew that small touches might make it more believable. *Romanita*: was he protecting whoever had been driving the car that night? Or whoever was planning to retrieve the rifle using the paint spots on the trees? Once he had made it back to his car, he said he drove to a nearby motel, booked into a room that was "the last one on the left." He'd rather not say the name of the place. Might get the owners there in trouble. The man who had rented it to him was the son-in-law of the East Indian couple who owned the motel. He had been in the military. The next day, when Kopp was on the road near Cleveland, he saw on the news that Slepian was dead. It was, he said, "the saddest day of my life."

He apologized to pro-lifers for initially denying he had pulled the trigger. "But I do not apologize to the FBI or law enforcement or the district attorney. They are intent on promoting and protecting the murder of children. They are my natural enemies. They can provide electricity to run suction pumps, to flush their children down after they run them through garbage disposals. They need help. I don't owe them any more straightforward an answer than the Gestapo a straight answer when they came up with the Jewish people in Holland."

He said that he had been telling the truth after his capture. He had not murdered Slepian, because he had no intention of killing him. "I was innocent of murder then. I am innocent of murder now." The Vatican smuggling Jews to safety. The mother of Moses hid her son. "Where would we be, Judge, if the mother of Moses had not hid him and deceived the Pharaoh and disobeyed him?" Mary and Joseph stealing away with Jesus in the middle of the night. "According to the prosecution, St. Joseph was carrying out a sinful deception by cover of night."

He took the court into the abyss that he felt so acutely: "I hate to mention this, Judge, an infernal supernaturality such as the bizarre case in Burlington, Vermont." Aborted late-term babies and their blood being drained for use in a Black Mass, "a satanic ritual in which the blood of children is offered to Satan and then drunk by participants in a chalice stolen from the Catholic Church. That ritual also explained the disappearance of some of the so-called milk carton kids …There is a supernaturally wicked drive behind abortion which brings back the medieval heresy of Albigensianism ... I hope the professional baby-killing industry will not be too offended when I say to them they are merely pawns in a much bigger choice."

His rambling address neared its conclusion. He had taken the court on a tour through his life and thinking, sliding from some relatively sober reflection to the fires of hell. Was it an act? It was surely not simply the usual *Romanita*. It was as though his psychological skin was peeling away. Had jail done that to him? Jim Kopp, Atomic Dog, had lived a life that was unusual in its scope, on a broad stage, taking him around the world, always on the move, pursuing a mission that knew no boundaries. But his life now was in a cage, his world confined to a small concrete room. And that was not going to change.

As Kopp wound down his comments, Judge D'Amico sat slumped in his chair, his cheek resting on his hand. He gets up and talks for, what, an hour and a half, almost two, and spends the entire time not on whether he intended to kill, but on why these doctors must be stopped? You've got your cause, fine, knock yourself out, thought D'Amico. But don't go around killing people, and don't tell me that it's OK.

"What would I do if I were let out in the street?" Kopp said. "This depends on the country, Your Honor. Will we, in America, still be killing children? If so, then I will stay duty-bound to do something about it ... I have always said, Judge, 'Show me—I'm from Missouri.' Show me a better way, but it better include a real chance for babies, not just rhetoric."

He said he had heard that several of the women who had planned to have abortions the morning after Slepian was killed had decided to keep their children. "Four or five children who are alive today because Dr. Slepian was unable to kill on Saturday, October 24, are now almost four years old. Two or three of them are black. They are all beautiful, happy, human lives. They are walking the streets of Buffalo, New York, and their mothers love them. Fifty years from now they will be taking care of their mothers in their old age. Is this such a terrible thing? Which of these children should be dead today? I say none of them."

His future? "My days of trying to save children are obviously over." But the number of doctors performing abortions has dropped, he said, from 2,300 in 1990 to 800 in 2002. "Every one that has quietly retired from mass murder is completely safe from me or anyone like me. Any mass murderer who is left still doing abortions, if you are concerned for your safety, then quit. Do you want to be the last abortionist doing abortions in America?"

Would others follow in his footsteps? "I am not aware of any conspiracy to use force to save children. My younger brothers and sisters in the movement may discover that independent simultaneous operation is the best way to save children ... They may soon come to realize if they don't do it, it doesn't get done."

Defiance and the rule of law? "The Supreme Court, I will not kneel and worship before them. I defy them. Anyone who provides protection to mass murderers, whether under the color of law or not, is participating in murder. Let me briefly suggest another way of looking at this. If the Supreme Court ruled tomorrow that black people show up at the local train station with an O-ring around their neck—'Bring a lunch, you are going for a long train ride, going back to Mississippi, sorry, the Supreme Court changes its mind again'— would you enforce the law? Would you throw Harriet Tubman in jail for trying to smuggle these slaves? I suppose if the court ruled tomorrow that Jewish people must report to the closest train station wearing the Star of David—'Bring a lunch, wear a coat, you are going for a ride'—would you enforce that law, too? You would not. You are morally obligated to refuse to punish me.

"I know that sounds laughable in the context of the review of this case. It isn't laughable to me, Judge. You are morally obliged to refuse to punish me just as surely as you are required to refrain from participating in sending Jewish people, or those who protect them, to their death. In any event, Judge, there are worse things than life in general. Jail—jail is not so bad, nowhere near as bad as being out of custody and constantly wondering what else could be done for the babies ... I do not see myself how God can bless a country which gives safe haven to child murderers, or to the practice of child murder. But even now He stands ready to forgive, if we will turn away from child murder. It's never too late to seek forgiveness, but first we must turn away from child murder. He will enable us to do that, if we ask Him to. Thank you, Your Honor."

CHAPTER 26—A COMPLEX MARTYRDOM

"Well," said the judge. "I guess we have heard a great deal of information this morning." Michael D'Amico did not typically say much at sentencing. Speech-making was not his style. But this time was different. James Kopp would not have the last word, not in his court. "You are not going to hear a speech or a sermon," said D'Amico. "Nevertheless, I feel compelled to say a few things."

First, he recognized the Slepians. "The letters I have received with regard to this sentencing indicate to me the depth of the loss that has been suffered and the fact that there are many in this community who share your grief." Second, he countered the shots taken by the defense at the FBI and police. "Mr. Barket has asked me to admonish them. I think the reverse is true."

Third, the judge addressed Kopp's intent. "It's clear the action was premeditated, there's no doubt about that. It is inconceivable to me that you did not expect your actions would result in the death of Dr. Slepian. I think that if Mr. Marusak or someone else could respond to what you said they would have a lot to say. Frankly, I don't want to hear it. But I think that there is one comment that you made that almost demands a response and you somehow equated the action of Dr. Slepian with some racial issue. Bald accusations are easy to make. Unfortunately, he's not here to respond to them and that's your responsibility. I guess in spite of all your education and all your intelligence, Mr. Kopp, there is one thing you haven't learned and that's that the pursuit of one's goal, your objective, that no matter how moral or just it may appear, does not permit the infliction of violence on your adversary. What may appear righteous to you may appear immoral to someone else. And obviously the reverse is true. The bottom line, I suspect, is that no civilized society can tolerate or excuse excesses that are tantamount to anarchy or to terrorism."

He issued a final rejoinder to Barket, who had said in his remarks earlier in the day that John Brown had been hung for fighting slavery but today was considered a hero, while the judge who sentenced him was nothing more than an historical footnote. "With regard to the comparison to the John Brown case, Mr. Barket, I will take my chances."

He looked at Kopp. "It is the judgment of this court, Mr. Kopp, that you be sentenced to an indeterminate sentence having a maximum of life imprisonment. The court hereby imposes a minimum period of 25 years." Kopp turned to Barket and smiled. D'Amico rose, the crowded courtroom followed suit. And James Charles Kopp was taken away.

"Shame on America! Shame on America!"

The voice of protest outside court belonged to a small black woman named Hettie Pasco. She had picketed for years at the clinic where Slepian had worked. "How about legalizing mass murder in America?" she shouted. "Abortion is a weapon of mass destruction!"

Joe Marusak left Courtroom Number One and strode down the corridor and out of the old building. He did about a half-dozen homicide trials a year. Nothing shocked him anymore, but this one had been the most bizarre trial he had ever worked. He had spent a lot of time analyzing Kopp's actions and building what in essence was a behavioral profile of the sniper to present in court. But in hindsight, Marusak still didn't quite know what to make of the man. He had been handed evidence to work with to prove that Kopp had intended to kill. But that was it. It wasn't his job to understand Kopp. He just needed to prove a fact, and he had done so.

Later, Judge Michael D'Amico relaxed in his office, the adjoining courtroom empty and quiet. He reflected on the case. Kopp was clearly a bright guy, educated. Who knows what forces someone like that into activism—and what throws the switch inside that turns him into Atomic Dog or whatever the hell his name was, he mused. There was something at some point that caused Kopp to surrender his life, essentially, to this cause, and ultimately it led to a martyrdom complex. D'Amico shook his head. Would that complex persist in Kopp's thinking for the rest of his life? He imagined the convicted man in jail. One day, down the road, it hits him: *I'm the one sitting in prison and everyone else is out there, free—my lawyers, allies in America and abroad. They're all back to normal, and I'm sitting here in prison.* And maybe, thought D'Amico, at that point he says, *Holy cow—what the hell have I done?* Maybe then he realizes he wasn't so smart.

On the other hand, concluded D'Amico, Kopp might carry his belief in the cause to his grave.

* * *

Buffalo Federal Detention Facility
Batavia, N.Y.
Spring 2003

Pitcher stands tall. Count is full. Checks the sign. Into his motion now, leg kick, the follow through, ball popping in the catcher's mitt. Strike! Jim Kopp sets again. Winds up. Zips his hand through the air, the imaginary ball whizzing over the imaginary plate.

Jim wore his red prisoner's jumpsuit, shoes with no laces, his face peppered with a sparse rust-colored beard, square metal-rimmed bifocal glasses. He worked on his pitching motion in a common room at the federal prison in Batavia, a town of 16,000. Pitching? Kopp's chronically bad back continued to bother him. He had discovered that going through the baseball pitcher's motions loosened him up. He did it for long periods while other inmates in the common room looked on.

Set. Pitch. Set.

Back in his cell, he stretched some more. And prayed. And worked on his book, the novel he was writing. Last night he crossed a barrier in plot development. It pleased him. He was also working on an essay about his father. He sang to himself. Joni Mitchell, of course. Time was something Kopp had plenty of. The next step in his legal journey was the federal trial, but that was still a long way off. Would they throw away the key on him? Or perhaps put the death penalty back on the table, in violation of the extradition agreement with France? As far as he was concerned, the executioner's needle would always be on the table for him, agreement or not. Frequently he had more time to write than paper to write on. On occasion he ran out, took to scribbling his letters in pencil on toilet paper. It's OK, he advised a correspondent. Just place the paper on a light table to make out the writing.

Some days were better than others. The jail was primarily used for immigration matters. He had been originally held there because his case involved extradition. He felt like a bug under a microscope in prison. The FBI was listening to his phone calls. Reading his mail. He wrote Latin acronyms on the envelopes of his outgoing mail so God might look over them, keep them safe from the Edgars. He had time to think about his life, his future. And his success, to the extent that it might be called success, he thought. Success? His campaign of terror had made an impact. There were doctors less willing to offer abortion services for fear of violence. The doctors Kopp had shot, and allegedly shot, no longer practiced medicine.

There was one notable exception, and it held a considerable irony that even Jim Kopp could appreciate on a certain level. In Vancouver, Dr. Romalis, allegedly one of Kopp's victims, continued to practice medicine, but had to alter his practice somewhat. He had always delivered babies as part of his practice. A major part, in fact. But delivering babies, like other surgeries, is a physically demanding job. After he was shot in the thigh, he no longer had the physical stamina to deliver babies—it can involve being on your feet a long time. Romalis couldn't stand long enough. The wound, the hole punched in his leg by the assault rifle, had put a stop to that. So Dr. Garson Romalis could only do procedures that required little time standing. He could perform what are called, in obstetrics phraseology, terminations. Abortions.

* * *

Starke, Florida
Summer 2003

Paul Hill awaited his appointment with the end. He had been on death row ever since admitting to murdering Dr. John Britton and a security guard in broad daylight outside a clinic in Pensacola in 1994. He had shown no remorse for his act. He was in good spirits. Radical pro-lifers who supported Hill's actions continued to keep in touch with him. He even corresponded on occasion with journalists. He returned a letter from a Canadian reporter:

> I appreciate your interest in the principles for which I stand. I would be glad to meet you and answer any questions you have ... I hope it all works out for you. I am currently in the final stages of writing a book. The working title is *Mix My Blood With The Blood Of The Unborn*. It presents the best case I can muster, I think it is rather convincing and compelling, for upholding the duty to defend the unborn with the means necessary (as required by the moral law, and as we would defend ourselves). At any rate, I look forward to meeting you.
> In Christ,
> Paul Hill

The date was set for September 3. He was scheduled to be the third inmate executed in Florida that year, and the 57th since the state reinstated capital punishment in 1979. Jim Kopp heard the news that a group of pro-lifers planned to gather at the site of the execution in Starke, to protest the death sentence and show their love and support for Hill, and the unborn. Kopp was excited. He wrote a long letter and had a friend post it on a website, urging pro-lifers to "join him" in Florida. It was titled, "I'm Going Back To Florida." In part the letter read:

> Sometime between now and when we die, we will have a different feeling about how we look at the whole, tragic pro-life capitulation which is taking place right now. And, grudgingly or not, just like Schindler, you will realize that there was something more you could have done, in between rescue and sidewalk work, and what Paul Hill did, and you will realize that you could have and should have done it. Be it forceful or not, "legal" or not, practical or not, efficacious or not. I assure you, the reasons we use to excuse ourselves will pale at the moment of our deaths … Come to Starke because you're a brand new pro-lifer and clueless. Come to Starke because you're a burnt-out, old curmudgeon (although I certainly have no direct experience in this matter). Come to Starke to look at blue herons. Just come to Starke. The Lord will take care of the rest … I'm looking forward to seeing you there. I'll be there in spirit. The rest of me will be very, very sad at a remote location, but my spirit will be with you and Paul and his beautiful and God-chosen family.

Five people had shot and either killed or wounded abortion providers or clinic workers in the United States: Michael Griffin, John Salvi—who committed suicide—Shelley Shannon, Hill and Kopp. Hill would be the first put to death. Five known shooters—shooters: a terribly crude word, really, Kopp mused in his letter, "but let's use it. Five known shooters. And now two of them, sadly, will be dead. And another [Griffin], sadly, and due to perhaps some unprecipitated—though not thereby necessarily unholy—action, essentially repented of his action. He took the 'aw shucks, I'm sorry, wish I hadn't done it' route."

On Tuesday, September 2, Paul Hill met with several reporters selected by the state. He smiled for the cameras and said he expected a great reward in heaven upon his passing. The next day he ate his last meal, alone: steak, baked potato, broccoli with hollandaise sauce, salad, orange sherbet, a glass of iced tea. He sat in the solitary-confinement cell. Outside, the sky turned black as a storm blew in. Hill had a final visit with his wife and son, his mother and father, and two sisters. His two daughters had visited earlier in the week. None of his family came to the observation room. The family of Hill's victims also stayed away. About 50 pro-lifers stood outside the prison gates, holding signs. There was a roll of thunder. IV tubes were inserted into both of his arms. He made his final statement: "If you believe abortion is a lethal force, you should oppose the force and do what you have to do to stop it," he said calmly as he lay strapped to a gurney, staring at the ceiling and speaking into the microphone that hung from it. "May God help you to protect the unborn as you would want to be protected."

Moments later, the chemicals pumped through his veins: first the sedative, then a paralytic agent and, finally, potassium chloride to stop his heart. Witnesses watched him gasp for air, swallow, lick his lips. His eyes fluttered, closed, and he went still. Hill was declared dead at 6:08 p.m. When the news reached Jim Kopp, his heart pounded, his mind trying to process it all, sort through his feelings. "I never knew of anyone dying on a predictable day and hour," he wrote. "I don't know how to deal with it. I can't deal with sudden death, either, though."

* * *

Miami Beach, Florida
November 11, 2003

A former soldier reading verse from the Army of God Manual. He wasn't going to be another Paul Hill. Stephen Jordi admired Paul, he had flown north to Starke to protest at Hill's execution. Hill had sent Jordi a letter, thanking him for his moral and financial support. Tactically, perhaps he would be more like Jim Kopp. Details of the story appeared later in news reports, quoting an affidavit filed in court. Stephen Jordi bought gasoline cans, flares, starter fluid, propane tanks. He wanted to blow up an abortion clinic. C-4 plastic explosives might be his best bet. But there were other ways to do it, too. A propane tank bomb. Pipe bomb.

He met again with his new friend. The friend shared Jordi's views on the need to use force in the abortion war. Was the time ripe to strike? Jim Kopp had been sentenced to life in prison, Paul Hill executed, and Eric Rudolph, who bombed a clinic in Alabama, arrested—all within the space of five months. If Jordi decided to hit a clinic, he would be a marked man. On the other hand, George W. Bush, a pro-life Republican, was in the White House, and the FBI's focus was now on al-Qaeda. He had no intention of ending up strapped to a gurney like Hill, or getting caught like Rudolph or Kopp. "As long as I keep hitting places, they'll keep after me," he told his friend. "But it's like trying to catch a cockroach in a house. They won't get me."

Jordi's friend sold him a .45-caliber pistol with an attached silencer and two empty magazines. Jordi tried to liaise with others on the fringe of the pro-life movement. One warned Jordi to be careful. In the current climate, he was playing a risky game. And one more thing: always assume that anyone you might be talking to could be a cop. On Tuesday night, Jordi met again with his friend, who lived on a houseboat at a Miami Beach marina. Perhaps Jordi felt especially safe talking with him, under cover of darkness, water lapping gently against the sides of the boat. Safe, until FBI agents emerged from the shadows to arrest him. Jordi's friend had been an informant. He had told the feds everything. Jordi plunged into the water to escape, managed to pull away from the boat. Half an hour later he was pulled from the water by the U.S. Coast Guard. He was charged with solicitation to commit a crime of violence, distribution of information relating to making and using explosives for arson, and possession of an unregistered firearm or destructive device. The FBI's Joint Terrorism Task Force had been investigating Jordi for four months, after getting a tip from his own brother.

One of Jordi's relatives told reporters that he was a loner, had a strained relationship with his family. Jordi was "overzealous about the Lord, but not a violent person." Four days prior to the arrest, the pastor at the Baptist church Jordi attended had faxed a letter to police, warning that the parishioner had violent views on stopping abortion. Clearly, in contrast to Kopp, Stephen Jordi stood out, with a shaved head and religious tattoos on both forearms. He was described in the press as a devout evangelical Christian who had four kids named Noah, Elijah, Charity and Trinity.

And Jim Kopp? A chameleon. Had seemed to one and all gentle, spoke like a devout Christian—and carried inside him a capacity for violence like a concealed shiv. Kopp knew the media would, "in its infinite wisdom," try to answer the puzzle of his life by finding some old lady somewhere who had known him, "and she would stand there for the camera, rub rosary beads in her hands, and say: 'Oh, dear, yes, Jim was such a nice boy. Can't believe he'd ever do anything wrong to anyone.'" Oh, Kopp mused, they'd trot out the old Jekyll-and-Hyde explanation for his behavior.

It was a bit more complicated than that, he reflected. Wasn't the FBI still trying to construct a psychological profile of him for the federal case? Why else would they, in the spring of 2004, with the federal trial still pending, fly him all the way to San Diego for a psychiatric evaluation? Federal prosecutors had asked for the evaluation to determine Kopp's fitness to stand trial. Was that the only reason? Why move him all the way from Buffalo to San Diego, near his boyhood home in Southern California? Perhaps they were trying to jog some old memories, shake him up a little bit? But of course. They wouldn't get inside him, though. He was sure the Edgars still hadn't figured out the code he had used in his letters to Loretta when he was on the run.

Stephen Jordi's lawyer accused the FBI of entrapment. His big mistake had been talking and trusting too much. The lesson of Jordi's capture, said a commentary on the Army of God website, is that "your family, pro-lifers and your church 'friends' will rat you out in a heartbeat, thinking they are doing God's will. Do not tell anyone, before, during, or after you are planning on taking action."

Jordi had military training, but he lacked Jim Kopp's guile. Kopp would have never been fooled by an informer, would never have talked like that. His advantage was that no one could see him coming. He used deception in every facet of his life, the *Romanita*. Yet in the end, the reason Kopp was caught and convicted was that he, too, had trusted, had talked too much—to the woman he loved. Loved? He never married, never had serious relationships. It had to be that way. His connections with adults were weak at best. Perhaps he eventually became so desensitized to grown humans that it created in him the soul of a killer, enabling him to shoot doctors, play Russian roulette with lives, shatter whole families for his cause. And yet he chose to shoot from a distance, ran after he pulled the trigger. He gave himself a buffer zone from the carnage, did not have the certainty of the up-close killer. In the end he was not completely desensitized, not quite enough. His connection with the fetus, his mission to save the unborn, wasn't enough, not when he was tired and vulnerable, "sleeping" on the run. It was then that Kopp reached for perhaps the only person he could connect with, and that was Loretta Marra.

Loretta was his blind spot, the chink in his psychological armor. His contact with her led directly to his capture. And, while few knew it at the time, she also led to his conviction. When he shocked everyone by confessing to shooting Bart Slepian, Jim Kopp was trying to sacrifice himself for Loretta's freedom. That fact all became clear one day in a Brooklyn court.

CHAPTER 27—FREE CONSCIENCE

Marra-Malvasi Sentencing Hearing
Brooklyn Federal Courthouse
Wednesday, August 20, 2003

Loretta Marra had labored over the speech in her cell. She had spent much of her adult life proselytizing, debating philosophy and morality, and now she was preparing the argument of her life. She was to make her case before federal judge Carol Amon. Marra's mission was nothing less than freeing herself and her husband, Dennis Malvasi, returning to their two young sons. They had been in custody for 29 months, since March 29, 2001, repeatedly denied bail. And now, having pled guilty to conspiracy to harbor a fugitive, Amon would decide their punishment. The maximum sentence was five years in prison and a $250,000 fine.

In Judge Amon's courtroom, Marra's lawyer, Bruce Barket, would argue for leniency. But Loretta would also speak. She could not try to make a pro-life argument to the judge, cite the feds' bigotry against pro-life Catholics—even though she believed that to her core. Why else had they been denied bail, labeled a flight risk? No, she had to make a legal argument. No one knew her case better than she did, no one knew what had gone on behind the scenes. Few knew the real reason why Jim Kopp had confessed. Now was the time to tell the whole story.

The morning broke clear and sunny. The courthouse sat on the other side of the Brooklyn Bridge from Manhattan. Spectators filed into the room, took their seats and waited: Loretta's friend Luanne, who loved Loretta, considered her a saint; old acquaintances of Loretta's late father; friends from the movement, like Joan Andrews with two of her five adopted children, one of them a child of Chernobyl born with physical disabilities; Jim Kopp's friends James Gannon and Betty Lewis, both of whom still lived in the Crestwood Village retirement community in Whiting, New Jersey; a priest who had been arrested many times for protesting and had met with Kopp in jail. The priest knew what he would have done if he had been in Loretta's shoes—he would have helped Jim, too. Any one of them would have taken in an old friend.

An activist named Bill Koehler was there. He supported the use of force against abortion providers, wished he had the nerve to actually pull the trigger. He actually hoped Kopp was not the lone sniper. That would mean there was more than just one man willing to defend the unborn. There was Luis, nickname Lifeboat, who looked as though he had hiked to the court through time from Woodstock, 1969, a long scraggly gray beard and a huge wooden cross hanging on his chest clicking against an assortment of pro-life pins. Lifeboat was 61, had been at the siege of Atlanta in '88.

Marra's sister Julia was there, too. Julia had cared for Loretta's two sons while she was in jail. So was brother Nick. He looked like Loretta, the dark French complexion of their late mother. He came to watch his sister get hammered again by the courts. It is what the establishment does, beats up on people like her. She didn't stand a chance. He turned to a journalist outside the courtroom and flashed a broad, sarcastic grin. "Ah yes," he said, "The media is here, that paragon of truth and balance."

Marra and Malvasi were led into the courtroom in handcuffs, wearing scrubs and baggy white prison-issue T-shirts. Loretta carried a stack of papers, looked weary and pale, had lost weight in prison. But Dennis Malvasi looked alert, his arms and upper body lean and hard. Loretta smiled nervously at the crowd. Guards unlocked the cuffs; they sat side by side at a table, but never touched each other in. "I love you," she mouthed silently to her sons, who sat in the front row.

The lawyers entered. Bruce Barket would argue that Marra deserved leniency in her sentence for harboring a fugitive because she had convinced James Kopp to forgo his extradition battle and come back to the United States for trial. Marra deserved credit for that. But in fact Loretta Marra planned to make an even more powerful argument to the judge. But first, her husband faced a serious allegation in court.

FBI agent Michael Osborn strode into the courtroom, took his seat at a long table facing the judge. For his role in catching Kopp, Osborn—along with Buffalo-based special agent Joel Mercer —had been presented with Attorney General's Awards for excellence in law enforcement. And Osborn had been posted to the bureau's Violent Crime Major Offenders Unit in Los Angeles. But there was still work to clean up in New York. Sitting beside him in court was the federal prosecutor, a tall, slim man with a youthful face, hair brushed to one side, olive suit, deep purple tie, brown shoes. His name was Peter Katz. Judge Carol Amon entered, took her seat, and the sentencing arguments began. Osborn leaned over and talked quietly with Katz. Then the prosecutor rose. He wanted to present new evidence that would keep Marra and Malvasi in jail.

He said that early one morning back in November 1998, less than two weeks after Bart Slepian was murdered, a woman walking in the doctor's neighborhood noticed a man standing on a sidewalk near Williamsville East High School, perhaps 100 yards from Slepian's property. The man wore a black warmup suit. Small man, compact build. Had lots of gray hair. She had never seen him before. She looked him in the eye. He seemed to look right through her, his stare was so intense. She kept walking, told a friend later about the encounter, how much it bothered her, but said nothing more about it. Fast-forward 29 months. James Kopp is arrested in France, and on TV, the woman in Amherst sees the faces of Lorretta Marra and Dennis Malvasi on TV after their arrest in Brooklyn. Malvasi. She could never forget the face, the build. Very distinctive. She felt like she was going to pass out. She called the police.

"Your Honor," Peter Katz said, "the government would like to bring forward a witness who will say she saw Mr. Malvasi on November 4 or 5, within 100 yards of where the rifle was buried in a wooded area behind Dr. Slepian's house."

What was Malvasi—a convicted abortion clinic bomber—doing in the Slepians' neighborhood less than two weeks after the murder and within a matter of hours of the FBI issuing a warrant for Kopp's arrest as a material witness? It was a shocking revelation. Those who had argued that Kopp was either framed, or at the very least had not acted alone, had been dismissed as conspiracy theorists. But this evidence suggested there was indeed more to the story—detail that Kopp himself had perhaps wanted to keep secret.

Katz continued. There was no explanation for Malvasi's presence, he argued, other than he was trying to recover the rifle left at the scene. "The witness saw him on a sidewalk on a street which is adjacent to the wooded area. There is no other reason for him to be there, given the timing, right after the material witness warrant was issued."

"The witness saw him standing on the sidewalk?" repeated Judge Amon.

"Yes."

The sniper had left a complex pattern of paint marks on trees in the woods to help direct him to find his rifle. Had he in fact put the marks there to help someone else locate the weapon—someone who had the skills to interpret them? Perhaps a Vietnam vet like Dennis Malvasi? Loretta Marra was furious with Katz's suggestion. They had agreed to a plea bargain, and now here was The Government suborning perjury from a witness to swear this—this damnable falsehood—about her husband. This witness, years after the fact, suddenly "remembers" seeing him there? All to lock them both up for the maximum five years. Lies, lies, lies. But she didn't need to worry. Judge Amon made her ruling on the spot. She would not listen to the Malvasi evidence, would not allow the witness to come forward.

"I don't see the need for the hearing," she said. "It's too great a leap for me to draw from that that (Malvasi) was there looking for the murder weapon." Dennis Malvasi lifted the pitcher of water on the table in front of him, poured a glass and took a sip.

At his seat, Michael Osborn stared ahead. You conduct your investigation, gather evidence. Then let the courts do their job. But how could it not infuriate him? They had not sprung the evidence at the last minute, he reflected. The judge knew it was coming. What possible explanation could there be for Malvasi being near the woods? Did it not at least offer the possibility that Malvasi—and by extension perhaps his wife—had a greater role in the Kopp case than just harboring him?

Katz next tried to persuade the judge that the couple still deserved the maximum punishment for harboring Kopp. They had not merely provided monetary aid and emotional support to Kopp while he was a fugitive, but had offered up their apartment as a safe house for him when he returned to the States, and implicit in that was that they would help Kopp resume shooting abortion providers. Marra and Malvasi, he argued, had engaged in obstruction of justice when Marra told her husband over the phone to "clean up the computer" shortly before their arrest. Malvasi's lawyer, Thomas Eoannou, countered that "cleaning the computer" was open to interpretation. Amon was not impressed.

"'Clean the computer' does not mean wipe the keys with alcohol," she said.

Bruce Barket argued that Marra was not aiding a killer, because she believed Jim Kopp was innocent of Dr. Slepian's murder. Kopp was a "Gandhi of the pro-life movement," who raised "hundreds of thousands of dollars" for his legal fund after his arrest, he said. "The government would have to establish that Loretta and Dennis knew Kopp was guilty, and that has never been proven."

"It defies common sense to assume they didn't know," countered Katz. "Their conversations speak for themselves. They knew that Kopp was wanted for murder, they have to know the government is looking for them."

Barket suggested that as far as Marra knew, Kopp had tried to wound Slepian, not kill him. "The government has been saying Kopp shot five abortion providers, and four of them did not die. He maintained that his purpose was to wound them, and Slepian's death was unintentional."

"Why distinguish between first-and second-degree murder?" asked Amon. "Either she knew he was guilty or not."

"She didn't know he was guilty at all, of anything," said Barket. "It was all well publicized, he did this four or five times, supposedly." Again, as he had done in Kopp's murder trial, Barket had invoked the shooting of the Canadian doctors, something that had never been entered as evidence in court.

Katz and Barket finished their arguments. All that was left was for Marra and Malvasi to have their say. Judge Amon turned to Dennis Malvasi.

"Do you have anything to say, Mr. Malvasi?"

"No."

"I just want to make sure you know that you don't have to take the opportunity, but that it is your right to address the court."

"No, thank you."

The floor was now Loretta Marra's. She stood and moved to the podium with her papers. "I hadn't planned to go much beyond begging you to let me go home to our children," she began. But she had much more to say. She wanted to take the court back in time to a year earlier, to the days in Buffalo before Kopp confessed, when her friend was still professing his innocence while awaiting trial.

* * *

Erie County Holding Center
Buffalo, N.Y.
August 2002

Loretta Marra listened to Bruce Barket. He had something very important to tell her about Jim Kopp. Kopp's upcoming defense on the murder charge would be that he had never shot Dr. Barnett Slepian. It was a setup, he was never there. He told his friends he was innocent. Barket was not yet Kopp's lawyer. That wouldn't happen for another three months. But Barket had met with Jim, spoken with him in France and met him since then in jail in Buffalo.

"Loretta," Bruce said, "I believe that Jim shot Dr. Slepian. In France I told him so—told him I believed he was culpable and that I didn't think he was framed by anybody. But Jim was convinced he could beat it. The point is, Loretta, whether Jim is convicted or acquitted, he is not at peace with continuing to deny it. It's making him very unhappy."

Marra didn't know what to think, how to feel. Jim was such a dear friend. She could think of no one more scrupulously honest. And from a moral standpoint, she had no issue with Jim denying guilt even if he was guilty of the crime. That's the way the law works. No, the most disturbing thing from a moral standpoint was that if he was guilty, he was accepting money from pro-lifers under false pretenses. The entire discussion depressed her. But what could she do now? Jim had taken his stand that he did not shoot Slepian.

"Bruce," she said, "I have nothing to say about it. It's not my business."

"Loretta, it is your business," Barket said. "Jim is your friend, he's involved in this, and he'll listen to you. He trusts you. Focus on the moral question, Loretta."

She knew what Barket was saying. They were both Catholics, they spoke the same language. Even though Jim might be acquitted, he had moral obligations that superseded his legal interests. Loretta found her lawyer's argument powerful. She knew it was always better to shoulder any amount of suffering than do something morally wrong.

"If he shot Slepian and lied about it, from a moral standpoint, he needs to undo the harm he has done to his supporters," she finally said. "At a minimum, he needs to stop fundraising and tell the truth."

But Marra was also torn. If Jim came clean before her own case went to trial, she feared it would not only doom Jim to life in prison, but help convict her as well. She and Dennis would be finished. Barket started to smile.

"Actually," he said, "it would set you and Dennis free. You would go home."

Loretta stared at him, wide-eyed. She was stunned. She felt like lightning had struck her. She saw it all so clearly now, the release from prison, into daylight, the smiling faces of her two boys. "Bruce, what are you talking about?"

"I have broached, hypothetically, the subject of Jim admitting guilt, with Kathy Mehltretter. And Mehltretter said that if you can get Jim to confess, you will get a walk." Loretta's joy now switched to anger.

"You what?" she said. "You incriminated Jim to the federal prosecutor? You are not helping Jim, Bruce, you are hurting him."

"Loretta—"

"And against my—my expressed wishes, you try and negotiate a deal to benefit me at Jim's expense, without asking me first? And then you go and manipulate me, talking to me here for, what, an hour, raising the moral issues—all while you are playing some kind of lawyer game! Just a lawyer game where winning is the only goal? This isn't about morality, Bruce, this is about you trying to get your client out any old way."

Barket calmed her down. "These are hypothetical discussions I have had with her," he said. "It's a routine tactic in negotiations like this, and that will cause no harm to Jim. And by the way, through his lying, he's doing more harm to himself, morally, than anything the state can do to him."

Barket told Marra that if he could get a deal with the prosecution, she and Dennis could be released on bail immediately after Jim confessed, and later they could cop a plea and very likely be released on time served. Marra decided she wanted to meet with Jim to feel him out on the idea. A meeting was suggested to him and he agreed. But Kopp's legal team was opposed, for obvious reasons. Jim Kopp said he was not guilty, and that was going to be his position in court. Everyone knew how deeply he felt towards Loretta. What might she convince him to do? One of Kopp's lawyers told Loretta it was a bad idea, that she could hurt her friend by meeting with him. She could even lead him, inadvertently or otherwise, to make a decision against his best interests. She might betray her friend.

"You have to understand the hierarchy of values Jim and I share," Marra replied. "And also what we consider to be true harm. We are Catholics. The fundamental belief of Catholics is to undergo suffering for sin. If Jim engaged in immoral conduct, it would imprison him for life, spiritually."

Over the next several weeks, she wrote Kopp many letters, urging him to ignore his lawyers. Meet with me, please, she wrote. You are the one in charge, Jim. The lawyers work for you. Force them to let us meet. He seemed to be wavering, his lawyers continuing to press him not to meet with Marra. He wrote her a letter: Do not write me again or try to communicate with me in any way, he said. But did he mean that? Was it *Romanita*? Tell her what she needs to hear, what his lawyers need him to say? Loretta Marra couldn't believe his response. This couldn't be Jim speaking freely. She started to write a letter. She planned to lie, tell him that she would acquiesce, respect his decision, would not bother him anymore. No. She did not mail the letter. She wrote a different letter instead. "Jim," she wrote, "if we have ever been friends, you'll meet me." Finally, he agreed.

She entered the meeting room at the Erie County Holding Center and saw her friend. She was instantly struck by how thin and distraught Jim looked. He was not at peace. She sat down beside him.

Barket and one of Kopp's lawyers stood off to one side. He looked into her pale, thin face, the green eyes. Loretta Marra did not come off well in photos in the media. Mug shots are never flattering. But in person, her eyes mesmerized, drew you in. Jim's voice was a soft whisper, out of earshot of the lawyers.

"Loretta, I shot Slepian, but I didn't mean for him to die." Tears formed in his eyes.

"Jim, people donated money based on your denial that you were the shooter."

"I know, I know. I've been racked with guilt for so long. That's why I stopped making public denials, stopped fundraising. I know I'll have to tell the truth at some point. After all our trials are over—win, lose or draw—I will."

Kopp told her he still thought it was best to go through with his trial pleading innocent. It would be best for the pro-life movement if he were acquitted, and he wanted to nail the FBI to the wall for treating his friends badly, for stomping on everyone he had ever known or loved. "But don't you think a pre-trial admission would be better in principle?" she asked. He thought about that. Then he grew agitated. No, no, it was enough to confess after the trial. One of his lawyers interrupted them. It was time. The meeting was over. Marra got up to leave.

"Loretta," Jim said. "I want to tell the truth. But I just can't do it now. If I do, it will destroy you and Dennis. I know what they'll do, they'll say you two knew everything and you'll get slammed."

"Jim, no, that's not what will happen. In fact it will send us home. Mehltretter says we'll get a walk."

Kopp frowned. "Why didn't you tell me this right away—that it would benefit you?" he said. He sounded bitter.

"You're right. But I knew that if I told you about the potential for a walk, you would reflexively sacrifice yourself. I know you, Jim, that's what you would do. And I don't want you to lose your life for me."

Marra left the cell. Barket and Marra asked to meet with Kopp again. His lawyers continued to oppose it. But he met with Loretta a second time. And then a third. He agonized over what to do, still undecided. "When I'm with my lawyers it feels like I'm in hell," he told her. "I'm fine with them one on one, but when they double-team me I can't stand up to them. If not for you, Loretta, if you hadn't pushed for the meetings, they wouldn't have happened. I am just so grateful."

"Jim," she said. "You've got to fire your lawyers. Can you not see the pattern here? Every time we speak, it's like things used to be, you are your old self, you're ready to free your conscience."

At the fourth meeting, in November, he seemed relaxed, at peace. He was ready to admit to shooting Slepian. It would set Loretta free. But first he wanted to ask the court to let him change the defense team, go with Bruce Barket as his lawyer. And there was one thing that was still bothering him.

"Even if I confess," he told Loretta, "and they tell you you're getting a walk, you will still be in danger. I can't help but think you're being set up by the government."

"Bruce says —"

"If it's too good to be true, it probably is, Loretta. Are you sure they won't find a way to railroad you?"

"Bruce has an understanding with Kathy Mehltretter. It just needs to be formalized, technicalities worked out. Jim, the government stands to benefit so much from your admission. And what's the government going to do, stand up in court and try to tell a judge that your admission did not help their case? Bruce has this expression—he said that won't pass 'the straight face test.'"

Kopp said she was still in danger. She could be sacrificing her legal interests, and thus the interests of her family, by encouraging him to confess before trial.

"Jim, if I were not positive that your admission will release us, I would beg you to endure your own moral pain and speak after our case was done with."

Jim Kopp finally had his opportunity to save Loretta. Everything changed after that. He confessed to the *Buffalo News* reporters, in

Barket's presence. He put it all out there, why he shot Dr. Slepian, how he did it. But Bruce Barket had made a big mistake. He did not yet have a deal finalized with the prosecution that a Kopp confession would automatically release Marra and Malvasi. The *Buffalo News* waited eight days before splashing "KOPP CONFESSES" on the front page. But Barket still had no signed deal from the prosecution.

James Kopp, Barket's new client, had figuratively hung himself. And Loretta Marra, his other client, was still in jail with her husband, and would not get a walk as he had promised her. Barket was furious. He felt the *Buffalo News* had lied to him, thought he had an understanding that the *News* would wait even longer before running the story. But the newspaper countered that, in fact, Barket had been promised nothing about the publication timetable. *News* editors said they told Barket that they would need time to write and edit the story, which would give him a bit of time, but there was no deal on how long that would take. Barket had made a major miscalculation. And he knew it.

In November 2002, after Kopp's confession, Marra and Malvasi were returned to Brooklyn to face trial. In early December they were again denied bail. Loretta Marra had sat in court that day, watched Kathleen Mehltretter recommend to the judge that the couple be kept in custody because they were a flight risk—despite Jim throwing himself on his own sword! They had a deal! Marra seethed, called the prosecutor a "lying bitch." Turned out Jim had been right all along. It was too good to be true. They had been set up by the government.

CHAPTER 28—*THE MALTESE FALCON*

Sentencing Hearing
Brooklyn Federal Courthouse
August 20, 2003

Judge Carol Amon listened to Loretta Marra's story. Marra had spoken for a better part of the afternoon, flipping page after page of her speech, and was still not finished. "Ms. Marra, do you think you can summarize your last several pages for the court?"

"Yes, I will try," she said.

She told the judge the prosecutors had acted in bad faith, had made promises that she and her husband would be released if Kopp confessed—and had then gone back on their word. And now the prosecution was trying to put them away for five years. "I hope you won't let them get away with it," she said. "Because Jim would never in a million years have made these admissions prior to the disposition of my case. I beg you, please do not let them get away with this."

"To summarize, Ms. Marra," said Amon, "it is your position that Mr. Kopp made these admissions after conversations with you and that the motivating factor for him in making these admissions at the time he did was to benefit you and Mr. Malvasi?"

"Yes."

Now it was Peter Katz's turn. The prosecutor argued that in fact there had never been anything on the record, no "direct promise" for the release of Marra and Malvasi. And a newspaper was not the proper forum for Kopp to confess. Barket countered that Marra had been promised "credit" for delivering Kopp's confession. The fly in the ointment had been when the *Buffalo News* published the confession story before he had a deal from the prosecution. "The reporters essentially lied to me," said Barket. "They promised to hold the story."

Court adjourned until 9:30 the next morning. Judge Amon had come to a decision on the sentence. The government had tried to prove additional criminal conduct to maximize their punishment, to give them nearly three more years in jail. But Amon had decided the prosecution had not proved that sufficiently. "I'm not persuaded that the acts were anything more than harboring." She looked at Barket. "How much time has been served already?"

"Twenty-nine to 30 months, Your Honor. Since March 29, 2001."

Amon said that Marra's words convinced her that she had a role in eliciting Kopp's confession, and that she deserved some consideration for that. But, the judge continued, the bottom line was that Kopp's confession, and Loretta Marra's role in it, was mostly irrelevant. Based on a strict reading of the sentencing guidelines for harboring a fugitive, Marra and Malvasi had already technically exceeded the incarceration guideline for the crime. Barket's eyes lit up.

"Move time served, Your Honor," he said.

"Your Honor," Katz interjected, "if you impose time served, that would not be appropriate."

"The guideline is low, in light of their conduct," said the judge. "And Mr. Malvasi has a really disturbing background of violence." But she decided to release Loretta Marra and Dennis Malvasi. "You are free to return to your children," the judge said.

In the gallery, friends broke into tears. Amon added a cautionary note. "You helped a man the FBI claimed was a murderer. And he was a murderer. Ms. Marra, in part of your statement you said you will continue to admire Mr. Kopp, and that your moral concern was not centered on his admission of killing, but that he lied to his followers about it. I find that troubling. I hope you will use your considerable intellect to educate your children; don't poison them with any notion that you were political prisoners of an unfair system, because that was not the case. You are sentenced to time served, plus three years supervised release and a $100 fine. You must reside in the Eastern District of New York."

"West Milford, New Jersey, is where her family is, Your Honor," said Barket.

"Then she can go to New Jersey today. This court is adjourned."

After paying their $100 fine, Marra and Malvasi were officially released. They walked out the front door of the Brooklyn courthouse arm in arm into sunshine and a warm breeze. Their skin looked even paler outside, Marra looked fragile. Reporters surrounded them. Loretta didn't want any part of it. Malvasi didn't shy away.

Dennis, do you think this experience will change you as far as your involvement in the anti-abortion movement goes?

"I am an abolitionist. I have never been a member of the anti-abortion movement. So I don't know what you're talking about."

Dennis, did you know that Kopp had killed Slepian when you invited him to stay at your apartment?

"With this one, I was actually minding my own business. I have never met James Kopp, I have never spoken to the man. One thing I know is, if my wife ever asks permission again for someone I don't know to stay at our house, I'm going to say no."

Dennis, was the murder of Barnett Slepian wrong?

"I don't want to answer that. I'm on federal parole. You guys are asking me loaded questions."

They started to move slowly away from the reporters. Among friends and family, Loretta Marra broke into a smile. She had delivered the speech of her life in court. Funny thing, though. Marra had gone to great lengths to prove to the judge that she was the one who had convinced Kopp to confess. He had done so in order to free her. But Judge Amon would have freed her anyway. Kopp's confession was mostly irrelevant to the timing of Loretta's release. A reporter asked Marra about that.

Loretta, given that the judge released you and said the confession had little impact on her decision, do you regret, now, having convinced your friend Jim to confess?

The pale green eyes stared unblinkingly, her face now showing color from the flush of the moment, the heat. Tiny beads of sweat had popped out on her forehead. "That's a really good question," she said. "I'll have to think about that one for a while."

Loretta, will you still take part in anti-abortion protests?

"I just want to get back to my kids." Her kids. She had gone to Canada to give birth to both of her children. Why? She smiled at the question. "Yes, that's true. They were born in Canada because—"

Bruce Barket cut her off in mid-sentence. "Ah-ah," he said. "She's not answering that."

Loretta and Dennis walked away with friends and family, through a park and the shade thrown by towering trees. Celebrations would follow in the weeks to come, 150 pro-life friends would gather with the couple at a hall in New Jersey. But for now, a dozen family and friends gathered for lunch in the sun at a sidewalk café on nearby Chilton Avenue. It was wonderful, God smiling on them all. Louis, Loretta's seven-year-old, found a five-dollar bill on the sidewalk, used it to buy his mom and dad their favorite candy bars. Dennis and Loretta still wore their prison attire, the baggy white shirts, scrubs, but their appearance turned no heads, not in New York City. They finally tasted decent sandwiches, pickles. Sipped some Sangria. As they walked away, Loretta stopped and gave Louis yet another hug. And then her other son, the four-year old, ran into her thin arms. He was born in 1999 when Jim Kopp was on the run. Loretta picked him up, held him high, looked into his eyes, joy rippling through her. He was her baby. She had named him James.

* * *

Buffalo Federal Detention Facility
Batavia, N.Y.

The scene is black and white, classic film noir, 1940s fedoras and
trench coats. The movie was filmed in Jim Kopp's old hometown,
San Francisco, the action couched in fog and the dark corners of
the Tenderloin district. In the final scene, hard-boiled detective Sam
Spade, played by Humphrey Bogart, looks into the woman's teary
eyes. She had murdered Spade's partner, tried to get away with it.
And Spade had almost taken the rap for it—almost. And now he
was confronting her.

Jim's mind returned to the present. But not for long. Thoughts
overwhelmed him at times, crowding his mind, bouncing between
places and people and events he had known, common connections,
books, songs, Bible verse, Mother Teresa, preborn babies, his family,
Mom, Dad, Anne, Marty, Mary, Walt. The garish pink walls of Mary's
bedroom where she taught him to read "Jack and the Beanstalk." Back
to the present, looking into the face of a visitor on the other side of the
glass of the prison visitor's booth. Picking up the black phone to speak
to the visitor. Was the FBI listening today? Of course they were. He
looked beyond the visitor's face, into the corridor. Who is that woman
walking around out there? She looks like a federal prosecutor. What
was she doing here? He picked his glasses up off the table, pressed
them to his face, trying to make her out. No. It wasn't her.

The visitor mentioned Loretta Marra. Kopp had been overjoyed
when he first heard that she had been freed in Brooklyn. Oh, to have
been there to see it, he thought, to hear the music in the air—what
a scene that must have been! As always, he was preoccupied by
movies, novels. How would his own life, his story, unfold? What
was the next twist, the next irony? And how would it end?

So many of his reference points were related to pop culture,
Hollywood. He pointed out that Novato, a town north of where he
had lived in California, was where his mother and sister and grandmother were buried—and was next door, practically, to filmmaker

George Lucas's Luke Skywalker Ranch. And the hospital where he was born, South Pasadena Hospital? That was where a scene from the movie *Pay It Forward* was filmed.

He loved *Pay It Forward*, which starred Helen Hunt and Kevin Spacey. He thought about it all the time. You have to see it, he urged. The film had polarized critics. Some applauded it as feel-good and well acted. Others ravaged it as sappy, sentimental and ultimately manipulative. The story is about a teacher who challenges his young students to come up with an idea that can change the world. It is meant as a motivational mental exercise. You can't really change the world with an idea. Can you? But one boy, Trevor, takes the challenge seriously. He comes up with the "pay it forward" concept: he performs three acts of unsolicited kindness to three people, the only requirement being that each passes on the goodwill to three others. His teacher says it's a utopian idea. But it catches on—all these disparate people, with no connection, suddenly coming together, and humanity is redeemed.

Jim Kopp thought of the movie as the story of his life. But why? *Pay It Forward* has a surprisingly dark ending. Trevor is famous, the movement spreads. One day, he comes to the aid of a smaller child who is being picked on by schoolyard bullies, and is himself stabbed to death. Cue the candlelit vigil, soft music. Kopp had always seen himself as a victim soul. Suffer for the cause, for God, die, painfully. But Kopp was now almost 50, and still alive. But for how long? He was certain he still might face execution. Impossible, wasn't it? France and the United States had long ago signed the extradition deal in his case. There would be no death penalty. He grinned at that bit of conventional wisdom. His case was still wide open. The trial on the federal charges was still to come. They would make an example of him. He had seen this letter, signed by Jacques Chirac, the French president. Read it with his own eyes. It proved that nothing is in stone, and the needle was still on the table. He was sure of that.

But back to more immediate concerns. Goodness, how solitary confinement compressed his already busy mind, squeezed it all together! The federal trial was still weeks, months, away. And he did not want a date set any time soon. What was he planning to do at that trial? He had confessed already to shooting Dr. Slepian. But that meant nothing for the new trial. The government would need to prove his guilt all over again. Would federal prosecutors bring up his pattern of behavior to prove his crime? Not only had he shot Dr. Slepian, but he had very likely shot Dr. Hugh Short in Ancaster, had cased out the property at least a week in advance?

Canada was part of Jim Kopp's story. The visitor mentioned Ancaster to Kopp—Jim, they have your DNA from Dr. Short's backyard. They can put you at the scene. Kopp put his hand over his mouth as if gagging himself, shook his head. No, don't talk about Canada. Anything but that, he replied. He'll be on a slow boat to Siberia if he does—nothing against Siberia! It's better than prison!

In the movie that was his life, how did the next scene look? For him, for Loretta, for pro-life? Jim Kopp would have a surprise for everybody before he was done in court. Was he not a lawyer's son? The reporters, the prosecutors will all end up looking like idiots. He had even written it out.

"Imagine a letter, the very existence of which would send any number of lawyers, etc. etc. all scurrying and fussing yak yak."

What did that mean?

The black-and-white images returned. San Francisco. The cold dark heart of Bogart's Sam Spade, who, true to nothing or no one but his own code, is telling Brigid that her number is up. She is the real killer.

"Yes, angel, I'm gonna send you over," Spade said.

"Don't, Sam," she replied. "Don't say that even in fun. I was frightened for a moment there, you do such wild and unpredictable things."

"You're taking the fall. I hope they don't hang you, precious, by that sweet neck."

"You've been playing with me, just pretending you cared for me, to trap me like this. You didn't care at all! You don't love me!"

"I won't play the sap for you," he snapped.

"It's not like that! You know in your heart that in spite of anything I've done, I love you."

Spade stared at her, his eyes hard, unrelenting.

"I don't care who loves who," he said. "I won't play the sap. You killed Miles and you're going over for it."

"How can you do this to me, Sam?"

"Chances are you'll get off with life. If you're a good girl, you'll be out in 20 years. I'll be waiting for you. And if they hang you, I'll always remember you."

A classic scene. If Kopp had one "hot tip" it was to watch that final scene from *The Maltese Falcon*. He'd been thinking about it an awful lot lately. Anyway. If Jim Kopp could just finish the latest draft of the essay he was writing about Dad, his mind would be eased considerably. Still need to clean up a few things for publication. The reference to General Douglas MacArthur, for starters, as "Dugout Doug." Don't think that derogatory label would be appreciated by military types. But it should be a good read. He'd come to terms with his father. Dad had beaten his drinking near the end of his life, had made a comeback. Oh, and he still needed to find a new bridge in the narrative of the novel he was working on. Perhaps use a "sunset piano" touch. Sunset piano, he reflected, was the part that comes two-thirds of the way through every movie—every "classical" movie, not the dumb action stuff. There is a sunset, and gorgeous music washing over all of it. Yes.

Don't fret about the writing, Jim, you dope. As always, at times like this, just think about Joni Mitchell, Court and Spark. *Your guardian angel is writing for you. Just put the words on paper and everything will take care of itself.*

The discussion with the visitor returned to Loretta's release. What was it, he thought, about living in a cell—in a concrete room the size of a bathroom—that made one's emotions reverberate so acutely? It was all overwhelming. Just wonderful. God had watched over them, Loretta and Jim, the whole time. He really had. Jim had known it would unfold one petal at a time, and it had. Loretta was free to be with her children again. She was still in danger, though, he thought. Very much so. *Children*. The meeting with the visitor came to an end. Jim hung up the phone and picked up his stack of papers, stood to leave, knocked on the door for the guard to come and escort him back into the general population. Through the glass, the visitor raised his voice to ask one more question. Did Loretta name her son James after you? Jim Kopp stopped, his mouth breaking into a wide grin, eyes twinkling.

"You'll have to ask Loretta."

EPILOGUE

Buffalo, N.Y.
June 25, 2007

In the spring of 2007 a Buffalo jury found James Charles Kopp guilty on federal charges of violating access to reproductive services. On June 25 he was sentenced. That day in a Buffalo courtroom, Lynne Slepian sat on the left side of the gallery, with her friends, and her sons—boys at the time of their father's murder, now young men. On the right side were faces from Kopp's past, among them pro-life veterans like Joan Andrews and a priest who had been meeting with him lately in prison. In the back row was a woman who had traveled several hours from her home, which is likely somewhere in New Jersey, at the wheel of an old beater of a car as thunderheads gathered above. Loretta Marra. She brought her two kids, who stayed with friends in town while she went to court as a spectator. Dennis Malvasi did not make the trip.

Kopp's court-appointed lawyer, John Humann, stood in court and argued before Judge Richard Arcara for leniency in the sentence. It was an unusual case, Humann said. Jim Kopp had not killed anyone for greed, or out of anger. "People kill for selfish motives, for money, contract killing, for evil reasons. In this case he meant to wound, not kill, because he felt a higher calling to stop abortions." Once again the sniper attacks on the Canadian doctors were floated in court, even though Kopp continued to maintain his silence about them. Those shootings "show intent to wound," Humann said. "The court should take that into account." He added that Kopp should get a break because the person who had helped him was a free person.

He was referring to Loretta Marra. Why should his client take the entire brunt of the punishment? The federal prosecutor, Kathleen Mehltrutter, stood and also invoked Marra, suggesting for the first time in a courtroom that Loretta had more direct involvement in the attacks than merely harboring a fugitive. She told the judge that Marra and Kopp crossed the border together, leaving British Columbia soon after Dr. Garson Romalis was shot in Vancouver. Outside court in the corridor, a writer from the *Hamilton Spectator* asked Loretta if that was true. Had she been in the car with Jim?

"We're not going there," she said with a smile. She appeared on edge during the entire hearing. Out in the hallway one of Bart Slepian's sons glared at Marra angrily. She stared back, her expression flat, saying nothing. Mostly she was upset that Jim, "an innocent man," was being condemned. An amazing man, she reflected. It was just a few months earlier that Marra had been officially released from being monitored by the authorities in her day-to-day life on the outside. She and Dennis were free. She could lead a normal life now, couldn't she?

"Normal? My life will never be normal," she said, the green eyes glowing with intensity, fighting to find the right words to express the fire inside that had not been tempered by doing time.

"Not when this country is bathed in the blood of millions of children." She very nearly spit the words out. "All I can smell is the stench—the *stench* of the blood. That means my life will never be normal."

Jim Kopp had one last chance to speak, to show remorse that might mitigate his federal sentence. Instead he defended shooting Bart Slepian, though adding that he had not intended to kill him. The physician died because of a "crazy ricochet." He had no regrets about the attack, though.

"If I see someone attacking a pregnant woman, or their children," he said, "I'm gonna do something."

"What made you so certain [Slepian] wouldn't be killed when you used a high-powered rifle?" Arcara asked.

"There's never 100 percent certainty. But I knew for certain he'd kill 25 children the next day." In his final words in court, off the cuff, Kopp showed that he was taking the long view on matters. "Judge, you may have a plan for me for 25 or 30 years, but Jesus has a plan for me for the next 30 billion years. I'll go with door number two."

By the end of the afternoon Arcara made his ruling. James Charles Kopp would receive the maximum sentence, life without any chance of parole. And he was rejecting Kopp's request that he be kept in a federal facility on the west coast. He would be housed wherever federal officials decided he should go. His possessions, such as they were, would be officially confiscated, Arcara added, including his tool box, the Euros found in his pocket in Dinan, and the infamous black Cavalier. It was the end of the line— almost, anyway.

In the courtroom gallery sat an Ontario Provincial Police detective taking notes. Canadian officicals still wanted to talk with Kopp in prison, try and get a statement from him. There was red tape to navigate, they needed to go through American justice channels, and if successul, inform families of the victims in Vancouver, Wininpeg, Ancaster what was going to happen. Perhaps, now that he was put away for life, Kopp would finally admit to what even his own lawyer had implied—that he was the Canadian sniper. He would almost certainly never be brought to Canada for trial to face attempted murder, but a confession would, finally, close the book on the case.

Among those continuing to follow the Canadian angle with great interest was the Brooklyn informant, code name CS1. Today the man who betrayed Marra and Malvasi lives under the FBI's protective umbrella, his identity erased, having been paid the $500,000 reward money offered by the U.S. Justice Department. Speaking to a journalist, he suggests calling him "Jack," the name he used with

FBI agents. (He thought of the name when he secretly met with an agent early on in the case and spotted a bottle of Jack Daniel's at the bar.) He keeps his whereabouts a secret, but allows that it's warm where he lives, and he has a nice view of the ocean. Jack wonders if there might be a book deal in the offing, perhaps a movie about his life. He felt he had been instrumental in catching Kopp, wouldn't his story be a fascinating one to tell?

Anyway, there was still the matter of the $547,000 in Canadian reward money. Jack called Canadian law enforcement officials asking about their progress getting an audience with Kopp, about closing the case. At times Jack has felt impatient, but is convinced it's not a matter of "if, but when", he gets paid again—and with the favorable Canadian–U.S. exchange on the dollar, he reflected, he stands to earn more now than if he had been paid when Kopp was first arrested. If it happens, no doubt he will be paid in cash, just as he was by the FBI. "How else do you pay someone who doesn't exist?"

As for Jim Kopp, was there any doubt he would appeal the federal sentence, try to get another day in court? He was a lawyer's son. He was cuffed, escorted out of the courtroom in his orange jumpsuit. He looked in the gallery on the way out. Several friends on the right side waved and smiled, the priest made a sign of the cross. Loretta made her way sideways along the back bench, as though negotiating her way along an empty church pew, to where they could see each other through a bulletproof glass partition near the prisoner's exit.

"God bless you, Jim. Good work," Loretta mouthed silently. Then she made a "call me" motion with her hand, and Jim smiled broadly just before he was led out and the door shut.

ACKNOWLEDGMENTS

I want to thank Dana Robbins and Roger Gillespie for their support and suggestions when I worked on the original "Sniper" story for the *Hamilton Spectator*; also lead editor Dan Kislenko, and Douglas Haggo. Special thanks to Scott Gardner who photographed the story and was an indispensable colleague and friend on the road. I thank Kirk LaPointe for giving me my first big career break and my first crack at long-form journalism.

I appreciate the support of the book undertaking from current *Spectator* editor-in-chief David Estok, publisher Ian Oliver, and especially managing editor Jim Poling, who stickhandled the contract. Thanks to Carmelina Prete, Pete Reintjes, and Scott Petepiece for suggestions and feedback. And of course I thank the people at John Wiley & Sons.

Most of all, I note the contributions of those who provided information that helped me craft the story. Chief among these were the Hamilton detectives who investigated the sniper attack on Dr. Hugh Short and who are referenced in the piece. The case, like all of the attacks, is a disturbing one. I thank them for their participation and candor. I also want to single out assistance from FBI profiler James Fitzgerald at the Behavioral Analysis Unit in Quantico, Virginia, and special agents Bernie Tolbert and Michael Osborn. Finally, I take advantage of this opportunity to thank my family for their love and inspiration. You mean everything.

Jon Wells